Words, Meaning and Vocabulary

Open Linguistics Series

Series Editor: Robin Fawcett, Cardiff University

This series is 'open' in two senses. First, it provides a forum for works associated with any school of linguistics or with none. Most practising linguists have long since outgrown the unhealthy assumption that theorizing about language should be left to those working in the generativist-formalist paradigm. Today large and increasing numbers of scholars are seeking an understanding of the nature of language by exploring one or other of the various cognitive models of language, or in terms of the communicative use of language – or both. This series is playing a valuable part in re-establishing the traditional 'openness' of the study of language. The series includes many studies that are in – or on the borders of – various functional theories of language – and especially because it has been the most widely used of these, Systemic Functional Linguistics. The general trend of the series has been towards a functional view of language, but this simply reflects the works that have been offered to date. The series continues to be open to all approaches – including works in the generativist-formalist tradition.

The second way in which the series is 'open' is that it encourages works that open out 'core' linguistics in various ways: to encompass discourse and the description of natural texts; to explore the relationships between linguistics and its neighbouring disciplines such as psychology, sociology, philosophy, and cultural and literary studies; and to apply it in fields such as education, language pathology and law.

Relations between the fields of linguistics and artificial intelligence are covered in a sister series, *Communication in Artificial Intelligence.* Studies that are primarily descriptive are published in a new series, *Functional Descriptions of Language.*

Words, Meaning and Vocabulary

An Introduction to Modern English Lexicology

Howard Jackson
Etienne Zé Amvela

continuum
LONDON • NEW YORK

Continuum
The Tower Building, 11 York Road, London SE1 7NX
370 Lexington Avenue, New York, NY 10017–6550

First published 2000
Reprinted 2001

British Library Cataloguing in Publication Data
A catalogue record for this book is available from the British Library.

ISBN 0-304-70395 8 (hardback)
0-8264-6096-8 (paperback)

Library of Congress Cataloging-in-Publication Data
Jackson, Howard, 1945–
    Words, meaning, and vocabulary: an introduction to modern English lexicology/Howard
Jackson, Etienne Zé Amvela.
        p. cm. — (Open linguistics series)
    Includes bibliographical references and index.
    ISBN 0–304–70395–8. — ISBN 0–8264-6096-8 (pbk.)
    1. English language—Lexicology. I. Zé Amvela, Etienne, 1948–.   II. Title.   III. Series.
PE1571.J33   2000
423'.028—dc21   99–31364
                                                                                    CIP

Typeset by York House Typographic
Printed and bound in Great Britain by The Cromwell Press, Trowbridge

Contents

Preface

This introduction to the words and vocabulary (lexicology) of English arises from courses that Etienne Zé Amvela and Howard Jackson have taught over many years at their respective universities, the former in Cameroon (Yaoundé and Buea) and the latter in Birmingham, UK (Birmingham Polytechnic/University of Central England). The study of vocabulary, by contrast with syntax, has been a rather neglected pursuit in English over recent years, and there are few textbooks in the area. It is our hope that this work will go some way towards redressing the balance.

Etienne Zé Amvela has been responsible for the first four chapters and Howard Jackson for the last four, but we have commented extensively on each other's work, and we hope that the book reads as a seamless whole.

The book is aimed at students of English language/linguistics, taking courses in the analysis and description of the English language, possibly with little prior knowledge of linguistics. However, we do advise students to have a good up-to-date dictionary to hand, preferably of the desk-size or collegiate type. In order to encourage interaction with the material discussed in the book, each chapter is interspersed with exercises, some of which require dictionary consultation. A key to the exercises is provided at the end.

Howard Jackson
Etienne Zé Amvela

To Hilary and Mama Régine

1 What is Lexicology?

This book is about English lexicology. But before we begin to discuss the various facets of the subject, we need to suggest a definition of the term lexicology (1.1). The rest of the chapter will discuss lexicology as a level of language analysis (1.2), and explore the structure of the English vocabulary (1.3).

1.1 Lexicology defined

At this early stage, a definition of lexicology is best considered as a working tool for a better understanding of subsequent chapters. In fact, we believe that this whole book is an answer, or at least a partial answer, to the fundamental question, 'What exactly is lexicology?' We shall not have completed our definition until we reach the end. Even then, we cannot claim to have said everything about lexicology.

For the purpose of an introductory textbook of this nature, lexicology may be defined as the study of lexis, understood as the stock of words in a given language, i.e. its vocabulary or lexicon (from Greek *lexis*, 'word', *lexikos*, 'of/for words'). This working definition shows that the notion of 'word' is central in the study of lexicology. However, 'word' itself needs to be defined and discussed as a technical term. This is done in Chapter 3. Since our main focus in this chapter is on the definition of lexicology, and in order to avoid a lengthy digression, we use 'word' somewhat loosely, in the usual traditional sense of a sequence of letters bounded by spaces. A comparison of the words 'vocabulary', 'lexis', and 'lexicon' would show that the three items may be considered more or less synonymous. However, it must be added that the first is more colloquial, the third more learned and technical, and the second may be situated half-way between the other two. A distinction must, nevertheless, be drawn between the terms 'vocabulary', 'lexis' and 'lexicon' on the one hand, and 'dictionary' on the other. While each of the first three may refer to the total word stock of the language, a dictionary is only a selective recording of that word stock at a given point in time.

Lexicology deals not only with simple words in all their aspects, but also with complex and compound words, the meaningful units of language. Since these units must be analysed in respect of both their form and their meaning, lexicology relies on information derived from morphology, the study of the forms of words and their components, and semantics, the study of their meanings. A third field of particular interest in lexicological studies is etymology, the study of the origins of words. However, lexicology must not be confused with lexicography, the writing or compilation of dictionaries, which is a special technique rather than a level of language study.

To avoid possible confusion and in order to introduce some of the technical terms we need in our discussion of lexicology, we shall examine the four related fields mentioned above, viz. morphology, semantics, etymology and lexicography. Finally, we shall discuss lexicology as a level of language analysis.

EXERCISE 1/1

Examine the following definitions of 'lexicology'. What do they agree on as the scope of lexicology? And where do they disagree?

1. An area of language study concerned with the nature, meaning, history and use of words and word elements and often also with the critical description of lexicography. (McArthur, ed. 1992)

2. The study of the overall structure and history of the vocabulary of a language. (*Collins English Dictionary* 1998)

3. A branch of linguistics concerned with the meaning and use of words. (*Longman Dictionary of the English Language* 1991)

4. The study of the form, meaning, and behaviour of words. (*New Oxford Dictionary of English* 1998)

1.1.1 Morphology

Morphology is the study of morphemes and their arrangements in forming words. Morphemes are the smallest meaningful units which may constitute words or parts of words. They are 'smallest' or 'minimal' in the sense that they cannot be broken down further on the basis of meaning, as Katamba (1994: 32) puts it: 'morphemes are the atoms with which words are built'. They are 'meaningful' because we can specify the kind of relationship they have with the non-linguistic world.

Consider the following items: cat, child, with, sleeping, armchairs, farmer. A close examination shows that *cat, child* and *with* cannot be analysed further into meaningful units. However, *sleeping, armchairs* and *farmer* can be analysed as 'sleep + ing', 'arm + chair + s', and 'farm + er'.

The items *cat, child, with, sleep, -ing, arm, chair, -s, farm,* and *-er* are all morphemes. Some are simple words such as *cat, child, with, sleep, arm, chair,* and *farm,* while others are only parts of words such as *-ing, -s,* and *-er.* But both types meet our definition of morpheme. On the one hand, they are minimal, since they cannot be broken down into further meaningful units; on the other hand, they are meaningful, because we can establish a stable relationship between each item and the non-linguistic world of experience. For example, the references of *cat, farm* and *chair* can be explained by pointing or acting out the meaning as in 'This is a chair', or 'That is a farm', 'It is a domestic animal that goes "miaow", "miaow"'. The meaning of *with* may be given as 'in company of', 'in antagonism to'; that of *-s* as 'plural'; while that of *-er* may be expressed as follows: '*-er* combines with the preceding lexical item to designate things or persons with a function describable in terms of the meaning of the preceding morpheme'. For example, the meaning of *-er* in *farmer* and *dreamer* is describable in terms of those of *farm* and *dream* with which the morpheme *-er* is combined.

Morphemes that can occur alone as individual words are 'free' morphemes. Those that can occur only with another morpheme are 'bound' morphemes. Thus, the morphemes 'cat', 'chair', 'farm' are free, while '-ing', '-s', and '-er' are bound, indicated by the hyphen (-). Any concrete realization of a morpheme in a given utterance is called a 'morph'. Hence, the forms *cat, chair, farm, -ing, -s,* and *-er* are all morphs. Morphs should not be confused with syllables. The basic difference between the two is that while morphs are manifestations of morphemes and represent a specific meaning, syllables are parts of words which are isolated only on the basis of pronunciation.

An examination of a number of morphs may show that two or more morphs may vary slightly and still have the same meaning. For example, the indefinite article may be realized either as *a* or as *an,* depending on the sound (not the letter) at the beginning of the following word. Morphs which are different representations of the same morpheme are referred to as 'allomorphs' of that morpheme (from Greek *allo* 'other' and *morph* 'form'). For example:

a context vs. *an* index
a battle vs. *an* apple
a union vs. *an* onion.

The last pair of words deserves some comment. Its members begin with *u* and *o,* which are classified as vowel letters. However, while *union* begins with the same sound as *yes* which is treated as a consonant, *onion* begins with the same sound as *onwards,* which is a vowel; hence '*a* union' vs. '*an* onion'.

The use of 'vs.' (versus) highlights the point that where the allomorph *an* occurs, its counterpart *a* cannot occur and vice versa. They are therefore mutually exclusive and are said to be in complementary distribution. It should be pointed out that as a descriptive term, 'distribution' refers to the total set of distinct linguistic contexts in which a given form occurs, sometimes under different morphological shapes. For example, the distribution of the indefinite article described above may be defined as: *a* before consonant sounds (e.g. *a* battle) and *an* before vowel sounds (e.g. *an* apple).

We now turn our attention to the relation between morphology on the one hand, and simple, complex and compound words on the other. Simple words such as *door, knob, wild, animal* are all free morphemes. They are therefore morphologically unanalysable. Complex (or derived) words such as *spoonful, wildish, reanimate, mentally, farmer* are formed from simpler words by the addition of affixes or some other kind of morphological modification. The limiting case for complex words is that of zero modification or conversion as in *answer, call* and *question,* which may be either nouns or verbs, or *clean, dirty,* and *dry,* which may be either adjectives or verbs, without the addition of further sounds/letters. Compound words, or simply compounds, are formed by combining two or more words (free morphemes) with or without morphological modification, e.g. *door-knob, cheeseburger, pound saver, wild-animal-tamer.* It should be pointed out that the distinction between word compound (solid and hyphenated) and phrasal compound (open) is not very clear in English. This fact is reflected by the inconsistency with which spaces and hyphens are used with compounds in written English.

This brief discussion shows the importance of morphology in lexicology. In fact, the construction of words and parts of words, and the distinction between the different types of words are all based on morphological analysis. As will be seen later in Chapter 4, morphology is particularly relevant in the discussion of word formation.

1.1.2 Semantics

Semantics is generally defined as the study of meaning. Its aim is therefore to explain and describe meaning in natural languages. The term 'meaning' is used here in the ordinary, non-technical sense, without reference to any particular theoretical framework. Most linguists agree that meaning pervades the whole of language. However, they are not always unanimous on the terms to be used in the discussion of semantics. For our purpose in this book, we adopt the terminology presented and the theoretical distinctions made by Jackson (1988: 244–7) in his brief treatment of semantics.

To highlight the pervasive nature of meaning, Jackson states that if we are to talk about semantics at all, then we should identify several kinds of semantics: pragmatic semantics, which studies the meaning of utterances in context; sentence semantics, which handles the meaning of sentences as well as meaning relations between sentences; lexical semantics, which deals with the meaning of words and the meaning relations that are internal to the vocabulary of a language. Semantics is usually approached from one of two perspectives: philosophical or linguistic. Philosophical semantics is concerned with the logical properties of language, the nature of formal theories, and the language of logic. Linguistic semantics involves all aspects of meaning in natural languages, from the meaning of complex utterances in specific contexts to that of individual sounds in syllables.

Consequently, since semantics covers all aspects of human language, it must be considered not only as a division of lexicology, but also as part of phonology, syntax, discourse analysis, textlinguistics, and pragmatics. But for our purpose in this book, it is enough to assume that lexical semantics is relevant to lexicology.

It will also be useful to introduce two terms which belong more to the area of sentence semantics, but which are equally relevant to our discussion of lexicology, viz. 'acceptability' and 'meaningfulness'.

'Acceptability' and 'meaningfulness' are distinct but related concepts. They are important in our discussion of lexicology because we may have utterances that are meaningless but acceptable, while others may be meaningful but unacceptable. Consider the following:

> That woman is a man.
> That doll is a bomb.
> That walking-stick is a gun.

They may be considered meaningless in the sense that a human being cannot be both 'a woman' and 'a man' at the same time. Similarly, it may be argued that an object cannot be 'a doll' and 'a bomb', just as the same object cannot be simultaneously 'a walking-stick' and 'a gun'. But with a bit of imagination, one can think of contexts where such utterances, and others like them, can be considered acceptable. For example, in a play, a character may be a man biologically and play the role of a woman; in a film, an actor could be carrying a doll or a walking-stick which in fact could be deadly weapons such as a bomb or a gun. To paraphrase Leech (1969: 13), the 'effective message' in all such utterances is: 'What appears as an "x" is in fact a "y".'

There are other types of meaningless utterance that may be acceptable for various reasons. Some may involve 'slips of the tongue', 'typographical errors', 'sarcasms', 'different figures of speech', etc. Others may be considered deviations from the norm of the language under study. Still others may have different origins or justifications. For example, if a person who has a bad cold and a completely blocked nasal cavity says 'It's dice beeting you', after he/she has just been introduced to someone, this utterance may be considered meaningless, strictly speaking. However, the 'effective message' it conveys in this context would be something like 'It's nice meeting you but I have a bad cold.'

The important point here is that there are several factors that contribute to the meaningfulness and the acceptability of utterances. As opposed to utterances that are meaningless but acceptable, others are meaningful but unacceptable. The latter category includes assertions that are false because of our knowledge of the real world, rather than for purely semantic reasons. Consider the following:

Crocodiles can fly.
The basket ate the vegetables.
John's behaviour pleased the *bananas*.

We may use different criteria to account for such utterances. For example, they may be explained by logical argument to highlight the contradictions, inconsistencies or incompatibilities in the message. From a syntactic point of view, such utterances are treated as errors in predication, meaning that the subject or object noun phrases are syntactically unsuitable to the corresponding verb phrases. Hence, the subjects *crocodiles* and *the basket* are syntactically unsuitable to the verb phrases *can fly* and *ate* respectively. Such examples point to the fact that all of syntax, semantics and lexicology contribute to a comprehensive study of language.

1.1.3 Etymology

A third field which should be of particular interest in lexicological studies is etymology, which may be defined as the study of the whole history of words, not just of their origin. The term 'etymology' was coined by the Stoics, a group of Greek philosophers and logicians who flourished from about the beginning of the fourth century BC. They noticed a lack of regularity in the correspondences between the forms of the language and their respective contents. In other words, they found no necessary connection between the sounds of the language on the one hand and the things for which the sounds stood on the other. Since they were convinced that language should be regularly related to its content, they undertook to discover the original forms called the 'etyma' (roots) in order to establish the regular correspondence between language and reality. This was the beginning of the study known today as etymology.

One of the difficulties faced by etymological studies is that some words are not etymologically related to ancient forms. It is therefore difficult to establish and indicate their origins. Consequently, the forms from which such words are said to derive can only be produced by analogy. Another difficulty is that while it is possible to specify the exact time when some terms entered the language, for example through borrowing, it is clearly impossible to say exactly when a form was dropped, especially since words can disappear from use for various reasons.

The most crucial difficulty faced with etymological studies is that there can be no 'true' or 'original' meaning, since human language stretches too far back in history. To paraphrase an example given by Palmer (1981: 11), one may be tempted to say that from the etymological point of view the adjective *nice* really means 'precise' as in 'a *nice* distinction'. But a study of its history shows that the word once meant 'silly' (Latin *nescius*, 'ignorant'), and earlier, it must have been related to *ne*, 'not' and *se*, probably meaning 'cut'. The form *se* is also used in the Modern English words *scissors* and *shears*. But at this level of analysis, one would still be left with the Latin items *ne*, 'not' and *se*, 'cut', the origins of which are still unknown. In other words, no matter how far back one goes in history, one cannot expect to reach the beginning of time. So, the Stoics' quest has proved fruitless.

As suggested in our definition, etymological information goes beyond the origin of the word. It also makes reference to cognates (i.e. words related in form) in other languages. Furthermore, in the case of borrowed words, it gives the source language, together with the date when the borrowing took place. Finally, it supplies any other information on the previous history of the word. In dictionary entries, such information is contained traditionally in square brackets. The amount of detail provided in etymologies varies from one dictionary to another. But in spite of its potentially wide range of coverage, etymological information is generally scanty in most monolingual dictionaries. In fact, it is totally absent from both bilingual and learners' dictionaries, presumably on the grounds that it is not helpful to language learners. However, as pointed out by Jackson (1988: 175), it could be argued that 'knowledge of etymology may help some learners to understand and retain new vocabulary items'.

Before we close this brief discussion of etymology, we should mention the expression 'folk etymology'. It is a historical process whereby speakers who cannot analyse an obscure form replace it with a different form which is morphologically transparent. Gramley and Pätzold (1992: 31) give good examples of this process with the noun 'bridegroom' and the verb 'depart'. In Middle English, the original spelling of the first word was 'bridegome' (*bride*, 'bride'; *gome*, 'man'). But the second element ceased to be understood and was altered to *groom* to make *bridegroom*. The etymology of *depart* is more complex. Initially, its use was restricted to wedding ceremonies to mean 'separate' in the expression 'till death us *depart*'. Later, the verb became obsolete and was analysed as *do* and *part*, hence the corresponding Modern English expression 'till death *do* us *part*'. Although a few other examples could be given, it must be acknowledged that folk etymology is not a very productive process in Modern English. See Chapter 2 for a discussion of the origins of English words; and Chapter 4 for the various word-formation processes.

EXERCISE 1/2

Etymology can be a fascinating area of study. Look up the etymology of *bridegroom* in your dictionary. Does it mention the folk etymology, i.e. the change from 'gome' to 'groom'?

Now look up the etymology of *adder*. Is there any folk etymology at work here?

Finally, look up the etymology of *snake*. What does your dictionary say is the origin? And does it give cognates?

1.1.4 Lexicography

The fourth and last field which is of special interest in lexicological studies is lexicography, which has already been defined as a special technique, the writing and compilation of dictionaries. This definition may be considered rather restrictive. In its widest sense, lexicography may also refer to the principles that underlie the process of compiling and editing dictionaries. Some of those principles are clearly lexical or lexicological in nature, while others stem from the specific domain of book production and marketing. But lexicographical compilation may be considered as derived from lexicological theory (Jackson 1988: 248). It is in this sense that lexicography can be regarded as 'applied lexicology'.

However, it should be acknowledged that it is only in recent years that the link between lexicography and linguistics has been clearly established. For example, the accuracy and consistency in the transcription of words and the adoption of a 'descriptive' as opposed to a 'prescriptive' approach to lexicography are direct applications of linguistic principles. It may be argued that initially, lexicography developed its own principles and tradition independently of linguistics in general; but this is no longer the case. In fact, since current dictionaries are compiled mainly by lexicographers who have been trained in linguistics, one should expect a more direct and more substantial input from lexicology. However, it should be pointed out that lexicology is not the only branch of linguistics which provides an input to lexicography. Clearly, morphology, syntax and phonology do. And sociolinguistics, too, contributes, not only in the study and selection of the language variety to be used in the dictionary, but also in the inclusion of information on style and registers. For a detailed discussion of lexicography as applied lexicology, see Chapter 8.

1.2 Lexicology as a level of language analysis

Lexicology is only one possible level of language analysis, others being phonology, morphology, syntax and semantics. Although an attempt may be made at treating any of these levels in isolation, it must be said that none of them can be studied successfully without reference to the others. All these different levels of analysis interact with one another in various ways, and when we use language, we call on all simultaneously and unconsciously. We briefly discussed morphology and semantics in 1.1; here we consider the relation of lexicology to phonology and syntax.

1.2.1 Lexicology and phonology

It may be thought at first sight that phonology does not interact with lexicology in any significant manner. But a close analysis will reveal that in many cases, the difference between two otherwise identical lexical items can be reduced to a difference at the level of phonology. Compare the pairs of words p*ill* and b*ill*, *sheep* and *ship*, *mea*t and *mea*l. They differ only in one sound unit (the position of which has been shown in each word) and yet the difference has a serious effect at the level of lexicology. As suggested by these examples, the sounds responsible for the difference may occur anywhere in the structure of the word; i.e. at the initial, medial, or final position. In some cases, the phonological difference does not involve discrete sound units but 'suprasegmental' or 'prosodic' features such as stress; and yet, even such differences are enough to differentiate otherwise identical items; e.g. *ex'port* (verb), vs. *'export* (noun). Note that the symbol (') is placed immediately before the syllable which receives primary stress.

Compounds provide another good example to show the relevance of phonology in lexicology. At first sight, the process of compounding may be viewed as a simple juxtaposition of two words. Thus, *green* and *house* may be put together to form *greenhouse*, 'a glass house for growing plants'. But such an analysis would be superficial, since the same items can be put together in the same order to produce *green house*, 'a house that is green'. The major difference between the two utterances is a matter of stress, which is a phonological feature. But this feature is enough to distinguish compounds from noun phrases containing the same words. Compare the stress pattern of the compound nouns in (a) and the corresponding adjective plus noun constructions in (b).

(a) *Compound*   (b) *Noun Phrase*
    'blackboard   ,black 'board
    'blackbird   ,black 'bird
    'greyhound   ,grey 'hound
    'White House   ,white 'house

Note: (') = main or primary stress, and (,) = secondary stress.

As a general rule, the primary stress falls on the first word of the compound as in *'blackboard* (a dark smooth surface in schools for writing on with chalk). The same rule applies to the rest of the words in (a). However, in the noun phrases in (b) like *,black 'board* (as opposed to any board that is painted green, red or yellow) both words can potentially receive stress. All the examples in (b) are phrases, not words. Consequently, they function as units at the syntactic level. They are therefore an indication that stress, which is a phonological feature, has a direct influence on syntax. The relation between lexicology and syntax is further explored in 1.2.2. This is a clear illustration of the interdependence of phonology, lexicology and syntax. However, since language is so complex that it cannot be studied all together, we must consider each level as if it were autonomous. But it must always be remembered that such an approach is only methodological and does not always reflect the way language operates when it is used by its speakers.

1.2.2 *Lexicology and syntax*

We use the term 'syntax' to refer to the particular knowledge which enables us to assemble words when we construct sentences. Syntax is also responsible, at least in part, for an appropriate understanding of the sentences we hear and those we read. That is, syntax is concerned with the relationships between words in constructions and the way these words are put together to form sentences.

As a basic assumption, we believe that we might know the meanings of all the words in a large English dictionary and still be quite unable to speak or understand the language. Consequently, to say that someone speaks English, or that they 'know' English, amounts to saying that they have somehow acquired a set of rules, among which are the rules of syntax, that enables them to produce English sentences as needed. The rules also enable them to understand the sentences of another person speaking the language. However, unless they have some special training in linguistics, the speaker and hearer cannot talk confidently about the nature of such rules.

In 1.2.1 above we saw how semantics and phonology are both relevant in any serious study of lexicology. We shall now investigate the relationship between lexicology and syntax. We assume that, although these two levels of language analysis are comparable, they may also be kept distinct. One argument in favour of the distinction between syntax and lexicology is the observation that a given sentence may be syntactic but unacceptable from the lexical point of view. One such example is the famous sentence 'Colorless green ideas sleep furiously', proposed by Chomsky (1957). This sentence is built according to the rules of English syntax but it is unacceptable on lexical grounds. If a sentence can satisfy the rules of syntax but be unacceptable lexically, this is perhaps an indication that the rules of syntax are different from those of lexicology; consequently, the two levels are distinct. In fact, the problem of the distinction between lexicology and syntax may be reduced to the distinction between sentences that are unacceptable on syntactic grounds and those that are deviant from the lexical point of view.

The essential difference between syntax and lexicology is that the former deals with the general facts of language and the latter with special aspects. It is in the main a question of general versus particular. Syntax is general because it deals with rules and regularities that apply to classes of words as a whole, whereas lexicology is particular because it is concerned with the way individual words operate and affect other words in the same context. Although borderline cases do exist in both lexicology and syntax, e.g. in the case of 'grammatical' or 'function' words (1.3.4), the distinction between the two levels is fairly clear.

At first sight, it may be thought that when judged in terms of how deviant they are, lexical restrictions are generally not a matter of well-established rules but of tendencies. In other words, it may be assumed that if asked whether or not a given lexical association is acceptable, one cannot answer by a categorical 'yes/no'; one is more likely to give an answer of the nature 'more/less', or 'it depends on the context'. Such an assumption is, however, an oversimplification. In syntax as well as in lexicology, there are cases of deviation which may be answered by yes/no, and others that can be answered only by more/less, though a 'yes/no' answer is more likely in syntax than in lexicology. For example, a sentence such as 'Sophisticated mice prefer to eat red elephants', though undoubtedly syntactic is lexically doubtful because it does not correspond to our experience of the world. Judging from our present knowledge of the natural world, the acceptability of this sentence is not a matter of 'more/less' but of a categorical 'no'. However, a sentence such as 'The flower gracefully walked away' may seem odd in the sense that 'flowers' are not normally associated with 'walking' but with some imagination, we can picture a context in which this sentence, which is already acceptable syntactically, is also acceptable lexically.

Similarly, some sentences are clearly ungrammatical, while others are clearly well-formed syntactically. For example, a sentence such as 'Did it he and I' is clearly deviant only on syntactic grounds and it could be corrected simply by changing the word order into 'He and I did it'. But there are also marginal cases such as 'Give it to whomever wants it' versus 'Give it to whoever wants it', where English speakers are not unanimous as to which alternative is grammatical. As a final observation, it should be pointed out that some sentences, such as 'Did it John and the table', are deviant on both syntactic and lexical grounds.

EXERCISE 1/3

Consider the following 'deviant' sentences. In which of them would an alternative selection of words (lexis) make an improvement, and in which does the arrangement of the words (syntax) need to be adjusted?

1. Visitors are aggressively requested to remove their shoes before leaving the temple.

2. You put can table the the on bread you bought have.

3. All mimsy were the borogroves and the mome raths outgrabe.

4. Anyone lived in a pretty how town, with up so many bells floating down.

5. Off you go, up the apples and pears and into uncle ned.

1.3 The structure of English vocabulary

As used in this book, the terms vocabulary, lexis and lexicon are synonymous. They refer to the total stock of words in a language (see 1.1).

Assuming the existence of some internal organization of vocabulary, the basic question we want to address here may be formulated as follows: 'How is the total stock of English words structured and organized?'

There have been a number of attempts to discover some of the general principles on which vocabulary is organized. These attempts have focused on three main areas: that of individual words and their associations, that of semantic or lexical fields, and lastly that of word families. We shall discuss these three approaches in turn. Finally, we shall also mention the notion of 'word class' as a way of accounting for the structure of the English vocabulary.

1.3.1 The word and its associative field

According to this approach, every word is involved in a network of associations which connect it with other terms in the language. Some of these associations are based on similarity of meaning, others are purely formal (i.e. based on forms), while others involve both form and meaning. In de Saussure's graphic formula, a given term is like the centre of a constellation, the point where an infinite number of co-ordinated terms converge. De Saussure tried to represent these associations in the form of a diagram using the French word *enseignement* ('teaching') (de Saussure 1959: 126). In Figure 1.1, we have not only modified the form of the diagram (by giving one word a more central position) but have also used English words to suit our discussion here. In this diagram, four lines of association radiate from the noun *lecturer*. (1) connects it with the verb forms *lectured* and *lecturing* by formal and semantic similarity based on the common stem *lecture*; (2) connects it with *teacher* and *tutor* by semantic similarity; (3) associates it with *gardener* and *labourer* because they all have the suffix *-er* forming agent nouns from verbs; (4) associates it with the adjective *clever* and the inflected adverb *quicker* by accidental similarity in their endings. The use of an arrow and that of *etc.* at the end of each line of associations suggests that the line has no limit and that an infinite number of words can be added to those suggested in the diagram.

Figure 1.1 also shows, among other things, that any word chosen from a given context will suggest other words to us, because they either resemble or differ from each other in form, meaning or both. Such relations are referred to as 'paradigmatic'. They are called relations 'in absentia', because the terms involved consist of a word present in the utterance and others that are not actually in the same utterance but that are substitutable for it in that context. For example, 'difficult' is paradigmatically related with 'easy', 'funny', 'silly', etc. in expressions such as 'an easy question', 'a funny question', 'a silly question', etc. Similarly, 'question' is paradigmatically related with 'problem', 'word', etc. in expressions like 'a difficult problem', 'a difficult word', etc.

Interesting as the notion of paradigmatic relations may be, it has one major difficulty: every other word in the language either resembles or fails

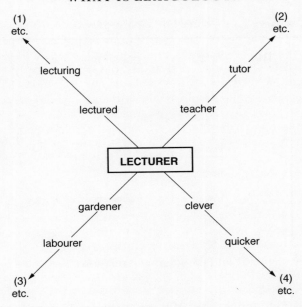

Figure 1.1 The word and its associative field

to resemble in form or meaning any given word. This difficulty notwith-standing, the notion has proved useful in language teaching and in the arrangement of words in a thesaurus. It has also been used to establish cross-references in the definitions of words in dictionaries.

This important notion was first introduced by de Saussure under the label 'associative relations'. But the term 'paradigmatic' has been substituted at the suggestion of the Danish linguist Hjelmslev (1963). Another notion which was also introduced by de Saussure was that of 'syntagmatic' relations. They are called relations 'in praesentia' since the words involved are actually co-occurent items. For example, the word *difficult* is syntagmatically related with the article *a* and the noun *question* in the expression 'a difficult question'.

Paradigmatic and syntagmatic relations may be represented in a diagram as in Figure 1.2. This shows that every word may be considered in terms of two dimensions or axes of structure. The 'horizontal' or syntagmatic and the 'vertical' or paradigmatic. It is precisely in terms of syntagmatic and paradigmatic relations that the meaning of English words can be deter-mined. However, our interest in constructions larger than the word is secondary, though see 5.6 on collocation.

1.3.2 Lexical fields

Some isolated attempts have been made to study the structure of some semantic or lexical fields, such as the hierarchy of military ranks, numerals,

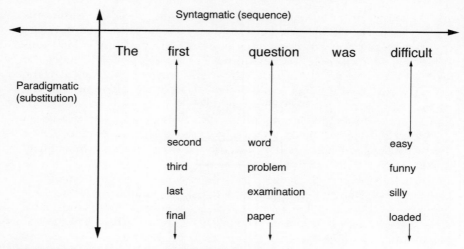

Figure 1.2 Syntagmatic and paradigmatic relations

colour and kinship terms. Most of these attempts are directly or indirectly connected with what has now come to be known as the theory of 'semantic fields' or 'lexical field theory'. 'Semantic field' or 'semantic domain' are used alternatively for the terms 'lexical field' or 'lexical set'. Crystal (1995: 157) defines a semantic or lexical field as a 'named area of meaning in which lexemes interrelate and define each other in specific ways'. For example, the lexical field of 'kinship terms' comprises the lexemes: father, mother, son, daughter, cousin, nephew, uncle, aunt, grand-father, grand-mother, etc.

Field theory was first put forward by a number of German and Swiss scholars in the 1920s and 1930s. However, according to Lyons (1977: 250) its origin can be traced back at least to the middle of the nineteenth century and more generally to the ideas of Humboldt and Herder. We shall not attempt a comprehensive treatment of field theory, nor shall we try to review the considerable body of descriptive work based on it. Instead, we shall discuss briefly how the theory may be used to account for the general organisation of the English vocabulary (see also 5.5.3).

According to lexical field theory, the vocabulary of a language is essentially a dynamic and well-integrated system of lexemes structured by relationships of meaning. The system is changing continuously by the interaction of various forces such as the disappearance of previously existing lexemes, or the broadening or narrowing of the meaning of some lexemes. The system is mainly characterized by the general–particular and part–whole relationships, which hold not only between individual lexemes and the lexical field within which they are best interpreted, but also between specific lexical fields and the vocabulary as a whole. One of the early theorists, Jost Trier, puts it like this: 'Fields are living realities intermediate between individual words and the totality of the vocabulary; as parts of a whole, they share with words the property of being integrated in a large structure and with the vocabulary the property of being structured in terms of smaller units' (quoted in Lyons 1977: 253). For example, the lexical field of 'colour terms' includes the lexemes: black, white, red, green, yellow, blue, orange, etc. Similarly, the lexical field of colour terms, together with those of kinship terms, military ranks, vehicles, among others are only parts of the whole English vocabulary. Furthermore, the general lexeme *red* for instance may in turn be considered a lexical field (or sub-field) within which the particular lexemes *scarlet, crimson, vermillion*, etc. may best be interpreted. These characteristics of field theory may be illustrated by Figures 1.3a and 1.3b.

As we would expect, the lexicologist who attempts to assign all the words in English to lexical fields is bound to face a number of difficulties. According to Crystal (1995: 157) these difficulties are of three kinds. First, some lexemes tend to belong to fields that are vague or difficult to define. For instance, it is not obvious to which field the lexemes *noise* or *difficult* should be assigned. Secondly, some may validly be assigned to more than one field, e.g. *orange*, either to the field of 'fruit' or to that of 'colour'; *tomato* as 'fruit' or 'vegetable'. The last difficulty concerns the best way to define a lexical field in relation to the other fields on the one hand, and its constituent lexemes on the other. To use Crystal's examples (1995: 157), one may ask such questions as the following: is it more illuminating to say that *tractor* belongs to the field of 'agricultural vehicles', 'land vehicles', or just 'vehicles'? Should the lexeme *flavour* be a member of the lexical field of 'taste' or is *taste* a lexeme in the lexical field of 'flavour' or should both be treated as lexemes in a broader semantic field such as 'sensation'?

The existence of these difficulties is a pointer to the fact that the English vocabulary is not made up of a number of discrete lexical fields in which each lexeme finds its appropriate place. Furthermore, it provides an additional proof that language usually cannot be analysed into well-defined and watertight categories. The analyst will always have to take a number of difficult decisions in order to accommodate fuzzy cases. However, it must be acknowledged that large numbers of lexemes can in fact be grouped together into fields and sub-fields in a fairly clear-cut manner. This is an indication of the usefulness of field theory in lexicology (see further 5.5.3).

1.3.3 Word families

The treatment of words in terms of 'word families' is a common approach in the lexicology of French (e.g. Lehmann and Martin-Berthet 1997: 109). This section, however, follows a recent treatment of English in such terms (Bauer and Nation 1993). Words are grouped into 'families' on the basis of their morphology, both their inflections and their derivations. A family consists of a base form, its possible inflectional forms, and the words derived from it by prefixation and suffixation (see Chapter 4), e.g.

(a)

Total English vocabulary

Lexical field (1) (vehicles)

Lexical field (2) (kinship terms)

Lexical field (3) (colour terms)

Lexical field (n)

(b)

Vehicles (lexical field)

Car/automobile (lexemes)

Lorry/truck (lexemes)

Bus (lexeme)

Cycle (lexeme and lexical sub-field)

Pedal cycle (lexeme)

Motor cycle (lexeme)

Train (lexeme)

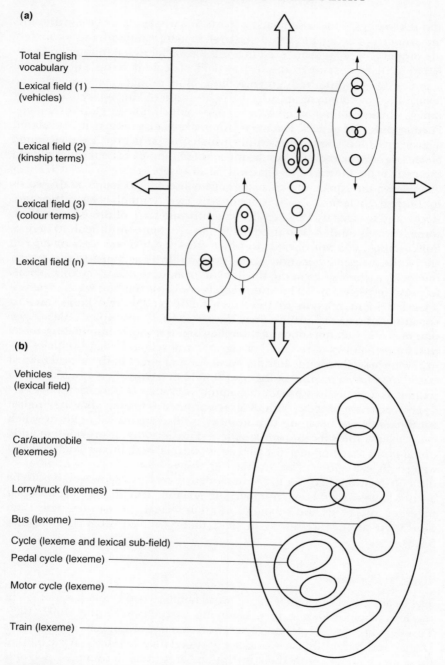

Figure 1.3a Lexical fields in the total vocabulary
Figure 1.3b Example of a lexical field

(a) state (verb)
    states, stated, stating (inflections)
    stateable, statement; misstate, restate, understate (derivations)
(b) skill (noun)
    skills, skill's, skills' (inflections)
    skilful, skilfully, skilfulness, skilless, skilled (derivations)

Bauer and Nation (1993) develop the notion of word families by proposing a set of levels into which families are divided. The levels are established on a number of criteria relating to the frequency, productivity, regularity and predictability of the affixes in English. The criteria are ordered in terms of their importance. The first concerns frequency, specifically the number of words in which an affix occurs; *-er*, for example, occurs far more frequently than *-ist* to form 'agent' nouns from verbs (*speaker, violinist*). The second criterion relates to productivity, the extent to which an affix continues to be used to form new words; *-ly* is still highly productive in deriving adverbs from adjectives (*stubbornly, speculatively*). The third relates to the predictability of the meaning of the affix; *-ness* is only used to form nouns from adjectives, with the meaning 'quality of' (*craziness, tiredness*), whereas *-ist* has a number of possible meanings. The remaining criteria concern regularity of spelling and pronunciation (of the base and affix) and regularity of the function of an affix in terms of the word class of the base to which it attaches.

Using these criteria, Bauer and Nation (1993) establish seven levels of family relationship. At the first level, each word form is regarded as a different word; so, there is no family. The second level groups words that have a common base but variant inflectional suffixes (plural and possessive for nouns; present and past tense, and present and past participle for verbs; comparative and superlative for adjectives), e.g.

Noun: road, roads, road's, roads'
Verb: fly, flies, flew, flying, flown
Adjective: great, greater, greatest.

At the third level are added words formed by the addition of 'the most frequent and regular derivational affixes', which are established on the basis of an analysis of a computer corpus (see Chapter 7), viz. *-able, -er, -ish, -less, -ly, -ness, -th, -y, non-, un-*. At level four are added forms with 'frequent, orthographically regular affixes': *-al, -ation, -ess, -ful, -ism, -ist, -ity, -ize, -ment, -ous, in-*. At level five come forms derived with some fifty 'regular but infrequent affixes', e.g. *-ary, -let, anti-, sub-*. The sixth level has forms derived by 'frequent but irregular affixes': *-able, -ee, -ic, -ify, -ion, -ist, -ition, -ive, -th, -y, pre-, re-*. Lastly, at level seven are included words formed using classical (Latin and Greek) roots and affixes, e.g. *bibliography, astronaut* and the common prefixes *ab-, ad-, com-, de-, dis-, ex-, sub-*. As an illustration, we borrow Bauer and Nation's example of the verb *develop*, which conveniently has examples at all of the levels two to six:

Level 2: develop, develops, developed, developing
Level 3: developable, undevelopable, developer(s), undeveloped
Level 4: development(s), developmental, developmentally
Level 5: developmentwise, semideveloped, antidevelopment
Level 6: redevelop, predevelopment.

The practical benefits of an analysis of vocabulary in terms of word families, especially one such as Bauer and Nation's (1993) with its carefully differentiated levels, can be found in language teaching and in lexicography. For language teachers there is a system of word building available both to pass on to their learners and to guide them in the selection of reading materials. For lexicographers, such an analysis provides a more secure basis for the treatment of affixes and derived words in dictionaries.

EXERCISE 1/4

For each of the following sets of words, say what the principle is that groups them into a set. Is the principle one of a common meaning, related forms of a lexeme, or something else (please specify)?

1.   dawdle, saunter, meander, wander, swan, tootle

2.   speak, speaks, spoke, speaking, spoken

3.   telephone, dial, number, answer, ring, engaged

4.   rich, wealthy, well-off, loaded, affluent, well-heeled, oofy

---

1.3.4 Word classes

The notion of word class may also be used to account for the structure of the vocabulary as a whole. Following an approach that can be traced back to Latin and Greek, traditional grammars of English distinguish eight parts of speech: noun, pronoun, adjective, verb, adverb, preposition, conjunction, and interjection. More modern grammarians have elaborated these parts of speech into further classes. For example, Quirk *et al.* (1985: 67) distinguish the following:

(a) closed classes: preposition, pronoun, determiner, conjunction, auxiliary verb;
(b) open classes: noun, adjective, verb, adverb;
(c) lesser categories: numeral, interjection;
(d) a small number of words of unique function: the particle *not* and the infinitive marker *to.*

The closed classes contain the so-called 'grammatical' or 'function' words, which generally serve the grammatical construction of sentences. They are small classes, with a restricted and largely unchanging membership. The open classes, by contrast, are large, and they are constantly being added to. The members of the open classes are the 'content' words, carrying the main meaning of a sentence; they are the words likely to be retained in a telegram or a headline.

It is assumed that without exception all English words must belong to one or more word classes. However, it is not generally possible to tell which word class a word belongs to, simply by looking at it, though inflections may provide a clue (e.g. a word ending in *-ing* is likely to be a verb, and one ending in *-est* an adjective). But to be sure, we need to study a word's behaviour in sentences. All words that function in the same way are deemed to belong to the same word class. For example, consider the following sentence:

> *on*
> The book was *in* the cupboard
> *under*

The words *on, in,* and *under* have the same function and express some kind of locational relationship between *the book* and *the cupboard.* Since they behave the same way in the sentence, they belong to the same word class, which we call 'preposition'. The notion of word class is therefore useful because it allows us to make general and economical statements about the way the words of a language behave. However, this notion is more useful in syntax (1.2.2) than in lexicology.

Traditional lexicology has been concerned mostly with open classes, but more recent descriptions, such as Jackson (1988) and Lipka (1990), attempt to discuss all classes of words. A close examination of the major word classes shows that they all have central and peripheral members and that they overlap. The boundaries between classes are therefore fuzzy. Moreover, a word may belong to more than one word class, e.g. *round* is an adjective in 'a round stone', a preposition in 'round the corner', an adverb in 'they all gathered round', a noun in 'you can buy the next round', and a verb in 'when we round the next bend'.

EXERCISE 1/5

(a) Closed word classes have a restricted membership: list all the personal pronouns in modern English.

(b) Attempt a definition of 'adjective'. Think of the kinds of general meaning adjectives have, their possible forms (inflections), and where they typically occur in sentence structure.

1.4 Summary

This chapter has given us at least a partial answer to the question 'What is lexicology?'. In so doing, it has established the distinction between lexicology as a level of language analysis and related fields such as phonology, morphology, syntax, semantics, etymology, and lexicography. It has also examined the various attempts made to account for the structure of the English vocabulary as a whole. Among other things, the chapter has revealed the central position of the notion of 'word' in lexicology, which we take up in Chapter 3.

2　Where Do English Words Come From?

This question calls for an investigation of the origin of English words. As useful preliminaries, we shall first place English in the context of world languages and discuss the historical development of English vocabulary from the Old English to the Modern English periods. We shall then examine in turn, native English vocabulary, and foreign elements in the English lexis. Finally, we shall discuss the creation of new words, before outlining the most important characteristics of modern English vocabulary.

2.1　The origin of English

The 5000 or so languages of the world can be grouped into about 300 language families, on the basis of similarities in their basic word stock and grammars. One of these families, the Indo-European, includes most of the languages of Europe, the Near East, and North India. One branch of the Indo-European family is called Italic, from which Latin, and later the Romance languages developed. Another is called Germanic, which had three branches: North Germanic, East Germanic, and West Germanic. It is not certain, however, whether North, East and West Germanic corresponded to actual languages.

The North Germanic branch is the linguistic ancestor of modern Scandinavian languages, viz. Danish, Swedish, Norwegian, and Icelandic. The East Germanic branch developed into Gothic, but it eventually died out. The West Germanic branch in turn developed into modern German, Dutch, Frisian, and English. Frisian, spoken in the north-west Netherlands and the island nearby known as Friesland, is considered the closest relative of English. Both languages derive from Anglo-Frisian, just as High and Low German derive from German.

2.1.1　How English came to England

The first people known to have inhabited the land that was later to become England were Celts. They are presumed to have come to the island around the middle of the fifth millennium BC. Their languages were yet another branch of the Indo-European language family.

The Celtic warriors withstood the initial attempt to add their land to the Roman Empire in 55–54 BC, but a century later they were overwhelmed by a much larger Roman army. Most of the island of Britain was occupied by the Roman legions, government officials, and their households, from about AD 43 until 410. When the Empire began to crumble, the military and government officials withdrew, leaving behind many settlements built around the installations of military government. These bore names such as *Doncaster, Gloucester, Lancaster,* and *Worcester* – all derived in part from the Latin word *castra* 'camp'.

The withdrawal of the Roman troops virtually invited the invasion of the rich lowlands by the Picts and Scots, two tribes in the north of Britain that the Romans had never conquered. The Celts appealed to bands of Germanic warriors from across the North Sea for aid in defending their land. Soon the Germanic tribes – called Angles, Saxons, Frisians, and Jutes – came in ever increasing numbers. The Celts found out too late that their new allies had become their conquerors. Although wars of resistance continued for the next 200 years, some of the Celts were pushed steadily to the fringes of the country, to Wales, Cornwall, Cumbria and the Scottish highlands. Others crossed the English Channel to join their relatives in French Brittany. Those who remained were subjected to the government of the newcomers and became assimilated to them by intermarriage. After a few generations, their identity was lost within Anglo-Saxon society.

2.1.2 *The name of the language*

The Germanic invaders referred to the native Celts as *Wealas* ('foreigners'), from which the name 'Welsh' is derived. The Celts called the invaders *Sassenachs* 'Saxons', regardless of their specific tribes, a practice which was followed by the early Latin writers. By the end of the sixth century, however, the term *Angli* 'Angles' was in use. For example, in 601, a king of Kent, Aethelbert, is called *rex Anglorum* (King of the Angles). During the seventh century, the usual Latin name for the country was *Angli* or *Anglia*. This became *Engle* in Old English, while the name of the language was referred to as *Englisc* (the *sc* spelling representing the sound 'sh'). The word *Englaland* (land of the Angles), which later gave *England*, did not appear until the beginning of the tenth century.

EXERCISE 2/1

Write a definition of the word 'English'. Then compare your version with that given in the Key to Exercises at the end of the book.

2.2 Historical development of English vocabulary

We shall discuss in turn the Old, Middle, Early Modern, and Modern English periods, with special emphasis on their respective characteristics at the lexical level. We shall also highlight the major contributions of each period to the development of English lexis as a whole.

2.2.1 The Old English period (450–1066)

The first Old English (OE) manuscripts were simply a few scattered inscriptions written around the fifth and sixth centuries in the runic alphabet brought in by the Anglo-Saxons. These scattered inscriptions give very little information on the language. The literary age began only after the arrival of the Christian missionaries from Rome in AD 597. The first OE manuscripts, dating from around 700, are glossaries of Latin words translated into Old English, and a few early inscriptions and poems. Unfortunately, very little material remains from this period. The most important literary work, which survived in a single copy, was the heroic poem *Beowulf*, written around 1000. But there were also a number of shorter poems concerned with Christian subjects or reflecting Germanic traditions and dealing with topics such as war, patriotism, travelling and celebration.

It is generally acknowledged that most OE texts were written in the period following the reign of King Alfred (849–899), who arranged the many Latin works to be translated, including Bede's *Ecclesiastical History* (Bede 731). But the total corpus is still considered relatively small. Crystal (1995: 10) points out that 'the number of words in the corpus of Old English compiled at the University of Toronto, which contains all the texts, is only 3.5 million – the equivalent of about 30 medium-sized novels'.

Since we are dealing with written records, it is important to say a word on OE letters and spelling. The OE alphabet was very similar to the one still in use today, but the absence of capital letters was a distinctive feature. Furthermore, a few letters had different shapes, while some modern letters were absent, e.g. *j, v, f, q, x* and *z*. Numbers were written only in Roman symbols. Several of the letters were used in combination (digraphs) to represent single sound units, just like modern English *th* and *ea*, as in 'tru*th*' and 'm*ea*t'. There was a great deal of variation in spelling, to such an extent that even with a single scribe in a single place at a single time, there could be variation. The same word could be spelt differently on the same page.

In most general terms, if we allow for the unfamiliar spelling and the unexpected inflections, we still notice a marked difference between the words used in prose and those used in poetic texts. While the majority of words in prose are very close to Modern English, words in poetic texts are different. For example, most of the prepositions and pronouns are identical in form (though not always in meaning): *for, from, in, he, him, his*. Modern English speakers can easily recognise *singan* as 'sing' or *stod* as 'stood'; *onslepte* is quite close to 'asleep', and *geleornode* to 'learned'. Omitting the *ge-*

prefix makes -*seted* more like 'seated', -*seah* like 'saw', and -*hyrde* like 'heard'. On the other hand, some of the words look very strange, because they have since disappeared from the language, e.g. *glimplice*, 'suitable', *swefn*, 'dream', *beboden*, 'entrusted', and some grammatical words such as *se*, 'the'.

The OE lexicon is characterized by its readiness to build up words from a number of parts, a feature that has stayed with English (see Chapter 4). As we might expect, some words may look familiar, but have a different meaning in Modern English; e.g. *wif* refers to any woman, married or not; *sona* meant 'immediately', rather than 'in a little while'; and *fæst* (fast) meant 'firm' or 'fixed', rather than 'rapidly'. These are 'false friends' when translating from Old into Modern English.

Old English is characterized by the frequent use of coinages known as 'kennings', a term from Old Norse poetic treatises referring to vivid figurative descriptions often involving compounds. Sometimes the interpretation is straightforward, sometimes it is obscure and a source of critical debate. Famous kennings include *hronrad*, 'whale-road' for the sea, *banhus*, 'bonehouse' for a person's body. Often, phrases and compound words are used. *God*, for example, is described as *heofonrinces weard*, 'guardian of heaven's kingdom', and as *mon-cynnes weard*, 'guardian of mankind'.

Kennings are sometimes a problem to interpret because the frequency of synonyms in OE makes it difficult to distinguish shades of meaning. For example, there are some twenty terms for 'man' in the herioc poem *Beowulf*, including *rinc*, *guma*, *secg* and *boern*; and it is not always easy to see why one is used instead of another. Naturally, when these words are used in compounds, the complications increase. Kennings were often chosen to satisfy the need for alliteration in a line, or to help metrical structure. In their compound forms, they also allowed a considerable compression of meanings, although many of these words, and of the elements they contain, are not known outside of poetry.

This discussion of the OE period shows that there are many differences between the way vocabulary was used in OE and the way it is used today. We shall comment on five of the most important differences. First, the Anglo-Saxon preference for expressions that are synonymous, or nearly so, far exceeds that found in Modern English, as does their ingenuity in the construction of compounds. Secondly, the absence of a wide-ranging vocabulary of loanwords also forces them to rely more on word-formation processes based on native elements. As a consequence, OE displays much larger 'families' of morphologically related words (1.3.3) than are typical of modern English. Thirdly, the latter period of OE was characterized by the introduction of a number of 'loan translations' (or 'calques'). Calques are lexical items that are translated part-by-part into another language, e.g. as *superman* was translated from German *Übermensch*. Calques are common in late OE, as can be seen from the following examples of loan translations from Latin:

Latin	Old English	Modern English
praepositio	foresetnys	preposition
conjunctio	gedeodnys	joining
unicornis	anhorn	unicorn
aspergere	onstregdan	sprinkle

Fourthly, grammatical relationships in OE were expressed mainly by the use of inflectional endings. In Middle English, they came to be expressed, as they are today, mainly by word order. This fundamental change in the structure of the language took place in the eleventh and twelfth centuries. The most plausible explanation for the disappearance of OE inflections is that it became increasingly difficult to hear them, because of the way that words had come to be stressed during the evolution of Germanic languages. By placing the main stress at the beginning of a word, it became difficult to hear the different endings, especially when they were phonetically similar, e.g. *en, on* and *an* as in *faren, faron, faran*.

Finally, the OE corpus is believed to contain about 24,000 different lexical items. However, this lexicon is fundamentally different from the one that we find in Modern English. About 85 per cent of OE words are no longer in use. Furthermore, only about 3 per cent of words in OE are loanwords, compared with over 70 per cent in Modern English. OE vocabulary was predominantly Germanic, which is no longer the case for Modern English.

Before we close this section, we must mention the Viking invasions of the eighth and ninth centuries. These invasions had a significant impact on the development of the English vocabulary (see 2.4.2 below).

EXERCISE 2/2

Examine the following lines from the Old English poem *Beowulf*. How many words can you recognize as still part of modern English vocabulary?

> Panon untydras ealle onwocon,
> Eotenas ond ylfe ond orcneas,
> Swylce gigantas, þa wið Gode wunnon
> Lange þrage; he him ðæs lean forgeald.

2.2.2 The Middle English period (1066–1500)

The Middle English period has a much richer documentation than is found in Old English. As Crystal (1995: 34) explains, this is partly due to the fact that the newly centralized monarchy commissioned national and local surveys which resulted in a marked increase in the number of public and private documents. However, the early material is of limited value, because it is largely written in Latin or French, and the only English data that can be extracted relates to places and personal names. Material in English began to appear in the thirteenth century, and during the fourteenth century there was a marked increase in the number of translated writings from Latin and French, and of texts for teaching these languages. This output increased considerably up to the 1430s.

Middle English poetry was influenced by French literary tradition, both in content and style. Much of the earlier Middle English literature is of unknown authorship, but by the end of the period the situation had changed. Among the prominent names that emerged in the latter part of the fourteenth century are John Gower, William Langland, John Wycliff, Geoffrey Chaucer, and later on poets who are collectively known as the 'Scottish Chaucerians'. It is this body of 'literature', in the modern sense of the word, that provides the final part of the bridge between Middle English and early Modern English.

The diversity in spelling was far greater than that found even in Old English. Even in an edited text, we still find variant spellings, e.g. *naure, noeure, ner, neure*, all standing for *neuer*, 'never'. This situation may be accounted for by a combination of historical, linguistic and social factors. Because of the spelling, several words look stranger than they really are. For example, *cyrceiaerd* would be close to the modern pronunication of *church-yard*, if we understand that the two *c* spellings represent a 'ch' sound, and that *i* stood for the same sound as modern *y*. Similarly, *altegaedere* is not far from *altogether*, and *laeiden* from *laid*. As the period progressed, so the spellings changed to approximate those of Modern English.

Middle English is particularly characterized by intensive and extensive borrowing from other languages. In particular the Norman conquest of 1066, which introduced French-English bilingualism into England, paved the way for a massive borrowing of French words into the English vocabulary (see 2.4.4 below). The effect of the borrowings on the balance of the vocabulary was unprecedented. In early Middle English, over 90 per cent of the lexicon was of native English (Anglo-Saxon) origin. By the end of the Middle English period, this proportion had fallen to around 75 per cent. However, loanwords were by no means the only way in which the vocabulary of Middle English increased. The processes of word formation, such as compounding and affixation, which were already established in Old English, continued to be used, and were extended in various ways.

EXERCISE 2/3

Make a modern English 'translation' of the following lines from William Langland's Piers Plowman (late fourteenth century):

Nau awaked Wrathe, wiþ two white eyes
And wiþ a nevelyng nose, and nypped his lippys.
'I am Wraþ,' quod þat weye, 'wolde gladely smyte,
Boþ wiþ stone and wiþ staf, and stel apon my enemy
To sle hym sleyliest sleʒthes Y þynke.

2.2.3 Early Modern English (1500–1800)

The transition from Middle English to Modern English would be too abrupt without the recognition of an Early Modern English period. However, there is no consensus about the beginning of this transitional period. Some consider an early date, around 1400 or 1450, others a later date, around 1500, to mark its beginning. But many consider the advent of the printing revolution as a determining factor. The year 1476, when William Caxton set up his press in Westminster, may therefore be a safe beginning point for the period. Printing played a major role in fostering the norms of spelling and pronunciation, in providing more opportunities for people to write, and in giving published works much wider circulation. As a result, more books were published, providing reliable evidence on the development of the language. Furthermore, in the sixteenth century, scholars began seriously to talk about their language, making observations on grammar, vocabulary, the writing system and style.

The period encompasses the 'Renaissance', which runs from the middle of the fifteenth century until around 1650. It is characterized by a renewed interest in the classical languages and literatures, and by major developments in the sciences and arts. It includes the Protestant Reformation, important scientific discoveries, and the exploration of Africa, Asia and the Americas. All these factors had a major impact on the English language, especially on its vocabulary. Writers began to borrow from other European languages to express the new concepts, techniques and inventions that first came from Europe. But as exploration developed worldwide, words came into English from North America, Africa and Asia. Some came directly, while others came indirectly via other European languages. Furthermore, thousands of Latin and Greek words were introduced, as translators of texts from these languages could not find precise equivalents in English, especially in fields such as medicine and theology.

The influx of foreign vocabulary attracted bitter criticism from purists, who opposed the new terms on the grounds that they were obscure and were interfering with the development of native English vocabulary. Some attempted to revive little known words from English dialects; others, such as Thomas Elyot, went out of their way to find new words in order to 'enrich' and 'credit' the language. Their objective was to bring the new learning within the reach of the English public, so as to make the English language fit not only for the street but also for the library. However, their efforts were not enough to stem the influx of new words. In fact, it is generally acknowledged that the increase in foreign borrowings is the most distinctive feature of the Renaissance for English (see Crystal 1995: 60).

It is generally agreed that the two most important influences on the development of the English language during the last decades of the Renaissance are the works of William Shakespeare (1564–1616) and the *King James Bible* of 1611. Shakespeare's work provides numerous instances of the way in which the language was developing at the time. It also gives abundant and reliable information on areas such as pronunciation, word formation, syntax, and language use. However, the Shakespearean impact on English was primarily in the area of the lexicon, because his poems and plays introduced or popularized thousands of new words in the language.

The *King James Bible* was appointed to be read in churches throughout the kingdom. Its influence on the population and on the language as a whole was therefore far-reaching. As the translators point out in the preface, they aimed for a dignified, not a popular style, opting for older forms of the language even when modern alternatives were available. Consequently, their style was more conservative than that found in Shakespeare, and unlike Shakespeare, they did not feel the need to introduce large numbers of new words. However, there are many phrases in the *King James Bible* that have entered the language as idioms, though sometimes with minor changes in grammar or emphasis, e.g. can the leopard change his spots, an eye for an eye, fight the good fight, if the blind lead the blind, a wolf in sheep's clothing, in the twinkling of an eye, money is the root of all evil, new wine in old bottles, the salt of the earth, the skin of my teeth, the straight and narrow, a thorn in the flesh. The frequency of occurrence of such phrases in both literary and everyday language is a clear indication of the impact that the *King James Bible* continues to have on contemporary English.

The period between 1530 and the Restoration in 1660 (of the monarchy, after the period of the Commonwealth) witnessed the fastest lexical growth in the history of the language. In addition to massive borrowing and the application of different types of word formation using native sources, there were also a great many semantic changes, as old words acquired new meanings. By the end of the seventeenth century, many critics felt that English was changing too rapidly and randomly. They considered the resulting language 'unruly', 'corrupt', 'unrefined' and 'barbarous'. It was therefore felt to be necessary to 'stabilize' the language, so that their works would be intelligible to future generations. However, neither Britain nor the United States chose the Academy solution for the stabilization of the language, as had the French and the Italians. The only part of the English-speaking world that has ever set up an Academy is South Africa. The debate on language corruption in the seventeenth century had the merit of drawing public attention to the need for 'preserving the consistency and stability' of the English language. Since the solution was not by means of an Academy, efforts were made to produce grammars, spelling guides, pronunciation manuals and dictionaries, from which it was expected that standards of correctness would emerge.

The importance of dictionaries had been felt long before the debate on language corruption. For example, Richard Mulcaster wrote the following in 1582: 'It were a thing verie praiseworthie if someone well learned and as laborious a man, wold gather all the words which be vse in our English tung ... into one dictionarie' (quoted in Crystal 1995: 73). In 1604, Robert Cawdrey published the first 'dictionary of hard words', which had about 3000 entries of 'hard vsuall English wordes', mostly borrowings, such as *abbettors*, glossed as 'counsellors', and *abbruiat*, glossed as 'to shorten, or make short'. It was in fact the first synonym dictionary, and it was followed by other compilations on similar lines. In 1721, Nathaniel Bailey published his *Universal Etymological English Dictionary*, which was a marked improvement on the previous 'hard word' dictionaries. Bailey gives more and fuller entries, but his definitions still lack illustrative support, and he gives little guidance on usage.

The English lexicon received its first really authoritative treatment in 1755, when Samuel Johnson published his *Dictionary of the English Language*. Although he has fewer entries than Bailey, his selection is considered more wide-ranging and his lexicological treatment more discriminating and sophisticated (Crystal 1995: 74). Another important feature of Johnson's *Dictionary* is that the alphabetical section is preceded by a preface in which he outlines his aims and procedures. The preliminaries also include a short history of the language, and a grammar, with sections on orthography and prosody. Johnson made a major departure from the prevailing prescriptive, to a descriptive approach in lexicography. In his preface, he stressed that his aim was to 'not form, but register the language'; and it is this principle that introduced a new era in lexicography. This work dominated the dictionary market for decades and appeared in several editions for much of the next century, when it began to receive a great deal of criticism. However, as Crystal (1995: 75) puts it: 'the fact remains that Johnson's *Dictionary* was the first attempt at a truly principled lexicography'. Among other things it was the first accurate description of the complexity of the lexicon and of word usage.

EXERCISE 2/4

Examine the following extract from George Fox's *Journal* (mid-seventeenth century). How does it differ in vocabulary from modern English?

> & before I was brought in before him ye garde saide It was well if ye Justice was not drunke before wee came to him for hee used to bee drunke very early: & when I was brought before him because I did not putt off my hatt & saide thou to him hee askt ye man whether I was not Mased or fonde: & I saide noe: Itt was my principle ...

2.2.4 The Modern English period (1800–present)

The Modern English period runs from the beginning of the nineteenth century to the present day. As in the case of the preceding periods, the change from Early Modern to Modern was equally gradual and imperceptible. For example, while it may be observed that many of the words used today had a different meaning in the eighteenth century, it would be very difficult to say exactly when the change of meaning occurred.

From the point of view of lexis, Modern English may be characterized by three main features: the unprecedented growth of scientific vocabulary, the assertion of American English as a dominant variety of the language, and the emergence of other varieties known as 'New Englishes' (see 6.2).

English scientific and technical vocabulary has been growing steadily since the Renaissance. But the nineteenth century saw an unprecedented growth in this domain, as a consequence of the industrial revolution and the subsequent period of scientific exploration and discovery. The steady increase in the level of education made the general public more and more curious about and interested in science and technology. Consequently, most discoveries, such as Faraday's, and theories, such as Darwin's, received widespread publicity. By the end of the nineteenth century, one could actually speak of 'scientific English' as a variety of the language (see 6.3). The characteristics of this variety are made explicit in grammar books and style guides of academic journals. Some sciences, such as chemistry, physics and biology, made spectacular lexical developments during this period.

The strong linguistic influence of American English as a dominant variety of the language can be explained, at least in part, by the emergence of the USA as the leading economic power of the twentieth century. This influence is felt directly in the areas of pronunciation and grammar, but more especially at the lexical level. Although there are still marked differences between American and British English (see 6.2.1), it must be acknowledged that the two varieties are becoming more and more alike, for several reasons: communication systems have improved greatly since the beginning of the twentieth century, the USA has become more and more involved in world affairs, the UK, just like the rest of Europe, is increasingly open to American culture, and finally the development of the mass media is playing an important role in this process. The assertion of American English is made even stronger by the Americans' numerical strength. In fact, the USA contains nearly four times as many speakers of English as a first language as the UK, and according to Crystal (1995: 106) these two countries comprise 70 per cent of all speakers of English as a first language in the world. Such dominance, with its political and economic correlates, makes American English a force to reckon with in any discussion of how the English language is likely to develop.

The concept of 'New Englishes' refers to new varieties of the language that have become localized not only through the influence of the other languages of the regions where they are used, but also through being adapted to the life and culture of their speakers. They are considered varieties of English in their own right, just like the 'older' Englishes, such as British and American English. These new Englishes have their origin in the colonial era. Well-known examples include Indian English, Philippine English, Singapore English, and African Englishes of such nations as Cameroon, Ghana and Nigeria. Vocabulary is the area in which these new Englishes best assert themselves.

In addition to new Englishes that are associated with a given geographical area, we must also mention the varieties of the language based on subject matter (see 6.3). These have also known an accelerated development during the Modern English period. Some, such as telecommunications and computing, are relatively new; others, such as religious and legal English, find their origins in earlier periods.

EXERCISE 2/5

Look up the history of the following words, preferably in the *(Shorter) Oxford English Dictionary*, otherwise in a dictionary with good coverage of etymology (e.g. *Collins English Dictionary, New Oxford Dictionary of English*). How has their meaning changed since their first entry into the language?

    cousin, hose, knight, nice, span, spell, starve, train

2.3 Native English vocabulary

Native English vocabulary is made up of Anglo-Saxon words; but we shall also discuss the influence of Celtic on English.

2.3.1 Anglo-Saxon words

This category consists of words that arrived with the Germanic invaders and are still used in modern English. Some are grammatical words, such as *be, in, that*, while others are lexical words: *father, love, name*. Most of them are the common words of the language. They constitute a nucleus or central mass of many thousand words with an undisputed claim to 'Anglicity' or English-ness. Some of them are only literary, some only colloquial, while the great majority are both literary and colloquial.

Anglo-Saxon words are generally short and concrete; e.g. parts of the body (arm, bone, chest, ear, eye, foot, hand, heart), the natural landscape (field, hedge, hill, land, meadow, wood), domestic life (door, floor, home, house), the calendar (day, month, moon, sun, year), animals (cow, dog, fish, goat, hen, sheep, swine), common adjectives (black, dark, good, long, white, wide), and common verbs (become, do, eat, fly, go, help, kiss, live, love, say, see, sell, send, think) (see Crystal 1995: 124).

2.3.2 *The influence of Celtic on English*

The conditions of cultural contact between the Celts and the invading Anglo-Saxons were such that the Celtic language could not have any serious impact on Old English. Only a handful of Celtic words were borrowed at the time, and just a few have survived into modern English, sometimes in regional dialect use: *crag, cumb,* 'deep valley', *binn,* 'bin', *carr,* 'rock', *torr,* 'peak' and *luh* (Scots *loch,* Irish *lough*), 'lake'. A few Celtic words of this period derive ultimately from Latin, brought in by the Irish missionaries, e.g. *assen,* 'ass', *ancor,* 'hermit', and possibly *cross*. There are a few Celtic-based placenames in what is now southern and eastern England. They include river names such as *Avon,* 'river', *Don, Exe, Ouse, Severn, Thames, Trent, Usk* and *Wye.* Town names include: *Bray,* 'hill', *Dover,* 'water', *Eccles,* 'church', *Kent, Leeds, London* (a tribal name), *York,* and the use of *caer,* 'fortified place' (as in *Carlisle*) and of *pen,* 'head, top, hill' (as in *Pendle*).

In more recent times, a few more Celtic words were introduced into English from Irish Gaelic in the seventeenth century – brogue, galore, shamrock, tory – and later on: banshee, blarney, colleen. From Scots Gaelic come: clan, loch, bog, slogan, whisky. And from Welsh: *crag,* occurring first in Middle English. Probably there are no more than two dozen Celtic loanwords in all. Consequently, Celtic has had a rather negligible influence on English. English is, thus, basically a Germanic language.

EXERCISE 2/6

(a) Take two pages from your dictionary, one from the letter 'h' and one from the letter 't', and count how many words have, according to the etymology, their immediate origin in Anglo-Saxon (A-S) or Old English (OE). What is the proportion of OE words on these two pages?

(b) Now take the first 100 words of a news article in a newspaper, and, by looking up the etymology of each word in your dictionary, calculate the proportion of OE words in the extract. If a word occurs more than once, include each occurrence in your count.

How do the two proportions differ?

2.4 The process of borrowing

By definition, when speakers imitate a word from a foreign language and, at least partly, adapt it in sound or grammar to their native language, the process is called 'borrowing', and the word thus borrowed is called a 'loanword' or 'borrowing'. There is a sense in which neither term is really appropriate, on the grounds that the receiving languages never return the borrowed words (Crystal 1995: 126). English may be considered an insatiable borrower, in the sense that, while other languages take special measures to exclude foreign words from their lexicons, English seems to have welcomed such words throughout its history, especially from the Middle English period onwards. It is estimated that over 120 languages from all over the world have been sources of present-day English vocabulary.

The history of a loanword may be quite complex, because such words may have come to English not directly, but via another language or two. According to Crystal (1995: 285), 'loanwords have, as it were, a life of their own that cuts across the boundaries between languages'. To give a stock example, *chess* was borrowed into English from Middle French in the fourteenth century. The French word (plural *esches*, singular *eschec*) came from Arabic, which had earlier borrowed it from Persian *shah*, 'king'. Thus the etymology may be traced from Persian, through Arabic and Middle French, to English. So, the direct or immediate source of *chess* is Middle French, but its ultimate source (as far back as we can trace its history) is Persian.

We shall now discuss in turn English borrowings from a number of languages, beginning with Latin.

2.4.1 Latin words in English

Latin has been a major influence on English right from the Germanic period up to modern times. The degree of this influence has varied from one period to another.

The Anglo-Saxons must have encountered Latin as used by the continental Roman armies; but only a few words have subsequently come into English as a result of these early contacts. In England, some early borrowings were concerned with the miltary domain, commerce and agriculture; others dealt with refinements of living, which the Germanic people acquired from their continental contacts with the Romans, e.g. words relating to clothing (*belt*, 'belt', *cemes*, 'shirt', *sutere*, 'shoemaker'), buildings and settlements (*tigle*, 'tile', *weal*, 'wall', *caester*, 'city', *straet*, 'road'), military and legal institutions, commerce and religion (*maesse*, 'mass', *munyc*, 'monk', *mynster*, 'monastery'). It is generally established that the total number of Latin words present in English at the very beginning of the Anglo-Saxon period is less than 200 items. Most of these items indicate special spheres in which the Romans excelled, or were believed to do so by the Germanic peoples. Many of these words have survived into modern English, including: *ancor*, 'anchor' (Lat. *ancora*), *butere*, 'butter' (Lat. *butyrum*), *caelc*, 'chalk' (Lat. *calco*), *cese*, 'cheese' (Lat. *coquina*), *disc*, 'dish' (Lat. *discus*), *mile*, 'mile' (Lat. *milia*), *piper*, 'pepper' (Lat. *piper*), *pund*, 'pound' (Lat. *pondo*), *sacc*, 'sack' (Lat. *saccus*), *sicol*, 'sickle' (Lat. *secula*), *weall*, 'wall' (Lat. *vallum*).

The labels 'popular' and 'learned' are often used to refer to the main categories of words borrowed during this early period (Pyles and Algeo 1993: 288). Popular loanwords were transmitted orally and constituted part of the vocabulary used in everyday, non-specialized communication, e.g. *plante*, 'plant', *win*, 'wine', *catte*, 'cat', *straete*, 'road'. Most speakers would consider these words to be native English words and are generally not aware of their foreign origin. As for learned words, they came into English either through the church or through more or less scholarly influences. Some learned words may in time have passed into general use, e.g. *clerk*, from Latin *clericus* or Old French *clerc*.

Borrowing from Latin during the Old English period increased over that during the earlier Germanic period, but the popular/learned distinction continues to apply. In fact up to 1000 AD, many words continued to be borrowed from spoken Latin, dealing with everyday practical matters. However, after 1000, owing to renewed interest in learning encouraged by King Alfred and the tenth century Benedictine monastic revival, borrowings came from classical written sources. Most of these terms were scholarly and technical.

Among the early English borrowings, some were acquired not directly from Latin, but from the British Celts, e.g. *candel*, 'candle', *cest*, 'chest' (Lat. *cista/cesta*), *crisp*, 'curly' (Lat. *crispus*), *maegester*, 'master' (Lat. *magister*), *mynster*, 'monastery' (Lat. *monasterium*), *port*, 'harbour' (Lat. *portus*), *sealm*, 'psalm' (Lat. *psalmus*, from Greek), *tilge*, 'tile' (Lat. *tegula*). Later borrowings are characterized by the fact that the English form is closer to the Latin word, e.g. *alter*, 'altar' (Lat. *altar*), *(a)postol*, 'apostle' (Lat. *apostolus*), *balsam*, 'balsam' (Lat. *balsamum*), *circul*, 'circle' (Lat. *circulus*), *demon* (Lat. *daemon*), *martir*, 'martyr' (Lat. *martyr*). Since Latin borrowed freely from Greek, some of the loanwords are ultimately of Greek origin, e.g. apostle, balsam, demon. During this period, a number of Old English words were given new 'Christian' meanings, under missionary influence: heaven, hell, God, gospel, Easter, holy, ghost, sin.

It is generally estimated that around 500 words in total were borrowed from Latin during the entire Old English period. This is a relatively small number compared with Latin borrowings in later times. Furthermore, many Latin loanwords, especially from the later OE period, were not widely used, and some fell out of use. Some were borrowed again at a later period, perhaps with a different meaning. For instance, modern English *sign* and *giant* are not survivors from Latin borrowings into Old English (*sign*, *gigant*), but more recent borrowings from French *signe* and *géant*.

In the Middle English period, French is undoubtedly the dominant influence on the growth of Middle English vocabulary, between the Norman conquest and 1500 (see 2.4.4). Many borrowings also occurred directly from Latin during that period, though it is often difficult to specify whether a word was borrowed from French or from Latin. For instance, on the basis of their form alone, the words *nature, register, relation* and *rubric* might be from either language.

Most of the Latin borrowings in this period were professional or technical terms, belonging to fields such as religion, law and literature, scholastic activities and sciences in general. Religious terms include: collect (short prayer), mediator, redeemer. Legal terms include: client, conviction, subpoena. Connected with scholastic activities are: library, scribe, simile. And scientific words include: dissolve, equal, essence, medicine, mercury, quadrant. Several hundred such words were borrowed before 1500. A more extensive list would include verbs (admit, commit, discuss, seclude) and adjectives (complete, imaginary, instant, legitimate, populous). Latin words were borrowed by some writers in a deliberate attempt to produce literary or elevated styles, but only a few such terms entered the language (e.g. mediation, oriental, prolixity), while most disappeared soon after borrowing (e.g. abusion, sempitern, tenebrous).

The simultaneous borrowing of French and Latin words led to a highly distinctive feature of modern English vocabulary: sets of three items (triplets), all expressing the same fundamental notion but differing slightly in meaning or style, e.g. kingly, royal, regal; rise, mount, ascend; ask, question, interrogate; fast, firm, secure; holy, sacred, consecrated. The Old English word (the first in each triplet) is the most colloquial, the French (the second) is more literary, and the Latin word (the last) more learned.

Borrowing continued into the Modern English period, both from Latin, and from Greek via Latin. The Early Modern period saw an avalanche of Latin words, including: abdomen, area, digress, editor, fictitious, folio, graduate, imitate, lapse, medium, notorious, orbit, peninsula, quota, resuscitate, sinecure, superintendent, urban, vindicate.

By contrast with the Early Modern period, when exisiting Latin words were borrowed, in the later Modern period, English has borrowed words or morphemes from Latin, but fashioned them into new words that Latin never knew. Such neo-Latin or neo-classical words (see 4.5.3) are used abundantly not only in the international vocabulary of science and technology, but also in other areas of modern life. Examples of such coinages are: *aleatoric*, 'dependent on chance' (from *aleator*, 'gambler'), *circadian*, 'functioning or recurring in 24-hour cycles' (from *circa diem*, 'around the day'), *pax americana*, 'peace enforced by American power' (modelled on *pax romana*), *vexillology*, 'study of flags' (from *vexillum*, 'flag').

This discussion of loanwords from Latin shows that Latin is not only the first major contributor of loanwords to English, but also one of the most important sources for the coinage of new English words.

2.4.2 Scandinavian loanwords in English

The second major influence on English lexis came as a result of the Viking raids on Britain, which began in AD 787 and continued at intervals for some 200 years. In fact, by the mid-ninth century, the Danes controlled most of eastern England, which became known as Danelaw. Further invasion in 991 resulted in the English king being forced into exile and the Danes seizing the throne. England was then under Danish rule for 25 years. The linguistic effect of this prolonged period of contact between the Anglo-Saxons and the Danish settlers was threefold. First, a large number of settlements with

Danish names appeared in England. Secondly, there was a marked increase in personal names of Scandinavian origin. And finally, many general words entered the language and became part of common English vocabulary.

Scandinavian placenames are particularly common in Yorkshire and Lincolnshire. Some end in -by, the Scandinavian word for 'farm' or 'town', e.g. Derby, Grimsby, Rugby, Naseby. Others end in -thorpe, 'village' (Althorpe, Astonthorpe, Linthorpe), -thwaite, 'clearing' (Braithwaite, Applethwaite, Storthwaite), -toft, 'homestead' (Lowestoft, Eastoft, Sand- toft). Although the word by, 'dwelling' existed in Old English, the -by ending is of Scandinavian origin. This is justified by the fact that placenames with this ending are almost entirely confined to the area of Danelaw (Crystal 1995: 25).

For personal names, a close examination of early Middle English records reveals a strong Scandinavian influence in the north and east, especially in Yorkshire and north Lincolnshire, where over 60 per cent of personal names seem to have been affected. Many of these names end in -son: Davidson, Jackson, Henderson.

With two cultures in such close contact for so long, we would expect extensive borrowing. However, most of the Scandinavian words in Old English did not actually occur in written records until the Middle English period. Because of the close relationship between Old Norse and Old English, many Scandinavian words resemble their English cognates so closely that it would be impossible to tell whether a given word was Scandinavian or English. Sometimes, if the meanings of obviously related words differed, semantic contamination took place, as when Old English *dream*, 'joy' acquired the meaning of the related Scandinavian *draum*, 'vision in sleep'.

Some of the commonest words in modern English came into the lan- guage at this time. They were made to conform wholly or in part with the English sound and inflectional systems. For example, Pyles and Algeo (1993: 294) note that the very common verbs *get* and *give* come to us not from Old English *gitan* and *gifan*, but from cognate Scandinavian forms. Even the personal pronoun system was affected, with *they*, *them* and *their* replacing earlier forms of the third person plural. One of the most remark- able borrowings relates to the verb *be*: 'the replacement of *sidon* by *are* is almost certainly the result of Scandinavian influence, as is the spread of the third personal singular *-s* ending in the present tense in other verbs' (Crystal 1995: 25).

A good many words with *sc-/sk-* are of Scandinavian origin: scathe, scorch, score, scowl, scrape, scrub, skill, skin, skirt, sky. Scandinavian loans some- times involve little more than the substitution of one word for another (such as *window* for *vindauga*), but some borrowings expressed new concepts (such as certain Scandinavian legal terms) or new things (for various kinds of Viking warship). A large number of duplicate words also arose from the contact. In such cases, both Old Norse (ON) and Old English (OE) provided ways of denoting the same object or situation. In some cases the

ON word was retained, e.g. *egg* vs. OE *ey, sister* vs. OE *sweoster, silver* vs. OE *sealfor*. In others the OE word survived, as in *path* vs. ON *reike, sorrow* vs. ON *site, swell* vs. ON *bolnen*. In a number of cases both words survived, but developed a useful difference in meaning:

ON		OE	
	dike		ditch
	hale		whole
	raise		rise
	sick		ill
	skill		craft
	skirt		shirt

Sometimes, where two forms have survived, one is considered standard and the other dialectal. In the following examples, the first word from OE is standard, while the ON equivalent is dialectal: cast/werpan, yard/garth, church/kirk, leap/laup, no/nay, true/trigg. As a final observation, it should be noted that a number of Scandinavian words continued to be borrowed even during the Modern English period: muggy, rug, scud, ski. More recent borrowings include: geyser, rune, saga, ombudsman.

2.4.3 Greek loanwords

As a classical language, Greek provided English, as well as other European languages, with a considerable number of technical terms in all branches of human knowledge. This need was perhaps most strongly felt by the English humanists, who wanted their language to be capable of expressing the most refined thoughts, just like Latin and Greek. Some Greek words were borrowed via Latin and French, some were derived from Greek and Latin elements, while others were taken directly from Greek.

Even before the Norman conquest in 1066, a number of Greek words had entered English by way of Latin, in addition to some very early loans such as *church*, which may have come into Germanic directly from Greek. From the Middle English period onwards, Latin and French were the immediate sources of most loanwords ultimately from Greek. But it was only in the Early Modern English period, from around 1500, that Greek influence became most noticeable. Greek words that came into English via Latin include: allegory, anaesthesia, chaos, dilemma, drama, enthusiasm, history, metaphor, paradox, phenomenon, rhythm, theory, zone. Those coming via French include: centre, character, chronicle, democracy, ecstasy, harmony, machine, pause, tyrant. The following came directly from Greek, though some are combinations unknown in classical times: acronym, autocracy, idiosyncracy, pathos, telegram, xylophone. Incidentally, the terms 'lexis', 'lexeme', 'lexical', 'lexicographer', 'dictionary' and 'vocabulary' are all derived from Greek and Latin elements.

Many of the Greek loanwords were considered learned, and some still are; but others have passed into the stock of more or less everyday vocabulary. Although Greek had considerable prestige as a classical language, it did not have the same influence as Latin, which was the language of literature, science, and religion, as well as the medium of instruction in European universities well into the seventeenth century and in some cases beyond. However, Greek studies received an enormous boost when Greek scholars fled to Europe following the conquest of Constantinople in 1453 by the Turks.

2.4.4 French loanwords

Borrowing from French has occurred ever since the Middle Ages, although not always on the same scale. Before 1066, there were close contacts between the English and French cultures following the exile to Normandy of Edward the Confessor, the son of Aethelred II and Emma, daughter of the Duke of Normandy. In fact, Edward lived there for 25 years, returning in 1041 with many French courtiers. When he acceded to the throne, several of the French nobles were given high positions. Furthermore, the monastic revival started in France, and many English monks would have studied there. The linguistic consequences of these contacts was the borrowing of some French words into Old English, e.g. *servian*, 'serve', *bacun*, 'bacon', *arblast*, 'weapon', *prisun*, 'prison', *castel*, 'castle', *cancelere*, 'chancellor'.

Following William, Duke of Normandy's accession to the English throne in 1066, Norman French became the language of government, the courts, and the new upper social classes. Within twenty years of the invasion, almost all the religious houses were under French-speaking superiors, and several new foundations were solely French. Such a context was favourable for the development of French-English bilingualism: many English people learned French to gain advantage from the aristocracy, while many Norman French learned English in their daily contacts with local communities.

As the period progressed, the influence of French vocabulary on English became increasingly noticeable. It is estimated that by the end of the thirteenth century, some 10,000 French words had come into English. These words were in part to do with law and administration, but they also included words from fields such as medicine, arts, fashion, and everyday life. According to Crystal (1995: 46) over 70 per cent were nouns, a great proportion of which were abstract terms constructed using French affixes, such as *con-*, *trans-*, *pre-*, *-ance*, *-tion*, *-ment*. Crystal concludes that three-quarters of these French loans are still in use in English today.

The following words, which have to do with lay and spiritual administration, are of French origin: government, administration, attorney, chancellor, court, crime (replacing OE *sin*, which is then confined to religious vocabulary), judge, jury. Words in the religious sphere include: abbot, clergy, preach, sacrament. Words designating titles of nobility include: prince, duke, marquess, viscount, baron – and their female equivalents. In military usage English borrowed: army, captain, corporal, lieutenant, sergeant, soldier. All the names of the best-known precious stones are French: amethyst, diamond, emerald, garnet, pearl, ruby, sapphire, topaz, turquoise. French names were given to various animals when served up as food: beef, mutton, pork, veal – and their OE equivalents are restricted to the live animal (cow, sheep, etc.). Words were also borrowed for culinary processes: boil, fry, roast, stew.

During the Middle English period, some words were borrowed from Norman French spoken in England (Anglo-Norman), others from Central French, which later became the standard in France. It is possible to tell by the form of a word whether it is of Norman or Central French origin. For instance, Old French *w* was retained in Norman French, but changed to *gw* and then *g* in standard French. Hence, the words *wage* and *warrant* were borrowed from Norman French, while *gage* and *guarantee* came from Central French. With similar sound changes, we may show that *chapter* and *chattel* came from Central French, while *cattle* is from Norman French.

It is reckoned that during this period the rate of adoption of French words by English was greater than it had ever been before or has ever been since. A statistical survey by Jespersen (1954: 86–7) of a thousand French loanwords from the *Oxford English Dictionary* shows that nearly half of the loanwords were adopted during the period. Many of the words borrowed duplicated words that already existed in English. In some cases, one of the words supplanted the other, in others both were retained but developed slightly different meanings or connotations. For example, *leod* gave way to *people*, *wlitig* to *beautiful*, and *stow* to *place*. Hundreds of Old English words were lost in this way. Cases where both OE and French words survive include: doom/judgment, hearty/cordial, house/mansion. Conscious of the difficulties caused by such doublets, specialists compiled bilingual word lists to aid intelligibility between English and French.

Borrowing from French continued during the Modern English period, though not on the same scale. There are cases where the same French word was borrowed at different times in the history of English. For example, *gentle, genteel* and *jaunty* are all from French *gentil*; the last two were borrowed during the seventeenth century. Similarly, *chief* first occurred in English in the fourteenth century, and *chef* in the nineteenth. Generally speaking, doublets show by their pronunciation the approximate time of their adoption. So, the pronunciation of the 'ch' shows that *chamber, champion, chance* were borrowed in Middle English times, while *chauffeur, chevron, chiffon* were borrowed in the Modern English period. Similarly, the position of the main stress is frequently evidence of the period of borrowing. Thus, *carriage, courage, village* came into English in the Middle English period and have acquired initial stress, following the normal English pattern, while more recent borrowings, such as *prestige, balloon, mademoiselle*, do not follow this pattern.

In general, French words borrowed since the seventeenth century are less completely naturalized than older loans, e.g. amateur, boulevard, crochet, detour, ensemble, liaison, massage, nuance, rapport, vignette. Later borrowings from French also reflect French dominance in the spheres of fashion, lifestyle, arts and sciences: gown, luxury, romance, tragedy, engineer, physician. And we must not forget gastronomic terms: casserole, crème brûlée, hors d'oeuvre, restaurant.

Let us also note, finally, that English has some loan translations from French, e.g. *marriage of convenience* (*mariage de convenance*), *that goes without saying* (*cela va sans dire*), *trial balloon* (*ballon d'essai*), *reason of state* (*raison d'état*).

2.4.5 German and Dutch loans

From the Middle Ages on, commercial relationships have existed between Flemish/Dutch and English-speaking peoples. In these contacts, English borrowed from Dutch and other forms of Low German. Because of the eminence of the Dutch in seafaring activities, their language has contributed many nautical terms to English, e.g. bowline, bowsprit, buoy, commodore, cruise, deck, skipper, smuggle, yacht. The Dutch and Flemish were also famous for their cloth making and associated commercial activities. England imported the goods together with the words denoting them, e.g. cambric, duck (cloth), jacket, nap, spool. Other commercial terms include: dollar, groat, guilder, mart.

Loanwords from other Low German dialects include: boor (lover), broke, isinglass, luck, skate, snap, wagon.

A number of loanwords came into English through contact between Americans and Dutch settlers, especially in the New York area, e.g. Dutch American food items such as *coleslaw* (*koolsla*, 'cabbage salad'), *cookie, cranberry, waffle.* The diversity of the contacts accounts for the wide range of loans: boodle, boss, caboose, dope, lowery, noop, Santa Claus (Sante Klaas, 'Saint Nicholas'), spook. From South African Dutch (Afrikaans), English has borrowed: apartheid, commandeer, commando, kraal, outspan, spoor, trek, veld.

When compared to Low German, High German has had comparatively little impact on English. Words have been borrowed in specialist fields such as geology and mineralogy, e.g. cobalt, feldspar, gneiss, nickel, quartz, seltzer, zinc. Some food and drink terms have accompanied their items: delicatessen, frankfurter, noodle, schnapps. Otherwise, it is a small miscellany of borrowings: angst, ersatz, Gestalt, hinterland, leitmotiv, rucksack, umlaut, waltz, Weltanschauung.

2.4.6 Romance loans other than from French

In addition to Latin and French, English has borrowed from other Romance languages such as Spanish, Portuguese and Italian.

Most of the borrowings from Spanish and Portuguese have occurred from the sixteenth century onwards. English has borrowed directly from Spanish, and to a lesser extent from Portuguese, but in addition many non-European words from the colonies found their way into English via these two languages. Many of these loanwords came from the New World: alligator (*el lagarto,* 'the lizard'), avocado, barracuda, canoe, chocolate, cigar, cockroach, domino, embargo, mosquito (little fly), peccadillo, potato, sombrero, tobacco, tomato, tornado, tortilla, vanilla.

In the nineteenth century it became fashionable for Americans to adopt words from Spanish, accounting for the following: bonanza, canyon, lasso, mustang, patio, ranch, sierra, siesta, stampede. The twentieth century is characterized by loan translations such as *moment of truth* (*momento de la verdad* – referring to the 'moment of kill' in a bullfight). Virtually all loanwords from Portuguese have entered English during the modern period, including: albino, copra, flamingo, madeira, mango, marmalade, molasses, palaver, teak.

Italian has had a particular significance for musical vocabulary, and other arts. Borrowing has occurred over a long period, starting in the sixteenth century with: duo, fugue, madrigal, violin. These were followed in the seventeenth century with: allegro, largo, opera, piano, presto, solo, sonata. But it was during the eighteenth century that interest in Italian music reached its peak in England, and there were numerous loanwords, including: adagio, andante, aria, cantata, concerto, crescendo, duet, finale, forte, obligato, oratorio, soprano, trio, trombone, viola. The process continued in the nineteenth century with the adoption of: alto, cadenza, legato, piccolo, prima-donna.

Other loanwords from Italian include: balcony, balloon, carnival, dilettante, fresco, ghetto, grotto, incognito, inferno, lagoon, malaria, miniature, portico, regatta, stiletto, studio, torso, umbrella, vendetta, volcano. Some Italian words came via French: cartoon, citron, corridor, gazette, porcelain. Italian food has also left its mark on English vocabulary, often by way of American English: lasagne, macaroni, pizza, scampi, etc.

2.4.7 Loans from the East

A number of words of Arabic origin were borrowed during the Middle English period, mostly to do with science and commerce. Some came via French or Latin. Examples include: admiral, amber, camphor, cipher, cotton, lute, mattress, orange, saffron, syrup, zenith. The Arabic definite article *al* is retained in one form or another in: alchemy, alcohol, algebra, algorithm, alkali, almanac, azimuth, elixir, hazard. Borrowing from Arabic has continued up to modern times, sometimes via Italian or French, including the following items: assassin, calibre, carat, garble, giraffe, hashish, lemon, magazine, sherbet.

Other Semitic languages have contributed little directly, though a number of Hebrew words have come into English, either directly (*kibbutz*) or by way of French (*amen, hallelujah, rabbi, sabbath*) or Yiddish (*chutzpah*).

A few words have been borrowed from Persian: caravan, bazaar, shah, shawl. Other Persian loanwords have come via Latin or French: azure, musk, paradise, scarlet, tiger.

From the Indian subcontinent, English has borrowed a few words from

Sanskrit (avatar, karma, mahatma, yoga), some from Tamil (curry, pariah), and a number from Hindi/Urdu: bangle, dungaree, jungle, pajamas, shampoo.

Words borrowed from the Far East and Australia are comparatively few in number, except in the local varieties (see 6.2). But there are some very common words from that area. *Silk* may ultimately be from Chinese, though there is no known etymon in Chinese languages. Also ultimately from Chinese are *judo*, *tycoon* and *kamikaze*, but they came into English via Japanese. Directly from Japanese are: kimono, samurai, soy(a). Australia has given English *kangeroo* and *boomerang*, among a few others.

2.4.8 *Loanwords from other sources*

English has borrowed a few words from West African languages, mostly via Portuguese and Spanish, e.g. *banana* and *yam*, which first appeared towards the end of the sixteenth century. Likewise, *voodoo*, with its variant *hoodoo*, which came in through American English, is of African origin. *Gorilla* is apparently African in origin. More recent borrowings from this source include: okro, chimpanzee, gnu, safari, zebra.

Most of the other borrowings have been made in modern times. *Sable*, however, came into English in Middle English times, via French from Slavic languages; *polka* came via French in the nineteenth century from Czech. *Mammoth* was borrowed in the eighteenth century directly from Russian. Other more recent borrowings from Russian have not become completely naturalized: bolshevik, czar, glasnost, intelligentsia (ultimately from Latin), perestroika, tundra, vodka. From Hungarian, English has borrowed directly *goulash* and *paprika*; while *coach* came via French from Hungarian *kosci*. Turkish words in English include: fez, shish kebab.

From Native American languages have come: moccassin, toboggan, tomahawk, skunk. And many American place names have their origin in these languages, e.g. Chicago, Michigan, Saratoga, Tallahassie.

2.4.9 *Sources of most recent loans*

English still borrows, and is likely to continue borrowing from other languages of the world. However, borrowing in recent times is characterized by two main factors: the frequency of borrowing is considerably reduced; and English seems to be spreading its tentacles to reach and borrow from less and less known languages. A study by Garland Cannon (1987) of more than a thousand recent loanwords from 84 languages shows that 'about 25% are from French, 8% each from Japanese and Spanish, 7% each from Italian and Latin, 6% each from African languages, German and Greek, 4% each from Russian and Yiddish, 3% from Chinese, and progressively smaller percentages from Arabic, Portuguese, Hindi, Sanskrit, Hebrew, Afrikaans, Malayo-Polynesian, Vietnamese, Amerindian languages, Swedish, Bengali, Danish, Indonesian, Korean, Persian, Amharic, Eskimo-Alent, Irish, Norwegian, and 30 other languages' (quoted in Pyles and Algeo 1993: 310).

French is still the largest supplier of words to English, which may be because of the geographical proximity of France and Britain. We would, therefore, expect more French words to enter via British English than American. Similarly, Spanish loanwords are often borrowed from American Spanish into American English. The increase in the importance of Japanese as a source of loans is probably a consequence of the increased commercial importance of Japan in the world generally. The decline of Latin as a source of loanwords may have a dual explanation: on the one hand, it may be argued that English has already borrowed so much of Latin vocabulary that there is relatively little left to be borrowed; on the other hand, rather than borrowing directly from Latin, English now often makes new Latinate words from English morphemes originally from Latin.

EXERCISE 2/7

The previous sections have illustrated just how many words in the modern English vocabulary are borrowed from other languages. Without going back over these sections, peruse the etymologies in your dictionary and list five words that have been borrowed into English at some time or other from each of the following languages:

French, Italian, Spanish, Latin, Greek.

2.5 Creating new English words

This section briefly reviews the processes used in creating new words in English, other than by borrowing. They are discussed in more detail in Chapter 4.

2.5.1 Root creation

'Root creation' refers to the building of a word that has no relationship whatsoever with any previously existing word. An often quoted example is *Kodak*, which was first used in print in the *USA Patent Office Gazette* of 1888. According to George Eastman, who invented the word and the device it referred to, *Kodak* is a 'purely arbitrary combination of letters, not derived in whole or part from any existing word' (quoted in Pyles and Algeo 1993: 258). Most tradenames, however, which may look like root creation, are usually suggested by already existing words. For example, *Vaseline* was created from German *Wasser*, 'water' and Greek *elaion*, 'oil'; *Kleenex* derives from *clean* and *curtex*. In the course of history, very few words have been coined by root creation.

2.5.2 Echoic words

'Echoic' or 'onomatopoeic' words find their origin in the specific sound that they are meant to represent, e.g. bang, burp, cuckoo, ping, splash, tinkle. Bloomfield (1933: 156) distinguishes two types of echoic words: 'imitative' and 'symbolic'. The first type intends to imitate the sound that it represents: meow, moo, bow-wow, vroom. The second has a less direct association with the sound: bump, flick. Symbolic words often come in sets, which either rhyme (bump, lump, clump, hump) or alliterate (flick, flash, flip, flop). Both imitative and symbolic words may be subject to the process of doubling, sometimes with a little variation, e.g. bow-wow, choo-choo, pee-wee.

2.5.3 Ejaculations

'Ejaculations' are words that attempt to imitate instinctive vocal responses to emotional situations (Pyles and Algeo 1993). They are also termed 'natural utterances', but they have become conventionalized and so become lexical items, e.g. *ha-ha* and its variant *ho-ho* for laughter. The words *pish* and *pshaw* express disdain, contempt, impatience or irritation. *Phew* imitates the reaction to a bad smell or to the avoidance of a disaster. To signify agreement, *uh-huh* is used.

2.5.4 Word formation

Word formation uses existing language material – words and morphemes – to create new lexical items. The processes were already well established in Old English. The major processes are compounding and affixation, which will be introduced here and elaborated on in Chapter 4.

The following nouns were produced by compounding, the combination of two words (free morphemes): birthday, craftsman, grandfather, highway. Compounds are also found among adjectives (newborn, red-hot, banana-flavoured, freeze-dried), verbs (download, safeguard, stagemanage), prepositions/adverbs (inside, inspite of, afterwards).

Affixation involves the use of prefixes and suffixes to form new words. As the language evolved, so the range of affixes increased, especially by borrowing from French and Latin. Here are some examples: celebrat-ion, duck-ling, forget-ful, green-ish, nap-kin, pre-figure, un-know-able.

2.6 Characteristics of modern English vocabulary

Among the characteristics of present-day English vocabulary, we shall discuss the size of the vocabulary, the frequency of occurrence of Anglo-Saxon words, before concluding with a discussion of the 'Englishness' of the vocabulary.

2.6.1 The size of the vocabulary

One way of answering the question, 'How large is the English lexicon?' would be to compare two of the biggest dictionaries of the English language.

David Crystal compared the unabridged *Websters Third New International* (1961), which claims over 450,000 entries, and the integrated second edition of the *Oxford English Dictionary* (1989), which claims over 600,000 entries. Crystal's sample comparison revealed a remarkable lack of identity between the headword lists: the *Websters* and *Oxford* dictionaries had only 21 headwords in common out of a possible 57, less than two-fifths. If this disparity were to be repeated across all the entries, then the combined lexicon of both dictionaries would exceed 750,000. The discrepancies observed may be accounted for by differences in editorial emphasis. For example, the *Oxford* has far more historical references and British dialect terms than *Websters*, which in turn has many more local American items. Furthermore, neither work would claim a comprehensive coverage of the 'New Englishes', used in areas such as India, West Africa, Singapore, where thousands of new lexemes are coming into the language. Finally, the tradition of lexicography, which gives preference to the written language as the test for inclusion, will exclude thousands of words and expressions that have never been recorded even if they are common in current spoken use.

Crystal argues that, even if we restrict the issue to standard vocabulary, there are many items that could be included as part of the lexicon, but which are not usually found in a dictionary. Many of the abbreviated forms and acronyms have a clear lexical status (e.g. BA, FBI, NATO, UNICEF), as well as fauna and flora local to diverse English-speaking areas. Crystal concludes his analysis by noting that it is difficult to see how even a conservative estimate of English vocabulary could go much below one million lexemes. More inclusive counts, to encompass all of scientific nomenclature, might easily double this figure. Only a small fraction of these totals is, of course, learned and used by any one of us (Crystal 1995: 119).

2.6.2 Frequency of occurrence and use of Anglo-Saxon words

In addition to being short and concrete, words from Anglo-Saxon have two other characteristics: they are the most frequent in the language; and they are considered 'warmer' than words of foreign origin.

The most frequent two hundred words in both British (BrE) and American English (AmE) consist overwhelmingly of one syllable. There are a few two-syllable words (40 in AmE, 24 in BrE) and a handful of trisyllabic forms (3 in AmE, 2 in BrE). Only AmE has a single four-syllable item, the word *American* itself. It has been estimated that for the 10,000 most frequent words in English, nearly 32 per cent have their origin in Old English (Crystal 1995: 18). In the one-million-word 'Brown University Corpus of Written American English' from the 1960s, the hundred most frequently used items are almost all from Anglo-Saxon. The exceptions are a few Scandinavian loans (e.g. *they*, *are*). The first words borrowed from Romance sources are *just* (at 105th) and *people* (at 107th) (Crystal 1995: 124). These statistics show the importance of the inherited Germanic vocabulary in the central core of

English vocabulary. However, it should be noted that the relative frequency of words varies not only according to the type of text but also according to the stylistic level. Generally speaking, formal style and specialized language use a greater proportion of foreign loans than does everyday conversation.

As regards the second characteristic, it is argued that native English words tend to be preferred in everyday speech because they are vague and convey many shades of meaning, as opposed to loanwords, which are more precise and restricted, and so are more difficult to handle. Furthermore, native English words are considered more human and emotional, whereas many polysyllabic loans from Greek, Latin or the Romance language are considered cold and formal. For example, in an informal everyday situation, when faced with the choice between *initiate, commence* and *start*, or between *nourishment, nutrition* and *food*, most people would opt for the short, Anglo-Saxon word. In formal situations, however, it may seem more appropriate to *allude* to a *nauseating odour* or even an *obnoxious effluvium* rather than a *nasty smell.*

2.6.3 'English' vocabulary

This chapter has shown the very cosmopolitan nature of English vocabulary, a prime example of a lexically mixed language. How then can we speak of the 'English' vocabulary in the face of this avalanche of words from other languages?

It should be noted, first, that the predominance of foreign words is felt only with reference to the total word stock, for example if we consider the 616,500 word forms in the *Oxford English Dictionary* (1989). But when we look at the items actually used in writing and speech, we find that the front-runners, i.e. the most common in the language, are all native English (Anglo-Saxon) words (see examples in 2.3.1 and Exercise 2/6). Moreover, a good many foreign words have been assimilated to the pronunciation and spelling of English, so they are no longer recognized as 'foreign' by native speakers. And the grammatical structures used have remained essentially the same throughout the various stages in the development of the language. English has, from Middle English times, been unable to afford to be purist in its attitude to the lexicon.

EXERCISE 2/8

Here are some English words that still betray which language they have been borrowed from. Without looking them up, make an intelligent guess at their language of origin. Then look in the Key to Exercises.

addendum (plural, addenda), baguette, cannelloni, con brio, criterion (plural, criteria), id est (i.e.), in loco parentis, mañana, sang-froid, vis-à-vis, zucchini

2.7 Summary

In this chapter we have examined the origins of English words. In the main, we have focused our attention first on the native English vocabulary, and second on words borrowed from other languages. Before discussing these main categories of words, it was necessary not only to place English in the context of world languages, but also to show how English vocabulary evolved from the Old to the Modern English periods. Finally, we touched on the creation of new words in English, before highlighting the most important characteristics of modern English vocabulary.

3   The Word

In Chapter 1, we defined lexicology as the study of the stock of words in a given language. In Chapter 2, we investigated the origin of English words. The 'word' is therefore of central importance in lexicology. This chapter deals first with the notion of 'word' in general, then with word meaning, before discussing in turn polysemy, homonymy and multiword lexemes.

3.1 The notion of word

The basic question we shall attempt to answer in this section is: 'What exactly do we mean by the term "word" in lexicology?' Before proposing the definition which we intend to adopt in this book, we shall first discuss the difficulties involved in the definition of the word. Then we shall discuss in turn the characteristics of the word and ambiguity in the notion of word.

3.1.1 Difficulties in the definition of the word

The term 'word' is used to designate an intermediate structure smaller than a whole phrase and yet generally larger than a single sound segment. However, the word may be defined differently depending on whether we focus on its representation, the thought which it expresses, or purely formal criteria.

The first type of definition relies mainly on writing traditions that separate by spaces sequences of letters or characters. It must be pointed out that these separations do not always correspond to functional realities. For example, in 'a new waste paper basket', the first two spaces do not have the same value as the last two because the group 'waste paper basket', although represented by three words, constitutes a semantic unit, while such a unit does not exist for the group 'a new waste'. Consequently, a definition based on writing traditions alone cannot be entirely satisfactory.

The second type of definition considers the indivisible unit of thought as the most essential criterion. The main problem faced by this view of the word is that of 'delimitation', which offers three possible alternatives.

(a) The word as represented in writing represents a thought unit or a psychological unit: this is the most common case, the easiest to observe and which, unfortunately, may make us forget the others. Examples are names of objects: *table, house*; abstractions: *courage, faith, intelligence*; adjectives: *tall, short*; verbs: *eat, sleep*.

(b) The word forms one block but includes two units of thought: e.g. *farmer, rethink, spoonful.*

(c) The psychological unit exceeds the limit of the graphological unit and spreads over several words; the word is only an element of the real unity, which is then a more complex unit: e.g. *all of a sudden, as usual, coconut.*

The third type of definition stems neither from writing traditions nor from thought units and relies only on purely formal criteria. Bloomfield was the first to suggest a formal definition of the word. He contrasted the word with other significant units: the morpheme or minimal meaningful unit and the syntagme or structure, consisting potentially of more than one word. For him, a minimal form is a morpheme; its meaning a sememe. A form which may occur alone is free. A form which may not occur alone is bound. For example, *book* and *man* are free; *-er*, and *-ing* as in *singer* and *writing* are bound forms. A word is a minimal free form. Hence, a word is viewed as a form which can occur in isolation and have meaning but which cannot be analysed into elements which can all occur alone and also have meaning (see Bloomfield 1933/5: 178).

From Bloomfield's analysis, it follows that lexis, which consists of an infinite number of elements, excludes relational words or grammatical morphemes. In fact, the latter may be considered as an integral part of the grammatical system of the language. Some of them occur as free forms, e.g. *and, by*, while others can only be bound forms, e.g. *-ing* as in *sleeping, -est* in *slowest.*

A further difficulty in the use of formal criteria is that the word may be defined from the phonological, lexical, and grammatical points of view. For example, the phonological word /'faɪndz/ and the orthographic word *finds* correspond to the grammatical word 'third person singular of *find*'. The word *find* as the base form without any modification is the lexical word. The lexical word is also referred to as a 'lexeme', e.g. *book, fast, open, student.* Lexical words are different from grammatical words. The latter are forms like *a, an, but, that*, which cannot usually occur alone as minimal utterances. For more details on the distinction between lexical and grammatical words, see 1.3.4, and 3.1.2 below.

3.1.2 The word defined

Most fluent speakers of English seem to know what a word is. They know, for example, that words are listed in dictionaries, that they are separated in writing by spaces, and that they may be separated in speech by pauses. But it is one thing to identify words and another to suggest a definition that will apply to all types of word in English. We shall not go into a theoretical discussion of how words can best be defined. Instead, we shall propose the following definition, which will serve as a working tool in this book. We shall consider the word as an uninterruptible unit of structure consisting of one or more morphemes and which typically occurs in the structure of phrases. The morphemes are the ultimate grammatical constituents, the minimal meaningful units of language. For example, the different forms of the verb *speak*, i.e. *speak, speaks, speaking, spoke* and *spoken* are separate words grammatically. Equally, *grave* (noun) and *grave* (adjective) are different grammatical words. So are the plural, the plural possessive, and the possessive of the word *boy*, all represented by the pronunciation /bɔɪz/, but spelt *boys, boys'* and *boy's* respectively. For further discussion of the different senses of the term 'word', see for example, Matthews (1974: 20–7), Quirk *et al.* (1985: 68–70), Jackson (1988: 1ff), Lipka (1990: 72–3).

We shall now come back to the distinction often made between 'lexical' and 'grammatical' words (1.3.4). In most general terms, lexical words are nouns, verbs, adjectives, and adverbs. They have fairly independent meanings and may be meaningful even in isolation or in a series. For example, *bottle* has an independent meaning; and so does the series *boy, break, bottle, stone*. On the other hand, a word such as *a, with*, or a series such as *a, the, to, with* does not automatically suggest any identifiable meaning. Classes of lexical words contain hundreds or even thousands of members, and they form open classes. For example, the English vocabulary has thousands of nouns, and new items can always be added to the list. Grammatical words are elements like prepositions, articles, conjunctions, forms indicating number or tense, and so on. Such classes contain relatively few members and the addition of new members is rather rare. They constitute closed classes or closed sets.

However, the distinction between grammatical and lexical words must be handled with care. There is no clear-cut dividing line between the two types of word. We should, in fact, speak of a continuum ranging from words with semantic content such as *exam, students*, to words devoid of semantic content such as *it* and *that* in a sentence like '*It* is obvious *that* some students will pass this exam.' However, although prepositions may be classed as grammatical words, they are not completely empty of semantic content. The sentence 'The book is *on* the table' has quite a different meaning when *on* is replaced by *under, near, off,* etc. Similarly, the co-ordinators *and, or,* and *but* are not mutually interchangeable, because they are not synonymous.

3.1.3 Characteristics of words

The following four characteristics are considered essential in our definition of the word in English.

First, the word is an uninterruptible unit. When elements are added to a word to modify its meaning, they are never included within that word. They respect the internal stability of the word and are added either at the beginning as prefixes of the word or at the end as suffixes. For example, the prefix *un-* and the suffix *-able* may be added to the words *aware* and *drink* and give *unaware* and *drinkable* respectively.

Note, however, that an affix may also occur not at the beginning or at the end, but simultaneously with the word; we then speak of a suprafix. Compare for example the words *'export* (noun) and *ex'port* (verb); they differ only in the position of the primary stress represented by the symbol ('). The stress pattern may be referred to as a suprafix. (We shall not discuss the use of infixes because such affixes do not occur in English.) The word to which affixes are added and which carries the basic meaning of the resulting complex word is known as the 'stem', which may consist of one or more morphemes. The label 'root' is used to refer to a stem consisting of a single morpheme.

Secondly, the word may consist of one or more morphemes. When it consists of one morpheme only, then it cannot be broken down into smaller meaningful units, e.g. *dog, hand, man, out, work*. These are called 'simple' words, which are typically 'minimum free forms', in the sense that they may stand by themselves and yet act as minimally complete utterances, e.g. in answer to a question.

When words consist of more than one morpheme, they may be either complex or compound. Complex words may be broken down into one free form and one or more bound forms: e.g. *dog-s, happi-ly, quick-er, work-ing*; whereas compound words consist of more than one free form: e.g. *birth+day, black+bird, candle+stick, coat+hanger*. We also need to mention cases which incorporate the characteristics of both complex and compound words: e.g. *gentle-man-ly* consists of the compound word *gentle+man* and the suffix *-ly*; *wind+shield+wip-er* consists of the compound word *wind + shield* and the complex word *wip-er*. For a general discussion of compounding, see 4.5.

However, it is not always obvious whether or not a given sound sequence should be considered a morpheme. For instance, should *window* and *woman* be said to consist of *wind+ow* and *wo+man* respectively? This would allow us to isolate *wind* and *man* as identifiable morphemes, but leave *-ow* and *wo-*, which are no longer morphemes in English. The morpheme may have ceased to be recognizable because of linguistic change, as in the case of *-ow* in *window* (related to 'eye') or the *-fer* of *refer* (from Latin *ferre*, 'carry'). In these cases, we shall say that unless a word can be completely analysed into morphemes, it should be regarded as unanalysable. It must also be noted that a sound sequence that is a morpheme in some words does not necessarily constitute a morpheme in all its occurrences. For example, the suffix *-er* is a morpheme in *gardener* and *speaker*, but it is not a morpheme in *never* or *consider*.

Thirdly, the word occurs typically in the structure of phrases. According to the hierarchy adopted in this book, morphemes are used to build words, words to build phrases, phrases to build clauses, and clauses to build sentences. This is the typical mapping of lower level into higher level units. However, in atypical mapping, a higher level unit may be used in a lower level unit. For example, a clause such as *who came late* may be used like an adjective (word) to modify the head noun *man* in a sentence such as 'The man *who came late* was my brother'. We shall still regard such a unit as a sequence of words; it has merely shifted levels.

Finally, it is also an important characteristic of each word that it should belong to a specific word class or part of speech (1.3.4). Where the same form appears in more than one class, as frequently happens in English, we regard the various occurrences as separate words (for example, *smoke* (verb) as distinct from *smoke* (noun)). It may even be suggested that a word is defined by two factors: its semantic 'nucleus' and the class to which it belongs.

EXERCISE 3/1

Count the number of words in the following sentence. You should ask: 'Which type of word am I to count?' Make a separate count of: (a) orthographic words; (b) grammatical word forms; (c) lexical words (lexemes).

In their conceptual world, words are at once containers, tools and weapons, just as in the physical world a bag is a container, a screwdriver is a tool, and a gun is a weapon. (Adapted from McArthur 1998: 38)

3.1.4 Ambiguity in the notion of word

No matter how careful we are in our definition of the word, we are bound to accommodate a certain amount of vagueness or ambiguity, which is inherent in the very nature of language in general and that of the word in particular. Following Ullmann, the most important sources of ambiguity are: the generic character of the word, the multiplicity of aspects in every word, the lack of clear-cut boundaries in the non-linguistic world, and the lack of familiarity with the referent of the words (see Ullmann 1962: 118ff). We shall discuss these various sources of ambiguity in turn, and close the section with a word on 'emotive overtones'.

In most general terms, a word can be regarded as 'generic' when it has 'abstract' reference, i.e. more schematic, poorer than particular words in its ability to distinguish specific features. Generic terms apply to a wide range of items but tell us little about them. The word *mammal*, for example, is more generic and therefore more abstract than *cow*, in the same way, *animal* is more abstract than *mammal*. The same relationship exists between the words *plant*, *tree*, and *acacia*, the last one being the least abstract and consequently the least vague.

Except for rigorously defined scientific or technical terms, proper names, and for a small number of common nouns referring to unique objects, the words denote, not single items, but classes of things or events bound together by some common element. There is always a certain amount of generalization, which inevitably involves an element of vagueness or some degree of ambiguity. In order to generalize, we must always discriminate between 'distinctive' and 'non-distinctive' features of words. For example, the word *table* will be used to refer to a certain class of objects, irrespective of certain non-distinctive features such as shape, size, colour, and number of legs. In other words, a table could be square, rectangular, oblong, round, etc.; it could have any dimension and/or any colour we wish to give it; it could have one or more legs, and yet it could still be a *table*, as opposed to a *chair* or a *bed*, for instance; provided it has a certain number of distinctive features which characterize all tables. From the above discussion, it may be said that most English words are generic to a lesser or greater extent.

The words we use are never completely homogenous in their meaning: all of them have a number of facets or aspects depending on the context and situation in which they are used and also on the personality of the speaker using them. Consider the word *table* again. Its significance will vary according to the context in which it occurs; e.g. a *table* for two in a restaurant, the *table* of contents in a book, a multiplication *table* at school, to give money under the *table*. It will also vary according to the user; e.g. a carpenter, a waiter, a member of parliament, a pupil.

With abstract words such as *democracy*, *equality*, *freedom*, *immortality*, such differences in application are even more marked. Note that even proper names, which may be considered the most concrete of all words, are also subject to such 'shifts in application': only the context will specify which aspect of a person, which phase in their development, which side of their activities we have in mind. Such shifts in application can easily lead to multiple meaning, ambiguity or even in extreme cases, misunderstanding.

The nature of the non-linguistic world itself may be a source of ambiguity. In our physical environment we are often faced with phenomena which merge into one another and which we have to divide up into discrete units. For example, the colour spectrum is a continuum; however, each language introduces into it a certain number of more or less arbitrary distinctions. This lack of boundaries is even more conspicuous when we consider abstract phenomena. Such phenomena involve distinctions that are largely imposed, because they have no concrete existence without the linguistic form used to refer to them. For example, while speakers may point at an object to specify the particular shade of *green* they have in mind, they would have no such alternative in order to specify the particular aspect of the word *equality* which they have in mind.

The specialists are aware of this difficulty and always strive to define their terms clearly and to distinguish them sharply from one another. The precise definition and limitation of abstract words can lead to endless and often heated discussions in philosophical works, in law courts and in conferences. A lawyer will avoid any confusion between *crime* and *offence*, a psychiatrist between *neurosis* and *psychosis*, and a linguist between *morpheme* and *allomorph*. For the layman, however, 'abstract' terms of ordinary language are far less precise than 'concrete' terms. One of the functions of the dictionary is to attempt to establish boundaries between the overlapping uses of words in order to reduce cases of potential ambiguity and misunderstanding.

Lack of familiarity with the 'referent' of a word is, of course, a highly variable factor, since it depends on the general knowledge and the special interest of each individual. For example, many university students and lecturers will have rather hazy notions about the meanings of tools and objects which will be perfectly clear to any mechanic. Similarly, town-dwellers will not be familiar with plant names or agricultural terms which will be common knowledge for any gardener or farmer. Since the vocabulary of any language is open-ended, i.e. new words can always be added to it, and since a single individual, no matter how learned, cannot be a specialist in all fields, nobody can pretend to be familiar with all the words in a given language. This lack of familiarity can therefore be another source of ambiguity and may in some cases cause a serious breakdown in communication.

Emotive overtones refer to the use of language either to express emotions or to arouse them in others. This use of language may be opposed to the purely communicative one, which is basically symbolic or referential. We assume that both the communicative and the emotive uses of language contribute to the meaning of all utterances. However, one of these uses may be particularly dominant in a given utterance. For example, some words are used purely for evaluative purposes, e.g. the adjectives *good* and *bad*, and the adverb *well*; but we cannot normally assume that such words have no cognitive meaning. As Delacroix (1924: 41) puts it in his book *Le Langage et la Pensée*: 'All language has some emotive value: if what I say were indifferent to me I would not say it. At the same time, all language aims at communicating something. If one had absolutely nothing to say one would say nothing' (quoted in Ullmann 1962: 128).

In lexicology, the consequence of this dual aspect of language use is that the meaning of any word may be modified by emotive overtones. Although this modified meaning may be considered secondary, it is nevertheless as important as the denotational meaning of the word. In certain contexts, it may even be the determining factor for the most appropriate interpretation of a given message. However, because emotive overtones may be added to any word, this aspect of language does not lend itself to objective analysis. Consequently, we shall not elaborate on the influence of emotive overtones in lexicology.

EXERCISE 3/2

What does the word 'bull' mean in each of the following sentences?

1. Beware of the bull!
2. I think the elephant is a bull.
3. Stop acting like a bull in a china shop!
4. There was a bull market on the stock exchange today.
5. Well done! You've hit the bull's eye.
6. Don't give me all that bull.
7. I'm afraid that you'll just have to take the bull by the horns.

3.2 Word meaning

Before we examine the most common terms used in the discussion of word meaning, we shall first define 'linguistic sign' and then discuss the word as a linguistic sign.

3.2.1 The linguistic sign

Following de Saussure (1959), the linguistic sign is a mental unit consisting of two faces, which cannot be separated: a concept and an acoustic image. The term 'sign' is quite a general expression which can refer to sentences, clauses, phrases, words, or morphemes. De Saussure later referred to 'concept' as 'signifié' or 'thing meant' and to 'acoustic image' as 'signifiant' or 'signifier'. These have since become accepted technical terms in modern linguistics. De Saussure pointed out that an alteration in the acoustic image must make a difference in the concept and vice versa. But this view does not appear to take homonyms into account (see 3.4 below). However, since the linguistic sign has both form and meaning, it follows that, when dealing with words, we can focus either on the form or on the meaning.

3.2.2 The word as a linguistic sign

Since the word is a linguistic sign, a discussion of 'word meaning' focuses on the relationship between the two faces of the sign, viz. the acoustic image or 'signifiant', i.e. the signifier, on the one hand, and the concept or 'signifié', i.e. the thing meant, on the other. A major difficulty in this task is how to accommodate both the fuzzy nature of meaning and the ambiguity inherent in the notion of word.

We cannot go into the intricacies of the various aspects of meaning in an introductory book of this nature. Instead, we shall limit our discussion to an examination of some of the most common terms associated with word meaning; those that will be useful not only in our discussion of the different types of relationship that exist between words, but also in our study of sense relations (Chapter 5). We shall consider in turn denotation, connotation, reference and sense. However, to ease comparison and cross-references, we shall discuss these terms in pairs as follows: denotation and reference, denotation and sense, and finally denotation and connotation.

3.2.3 Denotation and reference

We need the concept of 'lexeme' to clarify the distinction between denotation and reference. This concept, which was coined by Lyons in analogy to 'phoneme' and 'morpheme', is considered an abstract linguistic unit (spelt in capitals) with different variants (e.g. SING as against *sang, sung*).

Thus, the relation of denotation holds between a lexeme and a whole class of extra-linguistic objects. For example, Lyons defines the denotation of a lexeme as 'the relationship that holds between that lexeme and persons, things, places, properties, processes and activities external to the language system' (Lyons 1977: 207). It is therefore difficult to give concrete examples of denotation since this relation holds between an abstract linguistic unit and a whole class of extra-linguistic objects.

As opposed to denotation, the relationship of reference holds between an expression and what that expression stands for on particular occasions of its utterance (Lyons 1977: 207). Lyons further points out that reference depends on concrete utterances, not on abstract sentences. It is a property only of expressions. It cannot relate single lexemes to extra-linguistic objects, since it is an utterance-dependent notion. Furthermore, reference is not generally applicable to single word forms and it is never applicable to single lexemes (Lyons 1977: 197). For example, expressions such as *the computer, John's computer,* or *the two portable computers on the table* may be used to establish a relationship of reference with specific items as referents. In this case, the reference of these expressions containing *computer* is partly determined by the denotation of the lexeme COMPUTER in the overall system of the English language.

3.2.4 Denotation and sense

We have already defined denotation following Lyons (see 3.2.3). His definition of sense also evolved with time. Initially, he defined the sense of a word as its 'place in a system of relationships which it contracts with other words in the vocabulary' (Lyons 1968: 427). Later (Lyons 1977: 206), he defines sense as a relationship 'between the words or expressions of a single language, independently of the relationship, if any, which holds between those words or expressions and their referents or denotata'. It follows that sense is a relationship which is internal to the language system, i.e. a language-immanent relationship. Both individual lexemes and larger expressions have sense. However, the sense of an expression is a function of the sense of the lexemes it contains and their occurrences in a particular grammatical construction. The sense of the word *table* will vary in the following sentences: 'Don't put your feet on the *table*!' and 'It was finalized under the *table*.'

A comparison between denotation and sense shows that the two relations are dependent on each other. According to Lyons, some words may have no specific denotation and still have sense. To use an often quoted example, consider the following pair of sentences:

There is no such animal as a unicorn.
There is no such book as a unicorn.

While the first is perfectly acceptable, the second is semantically odd. Furthermore, this double observation proves that, whereas the lexemes *book* and *unicorn* are incompatible, *animal* and *unicorn* are somehow related in sense. Such examples can be multiplied easily. The important point here is that a word may have sense but have no denotation. (See further Chapter 5.)

3.2.5 *Denotation and connotation*

Specialists are not in agreement in their treatment of the distinction between denotation and connotation, or denotative vs. connotative meaning. Some, such as Ullmann (1962: 74) make a binary distinction between the two terms. Others, like Lyons (1977: 287) and Leech (1981: 12ff), do not accept the binary distinction and prefer to use denotation and connotation in a rather specific sense. However, these divergent views cannot conceal the fact that connotation is closely associated with synonymy. In other words, synonyms may have the same denotation, i.e. cognitive, or conceptual meaning, but differ in connotation. However, it is sometimes difficult to draw the line between 'connotation', which is essentially stylistic, and 'denotation'. To illustrate this point, Lyons (1977: 618f) argues that in Scots English, the word *loch* (vs. *lake*) can be regarded either as a dialectally marked variant of the Standard English word or as a different lexeme, with a specific 'descriptive meaning' or 'denotation', and a connotation of 'Scottishness'.

For the supporters of the binary distinction between denotation and connotation, denotative meaning refers to the relationship between a linguistic sign and its denotatum or referent. However, connotations constitute additional properties of lexemes, e.g. poetic, slang, baby language, biblical, casual, colloquial, formal, humorous, legal, literary, rhetorical. Denotation and connotation are both important in order to determine word meaning in a given context.

As a final observation, it must be acknowledged that words are not normally used in isolation, but are combined with other words to form larger units expressing various relationships. These units constitute the linguistic context in which a specific word operates.

EXERCISE 3/3

What are the connotations of the italicized words in the following
sentences?

1. We are away to sunnier *climes.*
2. I had to *fork out* a lot for that present.
3. Give mummy the *doggie* then.
4. If we do that, they'll call down *fire and brimstone* on us.
5. Let's get rid of this little *beastie.*
6. I suppose *muggins* will have to do it.
7. Let me get you the *aforementioned.*
8. We'll meet upon the *greensward.*

3.3 Polysemy

We shall first define polysemy in 3.3.1, before discussing some of the
problems inherent in the concept of polysemy in 3.3.2.

3.3.1 Definition

Polysemy refers to the situation where the same word has two or more
different meanings (from Greek *poly,* 'many' + *semeion,* 'sign'). For instance,
the noun *board* is said to be polysemous because it may mean: (1) a long thin
flat piece of cut wood, (2) a flat surface with patterns, used for playing a
game on, (3) a flat piece of hard material used for putting food on, (4) a flat
piece of hard material fastened to the wall in a public place to pin notices
on, (5) the cost of meals, (6) a committee or association, as of company
directors or government officials, set up for a special responsibility (*Longman Dictionary of Contemporary English* 1978: 105). Similarly, the word *flight* is
defined in at least the following ways: (1) the act of flying, (2) the distance
covered or course followed by a flying object, (3) a trip by plane, (4) the
aircraft making the journey, (5) a group of birds or aircraft flying together,
(6) an effort that goes beyond the usual limits, (7) a set of stairs as between
floors, (8) swift movement or passage (see LDOCE 1978: 421).

In most cases, only one of the meanings of a polysemous word will fit into
a given context, but occasionally ambiguity may also arise. For instance,
consider the words *bat* and *bank* in the following contexts:

  Look at that *bat* under the tree.
  Susan may go to the *bank* today.

Ambiguity results from the fact that *bat* may mean either 'flying mammal' or
'implement used to hit the ball in cricket', while *bank* may mean either 'river
bank' or 'the place that deals with money'.

3.3.2 Problems inherent in the concept of polysemy

Despite its apparent simplicity, the concept of polysemy is complex and involves a certain number of problems. We shall consider in turn the number of meanings, transference of meanings, and difficulty in recognizing polysemy.

Since one meaning cannot always be delimited and distinguished from another, it is not easy to say without hesitation whether two meanings are the same or different. Consequently, we cannot determine exactly how many meanings a polysemous word has. Consider the verb *eat*. Most dictionaries distinguish the 'literal' sense of 'taking in through the mouth and swallowing' and the derived meaning of 'use up, damage, or destroy something, especially by chemical action', which tends to suggest that the verb may have at least two different meanings. However, in the literal sense, we can also distinguish between eating nuts and eating soup, the former with fingers and the latter with a spoon. Moreover, we can talk of drinking soup as well as eating it. It may therefore be said that in this sense at least, *eat* corresponds to *drink*, since the latter involves the 'swallowing of liquids'. We can push the analysis further by asking whether eating an orange (which can involve sucking) is the same thing as eating an apple (which involves only chewing). It goes without saying that if we push this analysis too far, we may end up deciding that the verb *eat* has a different meaning for every type of food that we 'eat'.

The above discussion shows that there is no clear criterion for either difference or sameness of meaning. Consequently, it would seem futile to attempt an exhaustive count of the number of possible meanings which a given word may have. The point of view adopted in this book is that the meaning of a given word is bound to vary according to the specific context in a wide semantic field, part of which overlaps with that of other words. For instance, the semantic field of *eat* overlaps with that of *drink* when referring to a soup, since you can either eat or drink a soup, but there is no overlapping when dealing with nuts, since nuts can only be eaten, not drunk.

As suggested in the case of the verb *eat*, a word may have both a 'literal' meaning and one or more 'transferred' meanings, although we cannot determine with precision how many different meanings a given word may have altogether.

We shall first discuss metaphor, which is the most familiar kind of transference, before turning to other kinds of transference. The basic difference between metaphor on the one hand and the other types of transference on the other is that metaphor is 'irregular', because it applies to individual lexical items, whereas the other kinds may be considered more 'regular', in the sense that they do not apply just to individual lexical items but to several members of a specific class, e.g. a group of nouns or adjectives. These characteristics will be made more explicit below.

The term 'metaphor' refers to cases where a word appears to have both a 'literal' and a 'transferred' meaning. The words for parts of the body provide the best illustration of metaphor. For example, we speak of the *hands* and *face* of a clock, the *foot* of a bed or of a mountain, the *leg* of a chair or table, the *tongue* of a shoe, the *eye* of a needle, etc. Intuitively, we assume that words such as *eye, face, foot, hand, leg* and *tongue* apply first to the body, from which they derive their literal sense. This intuition is supported by the fact that the whole set of words applies only to the body, while only some of them can be transferred to certain objects. For instance, the clock has no *tongue*, the bed no *eyes*, the chair no *feet* and the mountain no *legs*.

It should, however, be said that metaphor is rather haphazard not only within specific languages, but also when we compare the use of the same metaphor across languages. It is from these two points of view that metaphor is considered 'irregular'. For example, it may seem obvious that *foot* is appropriate to a mountain, or *eye* to a needle, but a look at French will show that, although a mountain also has a 'foot' (French *pied*), the needle does not have an 'eye', but a 'hole' (*trou*); furthermore, a clock does not have 'hands', but 'needles' (*aiguilles*), chairs and tables do not have 'legs' but 'feet' (*les* pieds *de la table/chaise*).

The label 'metaphor' can also be applied to other cases of transference, but only in a rather loose sense, because it is not always clear which meaning should be considered literal and which transferred. However, this second kind of transference is fairly productive because it involves the transfer of meaning in a predictable manner. Thus, many adjectives may be used either literally for the quality they refer to or with the transferred meaning of being the source of the quality. For instance, in the literal sense, we may say that 'John is *sad*' (he feels sadness), 'a blanket is *warm*' (it is of a certain degree of temperature). But in the transferred sense, when we say that a book or film or story is *sad*, we do not imply that 'it feels sadness', rather, we mean that it causes someone else to feel sad. Note that this possibility of transfer of meaning may result in ambiguity. For instance, a blanket or a coat may be warm in two senses: either that it is of a certain temperature as mentioned above, or that it keeps one warm.

Similarly, many nouns may have a concrete and an abstract meaning. Thus, we may compare 'The *thesis* is on the desk' and 'The *thesis* is not supported by objective evidence'. The word *thesis* has, of course, a concrete meaning in the first sentence and an abstract one in the second. Similar contrasts may be established for *bible, book, score* and *table*, for instance.

When we refer to the difficulty in recognizing polysemy, we are dealing with the relationship between polysemy (i.e. one word with several meanings) and homonymy (i.e. several words with the same shape – spelling and/or pronunciation). The problem is to decide when we have polysemy and when we have homonymy. In other words, assuming that we have a written form with two meanings, should we consider it as one word with different meanings (polysemy), or as two different words with the same shape (homonymy)? Dictionaries have to decide whether a particular item is to be handled in terms of polysemy or homonymy, because a polysemous word will be treated as a single entry, while a homonymous one will have a separate entry for each of the homonyms. For a discussion of how dictionaries decide, see 8.3.

As a final observation, it must be said that far from being a defect of language, polysemy is an essential condition for its efficiency. If it were not possible to attach several senses to the same word, this would mean a crushing burden on our memory; we would have to possess separate terms for every conceivable 'object' we might wish to talk about, and be absolutely precise in our choice of words. Consequently, polysemy must be considered an invaluable factor of economy and flexibility in language.

EXERCISE 3/4

List all the meanings that you can think of for the lexemes *lemon* (noun) and *review* (verb). Then compare your list with that in the Key to Exercises.

3.4 Homonymy

Section 3.4.1 below defines homonymy, while 3.4.2 discusses the devices used to avoid homonymous conflicts in English.

3.4.1 Definition

Homonymy refers to a situation where we have two or more words with the same shape. Although they have the same shape, homonyms are considered distinct lexemes, mainly because they have unrelated meanings and different etymologies (see 8.3).

There is, however, some difficulty in the establishment of 'sameness' of shape, owing to the fact that we do not make the same distinctions in both speech and writing. Thus, *lead* (metal) and *lead* (dog's lead) are spelt the same but pronounced differently; while *right, rite* and *write* are spelt differently but pronounced the same. For the first case, the term 'homograph' (same spelling) may be used; for the second 'homophone' (same sound) is the appropriate term. In addition to the difference in meaning, homonyms may also be kept apart by syntactic differences. For example, when homonyms belong to different word classes, as in the case of *tender*, which has different lexemes as adjective, verb and noun, each homonym has not only a distinct meaning, but also a different grammatical function. The same observation applies to pairs of words such as *bear* (noun), and *bear* (verb), *grave* (adjective) and *grave* (noun), *hail* (noun) and *hail* (verb), *hoarse* (adjective) and *horse* (noun).

3.4.2 Homonym clashes

Because of the sameness of shape, there is a danger of homonymous conflict or clashes in the sense that two homonyms with totally different meanings may both make sense in the same utterance. For example,

> The *route* was very long
> The *root* was very long;
> Helen didn't see the *bat* (animal)
> Helen didn't see the *bat* (wooden implement).

However, there are at least two different safeguards against any possibility of confusion: the difference in word class and the difference in spelling, besides the difference in overall context.

Many homonyms exist only in theory, since in practice there is no risk of any confusion, because they belong to different word classes. Consider the pairs of homophones *knows* (verb) and *nose* (noun), *rights* (noun) and *writes* (verb). Apart from differences in meaning, it is difficult to imagine a context in which both members of a given pair might occur interchangeably. They are in 'complementary distribution', in the sense that where one occurs the other cannot occur. However, it must be specified that since the members of each pair differ in word class, the choice of one homonym instead of the other is determined mainly by the rules of syntax, not those of lexicology. Similar types of restriction also apply to pairs of homonyms which are identical in spelling and pronunciation, e.g. *grave* (adjective) versus *grave* (noun), *stick* (verb) versus *stick* (noun). This analysis shows that difference in grammatical class contributes to a substantial reduction in the number of 'effective' homonyms in English. However, it must also be acknowledged that difference in class alone does not automatically rule out all possibilities of confusion.

English has a non-phonetic writing system, in the sense that there is no absolute one-to-one correspondence between the letters of writing and the sounds in the pronunciation of words. Consequently, spelling will often help to differentiate between words which are identical in sound. This aspect also reduces the number of homonyms on the written and printed page; it may also be useful in spoken language because it provides a quick and easy way of removing confusion. For example, if there is any doubt in the listener's mind whether we mean *rite* or *write*, *route* or *root*, it may be much simpler to spell the words out than to define their meanings.

This discussion of the elimination of homonym clashes shows, among other things, that, in this respect, English writing is more intelligible than speech and that homonymy in the language as a whole, spoken as well as written, is reduced by writing conventions. It also shows that even if we focus on individual words, grammatical and graphological considerations play an important role in the distinction between homonyms. Before we turn to multiword lexemes, it is important to note that there is no clear-cut dividing line between polysemy and homonymy. The major difficulty, as we have seen, is that it is not at all clear how far meanings need to diverge before we treat the words representing them as separate. However, according to Lehrer (1974), the results of experiments suggest that native speakers are generally in agreement over a fair range of examples of homonymy and polysemy, although there is still a considerable residue of borderline cases (quoted in Lyons 1977: 550).

EXERCISE 3/5

As a test of Lehrer's thesis, which of the following pairs do you think are homonyms, and which are cases of polysemy? It is perhaps not always as easy as we think.

barge – noun (boat), verb (intervene); court – noun (entourage), verb (woo); dart – noun (missile), verb (move quickly); fleet – noun (ships), adjective (fast); jam – noun (preserve), verb (block); pad – noun (thick material), verb (walk softly); steep – adjective (of gradient), verb (immerse); stem – noun (of plant), verb (stop); stuff – verb (fill), noun (material); watch – verb (observe), noun (timepiece)

3.5 Multiword lexemes

In 3.1.1 the lexeme was simply referred to as 'lexical word' in opposition to 'grammatical word'. We also gave examples of lexemes consisting of single words. In this section we want to expand on the discussion in 3.1.1 by examining with appropriate examples two types of multiword lexeme. But first, let us revisit our definition of lexeme.

3.5.1 The lexeme

Following Crystal (1995: 118), a lexeme or lexical item is a 'unit of lexical meaning, which exists regardless of any inflectional endings it may have or the number of words it may contain'. Crystal adds that 'the headwords in a dictionary are lexemes'. This definition shows clearly that a lexeme may consist of one word, such as *big, boy, break, down, quick*; but it may also contain more than one word, e.g. *away from, brother-in-law, cut down on, hurry up, in front of, switch on, steam iron*.

For some words, such as adverbs or prepositions, which have no grammatical variants, the headword consists of only one form. But in most cases, the headword is considered as the base form or citation form of the word, from which all the other related word forms may be derived. For example, *speak* is the lexeme, the base form; while *speaks, spoke, speaking* and *spoken* are all derived forms. We shall come back to the way dictionaries treat multiword lexemes (8.3.5). For now, let us discuss two of the main types of multiword lexeme, viz. multiword verbs and idioms. For economy of presentation, the other main type of multiword lexeme, i.e. compounds (*steam iron*), will be dealt with in Chapter 4.

3.5.2 Multiword verbs

In multiword verbs, the main verb and one or two particles can be analysed as constituents of a single unit. Following Quirk *et al.* (1985: 1150), we shall make a distinction between 'phrasal verbs', 'prepositional verbs' and 'phrasal-prepositional verbs'. We shall first discuss the criteria for the classification of multiword verbs into sub-classes, then we shall examine these sub-classes in turn.

We shall use two main criteria in our identification of the different sub-classes of multiword verbs: first, the notion of 'transitivity' and the relative position of the direct object will establish the distinction between prepositional and phrasal verbs; secondly, the number of particles following the main verb will help distinguish between prepositional and phrasal verbs on the one hand and phrasal-prepositional verbs on the other.

Prepositional verbs are always followed by an object, i.e. they are all transitive, e.g. *call for* (John), *look at* (him). But they are all characterized by the fact that the object cannot occur between the particle and the main verb: hence '*call* John *for*', '*look* him *at*' are both ungrammatical (*has its usual meaning of an ungrammatical form or structure). Phrasal verbs may be followed by an object, i.e. they may be either transitive, such as *bring up*, *look up*, or intransitive, such as *give in*, *sit down*. By contrast with prepositional verbs, transitive phrasal verbs are characterized by the fact that the object may occur between the main verb and the particle without resulting in unacceptable structures, e.g. '*bring* them *up*', '*look* John *up*'. Phrasal-prepositional verbs constitute a bridge class between phrasal and prepositional verbs. Like all prepositional (and some phrasal) verbs, phrasal-prepositional verbs are transitive. But since they can easily be distinguished by the fact that they have two particles, transitivity is not used as a distinctive feature for this sub-group of multiword verbs; e.g. *check up on* (my friend), *get away with* (that), *stand up for* (your rights).

Other examples of prepositional verbs include *ask for, believe in, care for, deal with, refer to, write about*. Such verbs vary in the extent to which the combination preserves the individual meanings of verb and particle. In cases such as *ask for* and *refer to*, the meaning of the multiword verb can be derived from that of its constituents. But in cases such as *go into* (a problem), 'investigate', *come by* (the book), 'obtain', the multiword verb is best treated as an idiomatic expression.

Intransitive phrasal verbs consist of a main verb followed by a particle. Most of the particles are adverbials of place. Normally the particle cannot be separated from its verb. Hence, '*broke* again *down*' is ungrammatical. However, particles referring to directions can be modified by intensifiers, e.g. come *right* back, go *straight* ahead, go *straight* on. Other examples of intransitive phrasal verbs are: *blow up, catch on, get up, play around, stand up, take off, turn up*. This list is enough to show that phrasal verbs vary in the extent to which the combination preserves the individual meanings of the verb and particle. In several cases the meaning of the phrasal verb may be derived from that of its constituents; but in instances such as *give in*, 'surrender', *catch on*, 'understand', and *turn up*, 'appear', it is clear that the meaning of the construction cannot be predicted from the meanings of the verb and particle in isolation.

With most transitive phrasal verbs, the particle can either precede or follow the direct object, e.g.

They *switched on* the light.
They *switched* the light *on*.

However, the particle cannot precede personal pronouns, e.g.

They *switched* it *on*, and not
*They *switched on* it.

As a general rule, the particle tends to precede the object if the object is long or if the intention is that the object should receive end-focus.

Other examples of phrasal-prepositional verbs include *keep out of, stay away from, look down on*, 'despise', *look up to*, 'respect'. Like phrasal and prepositional verbs, some phrasal-prepositional verbs are more idiomatic than others. Some, like *stay away from* or *keep out of*, both meaning 'avoid', are easily understood from their individual elements, though many have figurative meaning, e.g. *stand up for*, 'support', *walk away with*, 'steal and take away'. Others are fused combinations and it is difficult, if not impossible, to derive the meaning of the multiword verb from that of its constituents, e.g. *put up with*, 'tolerate', *walk out on*, 'desert'. There are still others where there is a fusion of the verb with one of the particles. For example, *put up with* can mean 'tolerate' as in

I can't *put up with* heavy smokers

but it can also mean 'stay with' and in that sense *put up* by itself stands for the unit 'stay'. Similarly, *keep up with* (the Joneses) 'to compete with one's neighbours or stay level with social changes' may be analysed as consisting of the prepositional verb *keep up* plus the preposition *with*. Another example is given by the series *check, check on, check up on*, which consists of three transitive verbs of similar meaning, i.e. 'investigate'.

3.5.3 Idioms

Idioms may be treated as a type of collocation (see 5.6) involving two or more words in context. However, since the meaning of an idiom cannot be predicted from the meanings of its constituents, we may also consider idioms as a type of multiword lexeme. Before we discuss their characteristics, we will define and give appropriate examples of idioms in English.

In most general terms, an idiom may be defined as a phrase, the meaning

of which cannot be predicted from the individual meanings of the morphemes it comprises. For example, when we say that someone 'kicked the
bucket', we do not imply that they necessarily hit a certain type of container
for liquids with their foot; what we mean is that they *died*. Similarly, when we
say 'Don't beat a dead horse' we do not imply that the carcass of a certain
kind of animal is involved; what we mean is that the person should not waste
time harping on about an issue that has already been decided. When we say
that John used a 'red herring' in his argument, we do not imply that he
made use of a specific type of fish called 'herring'; instead we mean that
John introduced an irrelevant question to turn attention away from the
main issue. Other examples of idiom are 'bury the hatchet', 'come up
smelling like a rose', 'have an axe to grind', 'have a bone to pick with
somebody', 'have second thoughts', 'hit the nail right on the head', 'hit the
sack', 'let the cat out of the bag', 'on the straight and narrow', 'straight from
the horse's mouth', 'take the bull by the horns', 'wash one's dirty linen in
public'.

From the above examples, chosen at random, it is apparent that most
idioms are easily recognized as 'frozen' metaphors. However, once they are
established as fixed lexical units, frozen metaphors tend to lose their
vividness, and speakers often lose sight of their metaphorical origins. For
instance, the metaphorical origin of 'kick the bucket' is not readily apparent
to most speakers of modern English, and is in any case disputed.

Besides 'full' idioms, lexicologists also identify what are called 'partial
idioms'. In such idioms, some of the words have their usual meaning while
the others have meanings that are peculiar to that particular structure.
Thus, in 'red hair' the word *hair* has its usual meaning because it does refer
to the fine filaments growing from the human head; but *red* is idiomatic in
the sense that it does not refer to the strict colour term. Similarly, in 'to
make a bed', *a bed* is not idiomatic because it does refer to the piece of
furniture used to sleep on; however, *to make* is not used in the usual sense of
'to manufacture'. An interesting set of partial idioms involves the word
white, since 'white coffee' is brown in colour, 'white wine' is usually yellow,
and 'white people' are generally off-pink. While the words *coffee, wine,* and
people have their usual meanings, *white* is perhaps idiomatic at least to some
degree: it could be interpreted as 'the lightest in colour of that usually to be
found'. *Black* is, of course, used as its antonym for 'coffee' and 'people'
(though again neither is black in colour terms); yet it is not used for wine.
Thus, we may say that even partial idiomaticity can be a matter of degree and
may in some cases be little more than a matter of collocational restriction.
For instance, we can say that *black* collocates with *coffee* and *people* but not
with *wine*. (For more on collocation, see 5.1.2, 5.6, and 8.4.3.)

In conclusion, what is and what is not an idiom is, then, a matter of degree
(Fernando and Flavell 1981). Consider, for instance, 'make up a story',
'make up a fire', and 'make up one's face'. The first expression is used in its
literal meaning, the second is a partial idiom, while the last is fully idiomatic.

Idioms may be characterized by several features; but they may be summarized under two main headings: ambiguity, and syntactic peculiarities. Since most idioms are constructed from morphemes that are also used non-idiomatically, they may have either a literal or an idiomatic meaning; hence, their ambiguity. For example, if someone 'beats a dead horse', they may in fact be in the process of striking the carcass of an animal (literal meaning); or they may be wasting time discussing a matter that has already been closed (idiomatic meaning). Similarly, if someone 'hits the sack', they could be engaged in striking a sack (literal meaning) or they could be going to bed (idiomatic meaning). However, once a reader or hearer realizes that a given expression is an idiom, even if they are not sure of its exact meaning, they will automatically discard the literal meaning of the expression, and seek an idiomatic meaning (Abdullah and Jackson 1999). Furthermore, the context in which the idiom occurs also plays an important role in the reduction of this potential ambiguity.

In addition to the fact that idioms differ semantically from the corresponding strings of morphemes taken in the literal sense, idioms also have special syntactic properties. Consider 'John kicked the bucket'. In the literal sense, this expression has a passive variant, viz. 'The bucket was kicked by John'. But in its idiomatic use, i.e. when 'kicked the bucket' means 'died', the expression does not allow the use of the corresponding passive alternative. Also, as a general rule, in an idiomatic expression, none of the words may be replaced by a synonym. For example, in 'we look forward to meeting you', *look* cannot be replaced by *see* or *watch*, for instance. Hence '*we see/ watch forward to meeting you' is not idiomatic. Similarly, in 'wash one's dirty linen in public', *linen* cannot be replaced by *socks*, neither can *thought* be replaced by *idea* in 'have second thoughts'. Furthermore, none of the words in an idiomatic expression may normally be omitted. So, '*we look forward seeing you' is unacceptable because *to* is omitted. Similarly, '*straight from horse's mouth' and '*turn a new leaf' are both unacceptable because *the* and *over* have been omitted. There are other syntactic restrictions which characterize idioms. But we need not elaborate on such cases, especially as syntactic restrictions vary from one idiom to another, some idioms being more restricted or frozen than others (see Fernando and Flavell 1981).

EXERCISE 3/6

Examine the following definition of 'word' from *Collins English Dictionary* (1992):

> one of the units of speech or writing that native speakers of a language usually regard as the smallest isolable meaningful element of the language, although linguists would analyse these further into morphemes.

> In the light of the discussion in this chapter, what considerations have been ignored by this definition?

3.6 Summary

This chapter has shown the central importance of the word in lexicology. In so doing, it has first provided an answer to the fundamental question: 'What exactly is meant by "word" in lexicology?' Secondly, it has examined the notion of 'word meaning', before discussing two of the relationships that may be established between words, viz. polysemy and homonymy. Finally, it has revisited the notion of 'lexeme'; and with appropriate examples, discussed two of the main types of multiword lexeme, viz. multiword verbs and idioms.

4 Word Formation

Before we explore the different types of meaning relations that may exist between words in Chapter 5, we will examine the various processes of forming new words in English. We have already dealt extensively with borrowing and given a brief summary on the creation of new words in Chapter 2. We shall now examine two of the most general and most predictable processes of combining morphemes to form new words: inflection and derivation. Then, we shall deal with compounds, and finally with other word-formation processes such as conversion, blends and shortenings. However, our first question is: 'Why study word-formation processes?'

4.1 Why study word-formation processes?

By 'word-formation processes' we mean the different devices which are used in English to build new words from existing ones. Each word-formation process will result in the production of a specific type of word. Consequently, an understanding of these processes is one way of studying the different types of word that exist in English. In other words, if we know how complex lexical items are made by the association of different constituent morphemes, then we can also analyse any complex word into its various constituents. For example, if we know how the plural morpheme {-s} is added to singular nouns to make them plural, then we can also analyse any complex noun which is already inflected for plural into its constituent parts. Similarly, if we know how the comparative suffix {-er} and the superlative {-est} are added to adjectives, then given any inflected adjective, we can also analyse it into its constituent morphemes.

To give another example, if we know that *disturbance* and *payment* are made by the addition of the suffixes *-ance* and *-ment* to the verbs *disturb* and *pay* respectively, then we can also analyse any complex noun inflected by any of these suffixes into its constituent parts. However, not all instances of *-ance* and *-ment* are suffixes in English, for example *dance* and *comment*. As indicated in 3.1.3, what is left after the removal of a supposed affix must also be identifiable as a morpheme.

In our discussion of word-formation processes, we shall use the terminology already introduced in Chapters 1 and 3. It will be recalled that *free* forms are forms that occur alone; *bound* forms are those that cannot occur alone. *Stems* are forms that carry the basic meaning of the word; *affixes* add meaning to the stem. If a stem consists of a single morpheme it is also called a *root* or *base*. Roots constitute the innermost core of words and carry their basic meaning. Stems and roots may be bound or free but affixes are always bound. The affixes may be further classified as *prefix*, *suffix* or *suprafix*, depending on whether they occur before, after, or simultaneously with the stem.

We shall now turn to our next question: 'What is the difference between inflection and derivation?'

EXERCISE 4/1

Analyse the following words into their constituent morphemes. Remember, only analyse if all the parts of the word can be accounted for.

beadiness, coagulative, deactivators, forbearingly, half-deafened, left-handedness, noncombatant, readability, temporarily, weedkiller

---

4.2 Inflection and derivation

Inflection is a general grammatical process which combines words and affixes (always suffixes in English) to produce alternative grammatical forms of words. For example, the plural morpheme is an inflectional morpheme. This implies that the plural form *roses*, for instance, does not represent a lexical item fundamentally different from the singular form *rose*; it is simply an inflectional variant of the same word. Similarly, the addition of the comparative inflection {-er} to the adjective *cold* gives *colder*, which is not a different lexical item, but an inflectional variant of the same word.

On the other hand, derivation is a lexical process which actually forms a new word out of an existing one by the addition of a derivational affix. For instance, the suffixes *-ation* and *-ure* may be added to the verbs *resign* and *depart* respectively to derive the nouns *resignation* and *departure*, which are different words. Similarly, the suffixes *-dom* and *-ful* may be added to the adjective *free* and the noun *hope* respectively to derive the noun *freedom* and the adjective *hopeful*, which again are different words. Following Jackson (1985: 34), it may be said that 'strictly speaking, the term "derivation" refers to the creation of a new word by means of the addition of an affix to a stem'.

The above definitions and examples show that the distinction between inflection and derivation is mainly morphological. While the application of inflection leads to the formation of alternative grammatical forms of the same word, that of derivation creates new vocabulary items. This is the basic difference between inflection and derivation. However, each process does have additional characteristics which we shall now examine.

4.3 Inflectional affixes

We shall first define and give appropriate examples of inflectional affixes in 4.3.1, before discussing their characteristics in 4.3.2.

4.3.1 Definition and examples

Inflectional affixes may be described as 'relational markers' that fit words for use in syntax. This means that once the inflection or relational marker is added to a stem, that stem does not change classes, but its distribution is then limited in the syntactic structure. For example, the addition of the possessive suffix fits the inflected noun for use in syntax as noun modifier (i.e. like an adjective). The noun with the possessive marker can only be used as a modifier of another noun, never as a head or main element in a given structure. Thus, *John* + possessive becomes *John's* as in *John's book*. However, the word class of the noun has not changed. Note that although *John's* does function like an adjective, it is still not an adjective: it cannot take the affixes {-er} 'comparative' and {-est} 'superlative' which are characteristic of many monosyllabic members of that class.

Similarly, when the plural inflection is added to *dog* to form *dogs*, both *dog* and *dogs* are nouns and the addition of the plural inflection does not change the grammatical class of the word, but they do not have the same distribution in syntactic structures. Hence we say 'The *dog is* barking' but 'The *dogs are* barking'. To give another example, suffixing the past participle morpheme to the verb *speak* gives us *spoken*, which is still a verb; but both verbs cannot always occur in the same linguistic context. For instance, if we have the structure 'John could have spoken' we cannot replace the inflected verb form *spoken* by the corresponding uninflected form *speak*. Hence, '* John could have speak' is ungrammatical, i.e. not built according to the rules of English syntax.

4.3.2 Characteristics of inflectional affixes

One of the most important characteristics of inflectional suffixes is that they tend to lend themselves to paradigms which apply to the language as a whole. The paradigm of a major word class consists of a single stem of that class with the inflectional suffixes which the stem may take. The paradigm may be used as a suitable way of defining the word class in the sense that if a word belongs to that class it must take at least some of the suffixes characteristic of that set as opposed to suffixes characterizing other paradigms. However, to belong to a class, a word need not take every inflectional suffix in the paradigm. Inflectional suffixes of nouns, adjectives, and verbs may be tabulated and illustrated as follows (see Cook 1969: 122–3):

Nouns show the following inflectional contrasts:

Base form	stem + plural	stem + possessive	stem + plural + possessive
boy	boys	boy's	boys'
child	children	child's	children's
student	students	student's	students'

Adjectives (that are gradable and mono- or di-syllabic) show the following inflectional contrasts:

Base form	stem + comparative	stem + superlative
cold	colder	coldest
happy	happier	happiest
sad	sadder	saddest

Verbs (except the verb *be* and modals) show the following inflectional contrasts:

Base form	stem + 3rd person singular	stem + past tense	stem + past participle	stem + present participle
eat	eats	ate	eaten	eating
sing	sings	sang	sung	singing
work	works	worked	worked	working

Note that in some verbs, including all those formed regularly with *-ed*, the five-part paradigm has four parts only, because the past tense and the past participle inflections are identical in form. However, the past tense and the past participle inflections may be recognized as different morphemes which happen to have identical shape in such cases (they are homonyms).

English *pronouns* and *auxiliary verbs* may also be characterized by the noun and verb inflectional paradigms respectively, while some *adverbs* may be characterized by the adjective paradigm as shown in the following subsections.

Pronouns constitute a class of function words (1.3.4). They do not add suffixes which are inflections, but their respective forms fit the noun inflectional paradigm as shown below:

child	children	child's	children's
I, me	we, us	mine	ours
you	you	yours	yours
he, him		his	
she, her	they, them	hers	theirs
it, it		its	

The alternatives listed in each cell of the paradigm are mutually exclusive in the sense that where one occurs the other one does not occur (i.e. they are in complementary distribution). For example, *I* occurs before verbs (as grammatical subject), as in '*I* wrote a letter' whereas *me* occurs immediately after verbs (as grammatical object or indirect object), as in 'John wrote *me* a letter' or as the complement of a preposition as in 'John wrote a letter to *me*'. Similarly, *mine* replaces the whole structure consisting of '*my* + *noun*'. Thus *mine* could stand for 'my letter', 'my book', as in 'This book is mine.'

Auxiliaries constitute a closed sub-class of verbs. They can take certain forms of the verb paradigm but not all. While most verbs have five or four forms, the modal auxiliaries only have two. The English auxiliary *be* is the most polymorphic of all verbs, with eight different forms, while the modal auxiliary *must* only has one form whether it is used in the past or present tense (see paradigm below).

eat	eats	ate	eaten	eating
be	am/are/is	was/were	been	being
can	could			
may	might			
must				
shall	should			
will	would			

Note that although *must* has just one form, it is still considered to be a modal auxiliary verb.

Adverbs (some, and not usually -*ly* adverbs like *quickly*) of one or two syllables show the following inflectional contrasts:

Base form	*stem + comparative*	*stem + superlative*
fast	faster	fastest
soon	sooner	soonest

Since most adverbs consist of more than two syllables, this paradigm cannot be used as a definition of the class of adverbs in English.

Finally, under inflections, the distinction between 'regular' and 'irregular' inflections needs to be pointed out. Regular inflections are those that are formed according to a common pattern, e.g. -*s* for the plural of nouns, -*ed* for the past tense and past participle of verbs, -*er* for the comparative of adjectives. Irregular inflections are those that do not follow this pattern and which usually apply to only one or a small number of members of the word class concerned. For example, the following nouns form their plurals irregularly: child – children, man – men, mouse – mice, sheep – sheep, tooth – teeth. The number of verbs that form their past tense and past participle irregularly is much greater, e.g. begin – began – begun, buy – bought, give – gave – given, go – went – gone, hold – held, sing – sang – sung, split – split, throw – threw – thrown, write – wrote – written. Even the regular inflections may show some variation in spelling (e.g. dropping of *e* from *-ed*: *moved*; or the addition of *e* to *-s*: *masses*) and more usually in pronunciation: compare the pronunciation of plural *-(e)s* in *cats, dogs, horses*; and of the past tense *-ed* in *walked, jogged, glided*.

EXERCISE 4/2

Give all the possible inflections for the following words:

   bring, cow, forget, guest, have, high, stop, tall, tooth, weary

---

4.4 Derivational affixes

After a brief definition and a discussion of the main characteristics of derivational affixes in 4.4.1, we shall deal with the different types of derivational affixes in 4.4.2, before giving a recapitulatory table of English derivational affixes in 4.4.3.

4.4.1 Definition and examples

English has over sixty common derivational affixes, and there is no theoretical limit to their number. Derivations have a 'low functional load', in the sense that each single derivation occurs rarely and is limited to a few specific combinations with particular stems. In other words, they tend not to be paradigms which apply to sets of words as a whole. Even though derivational affixes do have characteristics which may enable us to distinguish them from inflectional suffixes, it should be noted that the distinction between the two types of affixes is not always clear-cut, e.g. the 'past participle' suffix *-ed* is used to form adjectives of the *red-haired* type.

Derivational affixes can change the word class of the item they are added to and establish words as members of the various word classes. They are inner with respect to inflections, so that if derivations and inflections co-occur, derivations are inner, closer to the stem, and inflections are outer, furthest from the stem, as shown in the table below.

Example	Base form	+ Derivation	+ Inflection
frightened	fright	-en	-ed
activating	active	-ate	-ing
payments	pay	-ment	-s
resignations	resign	-ation	-s

As a final observation, it must be said that derivational affixes do not always cause a change in grammatical class. The derivational affix *re-*, for example, derives *reconsider* from *consider*, yet both are verbs. Also, compare *populate/ depopulate,   intelligent/ unintelligent,   probable/ improbable*. Furthermore, a shift in grammatical class is not always signalled by an overt marker. Thus, *staff* and *star* are basically nouns, but they can also be used as verbs, with no affix as in the sentence 'The manager did not *staff* the restaurant properly' and 'I don't think Susan is the best actor to *star* in that new film'. A change in word class without the addition of an affix is known as 'conversion'. Sometimes a word consisting of two or more syllables may undergo a change of word class, with the only indicator being a change in the stress pattern. For example, in the following lists, stress distinguishes the nouns on the left from the verbs on the right. ('Stress' as used here means the impression of more energy in the articulation of the stressed syllable, which usually results in its sounding louder and longer than other syllables in the same word. The symbol (') occurs in front of the stressed syllable.) We shall regard 'stress' as a derivational affix (suprafix, see 4.1).

Nouns	*Verbs*
'contract	con'tract
'defect	de'fect
'import	im'port
'permit	per'mit
'present	pre'sent
'reject	re'ject

One exception to this rule is the word *effect* which is both a noun and a verb without any corresponding change in stress pattern.

4.4.2 *Types of derivational affix*

Derivational affixes are of two kinds: class-changing and class-maintaining. Class-changing derivational affixes change the word class of the word to which they are added. Thus, *resign*, a verb + *-ation* gives *resignation*, a noun. Class-maintaining derivational affixes do not change the word class of the word but change the meaning of the derivative (i.e. the word which results from the derivation). Thus *child*, a noun + *-hood* gives *childhood*, still a noun, but now an 'abstract' rather than a 'concrete' noun.

Class-changing derivational affixes, once added to a stem, form a derivative which is automatically marked by that affix as noun, verb, adjective or adverb. The derivations are said to determine or govern the word class of the stem. We shall discuss in turn noun, verb, adjective and adverb derivational affixes. Each of them has two distinct patterns of derivation depending on the word class with which the affix is associated.

For example, nouns may be derived from either verbs or adjectives; verbs from either nouns or adjectives; adjectives from either nouns or verbs; and adverbs from either adjectives or nouns. As will be shown below, English class-changing derivations are mainly suffixes.

Noun derivational affixes are also called 'nominalizers', e.g.

Verb	+	Affix	Noun
Leak		-age	leakage
Argu(e)		-ment	argument
Betray		-al	betrayal
Resign		-ation	resignation
Defen(d)		-ce	defence
Disturb		-ance	disturbance
Refer		-ee	referee
Depart		-ure	departure
Consult		-ant	consultant
Farm		-er	farmer
Enquir(e)		-y	enquiry
Brag		-art	braggart
Conclud(e)		-ion	conclusion
Im'port		(stress)	'import

Adjective	+	Affix	Noun
Accurat(e)		-y	accuracy
Social		-ist	socialist
Electric		-ity	electricity
Free		-dom	freedom
Good		-ness	goodness
Tru(e)		-th	truth
Social		-ite	socialite

Verb derivational affixes, also known as 'verbalizers', are used to form verbs from other stems. When compared with other derivational affixes, they are rather rare. This may be accounted for by the fact that verbs are the most basic forms in English: while they are used to derive other words, they themselves are not readily derived from other forms. Most English verbalizers are characterized by the fact that they are causatives.

Noun	+	Affix	Verb
Fright		-en	frighten
Pressur(e)		-ize	pressurize
Friend		be-	befriend
Glory		-fy	glorify
Title		en-	entitle

Adjective	+	Affix	Verb
Soft		-en	soften
Able		en-	enable
Pur(e)		-ify	purify
Legal		-ize	legalize

Adjective derivational affixes or 'adjectivizers' are used to form adjectives when added to a given stem. In English, adjectives are generally formed from nouns, more rarely from verbs.

Noun	+	Affix	Adjective
Season		-al	seasonal
Wretch		-ed	wretched
Care		-less	careless
Suburb		-an	suburban
Gold		-en	golden
Life		-like	lifelike
Hope		-ful	hopeful
Day		-ly	daily
Station		-ary	stationary
Fam(e)		-ous	famous
Passion		-ate	passionate
Child		-ish	childish
Cream		-y	creamy

Verb	+	Affix	Adjective
Argu(e)		-able	arguable
Creat(e)		-ive	creative
Depend		-ent	dependent
Sens(e)		-ory	sensory
Tire		-some	tiresome

Adverb derivational affixes or 'adverbializers' are affixes which form adverbs when added to a given stem. Adverbs, in English, are generally formed from adjectives, sometimes from nouns. Once it is formed, the adverb can no longer be used to form words of other classes such as nouns, verbs, or adjectives.

Adjectives	+	Affix	Adverb
Consistent		-ly	consistently
Slow		-ly	slowly
Obvious		-ly	obviously

-ly is the most productive of all derivational affixes.

Noun	+	Affix	Adverb
Home		-ward	homeward
Sky		-wards	skywards
Clock		-wise	clockwise
Shore		a-	ashore

Class-maintaining derivations refer to those derivations which do not change the word class of the stem to which they are added although they do change its meaning. Unlike class-changing derivations, which are mainly suffixes, English class-maintaining derivations are mainly prefixes.

Noun patterns:

Noun	+	Affix	Noun
Malaria		anti-	anti-malaria
Chief		-dom	chiefdom
Scholar		-ship	scholarship
Priest		ex-	ex-priest
Child		-hood	childhood
Duke		-y	duchy

Verb patterns:

Verb	+	Affix	Verb
Join		ad-	adjoin
Agree		dis-	disagree
Open		re-	reopen
Locate		col-	collocate
Judge		pre-	prejudge
Tie		un-	untie
Claim		pro-	proclaim

Adjective patterns:

Adjective	+	Affix	Adjective
Social		anti-	anti-social
Kind		-ly	kindly
Possible		im-	impossible
Green		-ish	greenish

As already pointed out, English adverbs are not used to derive words of other classes; consequently, we cannot speak of English adverb patterns to parallel the noun, verb and adjective patterns discussed above.

4.4.3 *Chart of English derivational affixes (adapted from Cook 1969: 129)*

For the purpose of this chart, the symbols *n, v, aj,* and *av* correspond to nouns, verbs, adjectives, and adverbs respectively. The derivational affixes are marked as input → output. Thus, D.n-n means a noun becoming a noun; D.v-aj, a verb becoming an adjective, and so on. In class-maintaining derivations both input and output consist of the same symbol (D.n-n, D.v-v, D.aj-aj).

Once formed, the derivative is treated as the simplest member of the same word class, both in syntax and in the addition of inflectional suffixes. Thus, *dog, argument,* and *childhood* behave similarly as shown below.

Stem class	→Noun	→Verb	→Adjective	→Adverb
1. Noun	D.n-n child-hood	D.n-v pres-surize	D.n-aj hopeful	D.n-av clockwise
2. Verb	D.v-n argu-ment	D.v-v pre-judge	D.v-aj creative	D.v-av no case
3. Adjective	D.aj-n soc-ialism	D.aj-v soften	D.aj-aj unreal	D.aj-av hardly

dog	dogs	dog's
argument	arguments	argument's
childhood	childhoods	childhood's

The { dog / argument / childhood } is ...   but   The { dogs / arguments / childhoods } are ...

EXERCISE 4/3

Identify the derivational affixes used in the following words. Give a meaning/function for each one, e.g. *-ment*: has the function of deriving a noun from a verb; *re-* means 'again'.

covariance, enactable, ungracious, preconnection, depressive, incriminatory, proconsulship, officialdom, declassify, trouble-some.

4.5 Compounds

After a brief definition of compounds in 4.5.1, we shall discuss the distinction between compounds and phrases in 4.5.2 before studying the parts of a compound in 4.5.3 and the classification of compounds in 4.5.4; finally, in 4.5.5 we shall give a recapitulatory chart of English compounds.

4.5.1 Definition

Compounds may be defined as stems consisting of more than one root. For example, *bedside, black market, car-wash, waste paper basket*. Note that the orthographic treatment of compounds is by no means consistent. Some are written as one word (with or without a hyphen between two roots), while others are written as two or more words. This observation tends to suggest that compounds have an intermediary status between phrases and words consisting of a single root. Note also that although most compounds consist of roots that are simply juxtaposed, in some cases, one of the roots of a compound may be modified by an inflection as in 'bird's-eye', 'driving-licence', and 'homing pigeon'.

4.5.2 Distinction between compounds and phrases

In English, compounds may be distinguished from phrases on phonological, syntactic, and semantic grounds.

In English, words are characterized by a single primary stress, so that compounds are often recognized by stress pattern and lack of juncture. (Juncture refers to the transition which characterizes adjacent syllables belonging to contiguous words.) For example, 'black 'board potentially has primary stress on each word and a juncture between the two words. On the other hand, 'black-board, the compound, has one primary stress and no juncture. The same observation applies to contrasts such as 'black 'bird versus 'blackbird; 'hard 'cover versus 'hardcover.

Compounds may also be distinguished from phrases in that they have specific syntactic features. But it must be added that the grammatical relations between the constituents of the compound are sometimes obscure. We shall consider in turn 'word order', 'interruptibility', 'modification', and 'inflectibility' of compounds.

Word order refers to the position of the different constituents of a compound in relation to one another. Some compounds are characterized by the fact that they use what may be considered ungrammatical or at least unusual word order in English. For example, the structure 'Noun + Adjective' is not the most usual phrase pattern in English but it occurs in compounds such as *sea-sick*. Similarly, the structure 'Verb + Preposition' is regular for verbs and unusual for nouns, but it does occur in the case of the compound *splashdown* which is a noun. Objects usually follow their verbs in sentence structure, but not necessarily in compounds, e.g. *knee-jerk*.

All compounds are non-interruptible in the sense that in normal use their constituent parts are not interrupted by extraneous elements, which confirms the assumption that compounds are indeed single lexical units. For example, the compound *dare-devil* cannot be used as 'dare *the* devil', which is a phrase. In general, once an extraneous element is inserted between the roots of a compound (see the insertion of *the* in *dare-devil* above), it destroys the stability of the whole structure to such an extent that the latter is no longer recognizable as a compound in English.

Modification refers to the use of other words to modify the meaning of a compound. Since the compound is a single unit, its constituent elements cannot be modified independently; however, the compound as a whole may indeed be modified by other words. For example, *air-sick* may occur neither as '*hot* air-sick', with *hot* modifying *air*, nor as 'air-*very* sick' with *very* modifying *sick*. However, if we say 'John was seriously air-sick', *seriously* modifies the whole compound, not just the first element.

Inflectibility refers to the use of inflections to modify the grammatical function of compounds. As a lexical unit, the compound may be inflected according to its grammatical class; however, its constituent elements may not be inflected. For example, *bottle-neck*, which is a noun, may not occur as *'bottle*s*-necks' with *bottle* inflected for plural. Instead, the form *bottle-necks* must be used to show the plural form of the compound. Similarly, we have *ash-trays*, *dish-washers*, *finger-prints*, *waste paper baskets*, *textbooks*. To give another example, consider *downgrade* as a verb: the corresponding past tense is not *downed grade* but *downgraded*. Similarly, we have *baby-sat* for *baby-sit*, *sweet-talked* for *sweet-talk*.

Compounds are characterized semantically by the fact that they tend to acquire specialized meanings, thus becoming very much like idioms. Only in rare cases is the meaning of a compound derived from that of its constituents in the literal sense. In most cases, the meaning of at least one of the constituents is somehow obscured. For example, a *dustbin* is not restricted to the collection of dust alone; a *blackboard* may be green and may be made of material other than wood.

To close this discussion of the distinction between compounds and phrases, it should be said that the phonological, syntactic and semantic features discussed above operate simultaneously and give the compound a strong binding force, thus making it quite distinct from the phrase.

4.5.3 Parts of a compound

We shall discuss in turn compounds consisting of two roots, and compounds in which one of the elements is complex.

Compounds consisting of two roots are the simplest type of compound. They also tend to be the most numerous in the language. To give an idea of the extent to which this type of compound dominates in English we have listed some of the initial roots. It is possible to verify them from any dictionary and see the vast number of compounds that may be formed from each initial root.

Nouns as initial elements: air, arm, ash, beach, bird, book, bull, car, cat, cow, door, duck, ear, eye, farm, foot, hair, hand, heart, house, lamp, lip, moon, mouth, rail, rain, rose, shoe, snow, suit, star, steam, sun, table, tea, time, wall, wind, wrist.

Verbs as initial elements: break, carry, cast, come, count, drive, drop, fall, feed, go, kick, line, pick, play, pull, push, print, read, run, set, shoot, show, sit, splash, stand, stick, swim, take, turn.

Adjectives as initial elements: big, black, blue, brief, cold, fair, far, green, grey, high, hot, left, long, low, near, quick, red, right, short, slow, small, south, straight, tight, white, yellow.

Adverbs as initial elements: about, after, back, by, down, fore, front, hind, in, off, on, out, over, under, up.

There is a rather special type of two-part compound which is not formed by the combination of two free root morphemes, but by the combination of two bound root morphemes. These are the so-called 'neo-classical' compounds, such as *astronaut, bibliography, xenophobia*. They are formed from Greek and Latin roots (*astro*, 'star', *naut*, 'sailor'; *biblio*, 'book', *graphy*, 'writing'; *xeno*, 'foreigner', *phobia*, 'fear'), which do not, for the most part, occur as simple words in English, and whose combinations are not generally compounds in classical Greek and Latin. They are 'learned' vocabulary and form much of the international vocabulary of science, medicine and technology. They are considered to be compounds because their parts are clearly roots rather than affixes, but they are unlike the usual compounds in English because their roots are not free morphemes.

As already pointed out in 4.5.1, the first element of a compound may be inflected, as in 'bird'*s*-eye', 'driv*ing*-licence', and 'hom*ing* pigeon'. The second element of the compound may also be complex. In such cases, the pattern of the compound and its underlying form are determined by the type of suffix associated with the second element of the compound. Note that we are interested here in cases where one of the roots of the compound must always occur with a suffix; not in cases such as *ash-tray(s)* and *textbook(s)* where the suffix is optional. We shall discuss the cases where the second element is suffixed by either *-er* or *-ed*.

Forms in *-er* that occur as second root function in the compound as simple forms. The construction should be analysed as Noun + Noun (*-er*). For example, *book-keeper, coat-hanger, dish-washer, house-keeper, left-winger*, are all analysable in terms of Noun + Noun compounds. The second noun is a derived form with the structure 'verb root + derivation'.

Forms in *-ed* which occur as second root are phrase derivatives, with *-ed* governing the whole phrase. Consequently, such constructions should be analysed as (Adjective + Noun) + *-ed*. For example, in *left-handed, left* modifies *hand* and the whole phrase is in turn governed by *-ed*. The same analysis also applies to *kind-hearted, red-haired, well-intentioned*.

4.5.4 Classification of compounds

It will be recalled that compounds must consist of more than one root, but the different roots need not belong to the same word class. When the two constituents of the compound belong to the same class (e.g. noun + noun, verb + verb), it may be assumed that the resulting compound also belongs to the same word class and functions as the simplest member of that class. But when the two constituents of the compound belong to different word classes, the classification of the resulting compound cannot be taken for granted.

We shall consider the classification of compounds according to the word class, and the syntactic relationship between the roots. Classification by word class is independent of the syntactic relation existing between the two roots and resembles an algebraic equation. As a general rule, the word class of the last element of the compound determines the class of the compound. We shall consider in turn noun, verb, adjective, and adverb compounds.

Noun compounds: Any root + noun = noun compound
The second root must be a noun while the first root may be a noun, a verb, an adjective or an adverb. Examples of noun compounds are as follows:
N + N (modifier-head): ash-tray, arm-chair, text-book
V + N (verb-object): dare-devil, pick-pocket
Aj + N (modifier-head): black-bird, blue-collar, hard-cover
Av + N (not syntactic): after-thought, back-talk, down-grade.

Verb compounds: Any root + verb = verb compound
The second root must be a verb and the first root may be a noun, a verb, an adjective, or an adverb.
N + V (object-verb): baby-sit, brain-wash, house-keep
V + V (co-ordinate): dive-bomb, drop-kick
Aj + V (not syntactic): dry-clean, sweet-talk, white-wash
Av + V (modifier-head): down-grade, over-do.

Adjective compounds: Any root (except verbs) + adjective = adjective compound
The second root must be an adjective and the first root may be a noun, an adjective, or an adverb. Verbs do not combine with adjectives in English.
N + Aj (not syntactic): earth-bound, ox-eyed, sea-sick
Aj + Aj (co-ordinate): blue-green, metallic-green, south-west
Av + Aj (modifier-head): near-sighted, off-white.

Adverb compounds: Adverb + adverb = adverb compound
Av + Av (co-ordinate): in-to, through-out.

Special noun compounds: Verb + adverb = noun compound
The first root is a verb and the second root is an adverb. The compound may be distinguished from the 'verb + particle = phrasal verb' construction only by the context in which it occurs. V + Av (derivation): blast-off, drive-in. This class of compounds is the only type which does not follow the general rule in English; that is, it is the only one composed of two roots in which the compound is not a member of the same class as the second root. So, *blast-off* and *drive-in* are not adverbs but nouns.

The type of syntactic relationship existing between the two roots of a compound is a reliable criterion for the classification of compounds into sub-groups. The first, which includes most compounds and is therefore the most important, consists of compounds in which the constituents are put together according to syntactic rules that also operate elsewhere in English phrase structures. The second, by far the smaller, consists of compounds in

which the association of roots violates syntactic rules. We shall discuss the
first sub-group under the label 'syntactic compounds' and the second under
'non-syntactic compounds'.

To parallel the different types of phrase that may be identified in English,
syntactic compounds may be classified as follows:

> *Endocentric:* one or both roots is the 'head' of the compound
>> co-ordinate: two head roots, e.g. *boyfriend,* i.e. a boy who is a friend, a
>> friend who is a boy
>> subordinate: only one head root; this is a modification structure, e.g.
>> *armchair,* i.e. a chair with arms
>
> *Exocentric:* neither root is the 'head'
>> e.g. *pick-pocket,* i.e. one who picks pockets.

Since non-syntactic compounds do not follow the rules of syntax, they
cannot be classified systematically like syntactic compounds. They include
structures such as:

> 'Noun + Adjective' and 'Adverb + Noun' instead of the more common
> structures 'Adjective + Noun' and 'Noun + Adverb' respectively:
> Noun + Adjective: *air-sick,* i.e. sick because of travelling by air.
> Adverb + Noun: *back-talk,* i.e. rude talk in reply to someone (derived
> from 'to talk back').

Both syntactic and non-syntactic compounds may be characterized by the
fact that the relationship between the constituents is highly condensed.
Compounds are thus interpreted as short-cuts for longer and more elaborate phrase structures. If the elaborate phrase structure is perceived, then
the meaning of the compound becomes more explicit. For example, in
noun compounds consisting of the structure 'noun + noun', we may
postulate the existence of relational words (e.g. prepositions) in the structure, as follows: *ash-tray* = tray *for* ashes; *armchair* = chair *with* arms; *sea-shore*
= shore *of* the sea; *sun-light* = light *from* the sun; *gas-mask* = mask *against*
gases.

4.5.5 *Chart of English compounds*

English compounds consisting of two roots may be represented conveniently in the chart shown below. As already stated above, it should be
noted that the grammatical class of the compound is the same as that of the
last element in its structure. The only exception is the 'verb + adverb'
construction in which the resulting compound is not an adverb, but a
noun.

To close this discussion of English compounds, it must be said that
although a number of regularities can be observed, the process of compound formation does not lend itself readily to general rules. All the various
regularities which may be formulated are coupled with many important
exceptions. Consider, for instance, English compounds consisting of an

Compound	+ Noun	+ Verb	+ Adjective	+ Adverb
1. Noun	N + N moon-light	V + V drop-kick	N + Aj sea-sick	N + Av No case
2. Verb	V + N pick-pocket	V + V dive-bomb	V + Aj No case	V + Av = N lift-off
3. Adjective	Aj + N black-board	Aj + V dry-clean	Aj + Aj blue-green	Aj + Av No case
4. Adverb	Av + N back-talk	Av + V over-do	Av + Aj off-white	Av + Av in-to

adjective and a noun. The following seem quite regular: *dirty-work, English-man, long jump, madman, wildlife*. They can all be paraphrased by an expression of the form 'NOUN that is ADJECTIVE'. Thus, *dirty-work* is a *work* that is *dirty*; *wildlife* is *life* that is *wild*, and so on. This is a recurrent pattern of compound formation in English; in other words, given the existence of an expression of the form 'NOUN that is ADJECTIVE' a corresponding adjective-noun compound can be formed.

However, a person learning English must learn more than this general rule of compound formation. They must at the same time learn a wealth of unpredictable, arbitrary facts about compounds of this type; otherwise, they will end up with compounds built according to the general rule suggested. For example, while *dirty-work* is an English compound, *clean work* is not a compound, neither are *dry work* and *wet work*. Why do we have *madman* but neither *saneman* nor *deafman*?

Furthermore, many compounds that are superficially of this type do not mean what we could predict on the basis of the regular pattern. Hence a *highbrow* is not a 'brow' that is 'high', but an 'intellectual'. A *blackboard* is not necessarily a *board* that is *black*. Other examples of this kind are *dumbbell, red-coat, sourpuss, tenderfoot*. Similar observations could be made for compounds other than those consisting of an adjective and a noun.

As shown in the above discussion, compounds have phonological, syntactic, and semantic features which account for their status as single words; on the other hand, since the meaning of a compound cannot always be predicted from that of its constituents, compounds also have features in common with an intermediary structure between simple lexical items on the one hand and idioms and phrases on the other. Note, however, that a discussion of English phrases has its place in the study of syntax, not in that of lexicology. As for the discussion of idioms, it comes under 'multiword lexemes', since each idiom consists of at least two words in a specific collocation (see 3.5).

EXERCISE 4/4

Return to the list of compound-initial elements in 4.5.3 and choose two elements from each of the noun, verb, adjective and adverbs lists. Create as many compounds as you can think of, and then check your lists against a dictionary.

4.6 Other word-formation processes

In addition to inflection, derivation and compounding, there are other word-formation processes in English. We shall discuss in turn conversion, blends and shortenings.

4.6.1 Conversion

Conversion may be defined as a process by which a word belonging to one word class is transferred to another word class without any concomitant change of form, either in pronunciation or spelling. It is a highly prolific source for the production of new words since there is no restriction on the form that can undergo conversion in English. In fact, this word-formation process occurs so regularly that many scholars prefer to consider it as a matter of syntactic usage rather than as word-formation (see Bauer 1983: 227). Pyles and Algeo (1993: 281) use the term 'functional shift' to refer to the same process and to highlight the fact that in such cases, words are converted from one grammatical function to another without any change in form.

Conversion may involve a change within the same word class as in the change from one type of noun to another or one type of verb to another. For example, the use of uncountable nouns as countable and vice-versa. Thus, in 'some beer/coffee/sugar/tea', the nouns are uncountable; whereas in 'two beers/coffees/sugars/teas', the nouns are countable. As a general rule, if the context is carefully chosen, it is possible to use almost any noun in either way. Even proper names can be easily used as common nouns as in 'Which Hilary do you mean?'. Similarly, intransitive verbs are often used as transitive verbs. Compare for instance the members of the following pair:

How long can a pigeon *fly* non-stop?
Can this little boy *fly* a kite?

The first is intransitive and the second transitive.

Conversion most often involves a change from one word class to another. The major kinds of conversion are noun → verb, verb → noun, adjective → noun, and adjective → verb. For example:

Noun → verb: to bottle, to commission, to data-bank, to network.

Verb → noun: a call, a command, a guess, a spy.
Adjective → verb: to better, to dirty, to empty, to wrong.
Adjective → noun: Such conversions are relatively rare and restricted in their syntactic occurrences; e.g. the poor, the rich (no plural), a convertible, a daily, a double.

Adverbs, prepositions, conjunctions, interjections and even affixes can all act as bases for conversion as in *to up* prices (preposition → verb), the *hereafter* (adverb → noun). Furthermore, many of these word classes can undergo conversion into more than one other word class, e.g. to go *down* (adverb particle), to *down* a beer (verb), to have a *down* on someone (noun). Finally, it should be noted that even a whole phrase may undergo conversion and act as a noun, e.g. a *forget-me-not*, a *has been*, a *don't know*, it may also act as an adjective as in a *Monday morning* feeling, a *not-to-be-missed* opportunity.

To close this brief discussion of conversion, we wish to point out that contrary to the position adopted by some scholars (e.g. Bauer 1983: 228–9), we do not recognize a class of 'marginal cases of conversion'. From the point of view adopted in this book, if there is any change in either spelling or pronunciation, as a word is transferred from one word class to another, we cannot speak of conversion (see 4.4.1).

4.6.2 Blends

A blend may be defined as a new lexeme built from parts of two (or possibly more) words in such a way that the constituent parts are usually easily identifiable, though in some instances, only one of the elements may be identifiable. Blends may also be referred to as 'telescope' or 'portemanteau' words (see Gramley and Pätzold 1992: 26). For example:

breakfast	+	*lunch*	→ brunch
channel	+	*tunnel*	→ chunnel
dove	+	*hawk*	→ dawk
motor	+	*hotel*	→ motel
sheep	+	*goat*	→ shoat
slang	+	*language*	→ slanguage.

These examples show that in the formation of blends, the first part of the first element is added to the second part of the second element. The resulting items are generally nouns, while a few are adjectives such as *glitzy* (glitter + ritzy), and verbs such as *gues(s)timate* (guess + estimate) and *skyjack* (sky + hijack).

Blends tend to be more frequent in informal style in the registers of journalism, advertising and technical fields. They give rise either to new morphemes or to folk etymology. In most cases, blending results in the creation of new morphemes or in the addition of new meanings to old ones. For example, *automobile*, taken from French, was originally a combination of

Greek *autos*, 'self' and Latin *mobilis*, 'movable'. The element *auto* became productive as evidenced by the words *autobiography, autodidact, autograph, autocar* and *autobus*. The second element of *automobile* also acquired a combining function as in *bookmobile*, 'library on wheels' and *bloodmobile*, 'blood bank on wheels'. Similarly, *hamburger* was blended so often with other words (e.g. cheeseburger, steakburger, chickenburger, and vegeburger) that the form *burger* acquired the status of an independent word.

Folk etymology (see 1.1.3) is viewed here as a minor kind of blending. It is a naive misunderstanding of a relatively esoteric word which gives it a new, but false, etymology. Pyles and Algeo (1993: 280) give interesting examples of such folk etymology: a certain ballet jump called '*saut de basque*' ('Basque leap') which was interpreted by American students as *soda box*, a lady who interpreted *chest of drawers* as *Chester drawers*, or a child too young to read who interpreted 'artificial snow' as 'Archie Fisher snow' because he knew a man called Archie Fisher, who displayed it in his shop window. However, it should be pointed out that we speak of folk etymology only when this sort of misunderstanding of words becomes sufficiently widespread, thus leading to the acquisition of a new item in the English vocabulary.

4.6.3 Shortenings

We have already discussed some of the processes used in the creation of new English words in 2.5. We shall now turn to the processes which come under the heading of shortening, viz. clipping, backformation, initialism and aphetic forms. Clipping involves the type of word-formation device in which only part of the stem is retained. The beginning may be retained as in *lab* (from laboratory), the end as in *plane* and *phone* (from aeroplane and telephone respectively), the middle as in *flu* (from influenza). Very often, the clipped form completely supplants the original full form. Thus, *bra, bus, car* and *mob* supplanted *brassière, omnibus, motorcar* and *mobile vulgus* respectively.

Backformation is the making of a new word from an older word which is mistakenly assumed to be its derivative. Backderivation is characterized by the fact that it involves the shortening of a longer word by the substraction of a morpheme. For example, it may be said that the verbs *peddle* and *televise* are derived from the corresponding nouns *peddler* and *television* by the subtraction of the suffixes *-er* and *-ion* respectively. But following Strang (1969: 231), backformation can better be interpreted as a means of completing a proportion. According to this interpretation, verbs such as *peddle* and *televise* arise from completing the proportions writer : write :: peddler : ?; revision : revise :: television : ?. In other words, *write* is to *writer* as *peddle* is to *peddler*. Similarly, *revise* is to *revision* as *televise* is to *television*.

Initialisms constitute an extreme kind of clipping since only the initial letters of words, or sometimes initial syllables, are put together and used as words. Usually, the motivation for initialism 'is either brevity or catchiness, though sometimes euphemism may be involved, as with BO and VD for "body odour" and "Venereal Disease" respectively' (Pyles and Algeo 1993: 273).

When initialisms are pronounced with the names of the letters of the alphabet, they may be called *alphabetisms* or abbreviations. But when they are pronounced like individual lexical items, they are *acronyms*: from Greek *akros*, 'tip' and *onyma*, 'name', by analogy with *homonym*. Examples of alphabetisms are: AI (*A*mnesty *I*nternational; *A*rtificial *I*ntelligence); ATV (*a*ll *t*errain *v*ehicle in AmE; *A*ssociated *T*ele*v*ision in BrE); BP (*b*eautiful *p*eople, AmE; *B*ritish *P*etroleum; *b*lood *p*ressure, BrE); VIP (*v*ery *i*mportant *p*erson). Examples of acronyms are: *laser* (*l*ight wave *a*mplification by *s*timulated *e*mission of *r*adiation), *scuba* (*s*elf-*c*ontained *u*nder *w*ater *b*reathing *a*pparatus), AIDS (*a*cquired *i*mmune *d*eficiency *s*yndrome), RAM (*r*andom *a*ccess *m*emory); ROM (*r*ead *o*nly *m*emory), NATO (*N*orth *A*tlantic *T*reaty *O*rganization), UNESCO (*U*nited *N*ations *E*ducation *S*cientific and *C*ultural *O*rganization).

There are also cases where alphabetisms are mixed with acronyms and the two systems of pronunciation are combined: e.g. VP (for *V*ice-*P*resident) pronounced like *veep* and ROTC (for *R*eserve *O*fficers *T*raining *C*orps) pronounced like *rotcy*.

Aphetic forms are a special kind of shortening characterized by the omission of the initial unstressed syllable as in *'scuse me* and *'cause* for *excuse me* and *because* respectively. This phenomenon has often resulted in the introduction of two different words in the language, as illustrated by the following pairs: fender–defender, fence–defence, cute–acute and sport–disport. The first member of each pair is said to be an aphetic form of the second.

To illustrate the difference between aphesis on the one hand, ellipsis and clipping on the other, consider the word *professor*. When pronounced casually, the first, unstressed syllable may be omitted, shortening the word to *'fessor* and giving an aphetic form. But when the word is shortened to *Prof*, it is an instance of clipping.

EXERCISE 4/5

During one day keep a notebook to hand and write down from your newspaper reading and listening to the broadcast media all the word formations that strike you as new or unusual. Attempt to make an anlysis of them in terms of derivation, compounding and other processes.

4.7 Summary

In this chapter, we have examined English word-formation processes. In the main, we have focused our attention on derivation and compounding, two of the most general and most predictable processes of combining morphemes to form new words. Before discussing these major processes, it was necessary not only to define word-formation processes, but also to answer the question 'Why study word-formation processes?' Finally, we dealt with other word-formation processes such as conversion, blends and shortenings.

5   Meaning Relations

In this chapter, we are going to explore various types of semantic relationship that may hold between words, both within the vocabulary as a whole and in use in sentences.

5.1 What are 'meaning relations'?

A discussion of meaning (e.g. Lyons 1977, Palmer 1981) often begins by drawing a distinction between the 'reference' of a word and the 'sense' of a word. Reference is an external meaning relation; it is the relationship between a word and the entity that it 'refers to' in the physical world, in our mental world, or in the world of our experience. The reference of *tree* is a particular plant which has a trunk, branches, twigs and leaves; the reference of *hostility* is a particular attitude displayed especially by humans and animals that signals hatred and enmity.

5.1.1 Sense relations

Sense is an internal meaning relation. Sense relations hold between words within the vocabulary. The two most obvious sense relations are those of 'sameness' and 'oppositeness', called synonymy and antonymy respectively. Other sense relations – hyponymy, meronymy – relate words hierarchically, showing how a word with a general meaning includes the meaning of other words with more specific meanings. *Hostility* has a relation of synonymy with *antagonism* and *enmity*, and a relation of antonymy with *friendliness*. *Tree* is in a hierarchical relation with *plant*, a more general term, and with *beech* and *oak*, more specific terms.

5.1.2 Collocation

Sense relations are paradigmatic. They are about the choice between words, the substitution of one word for another in a particular contextual slot in a sentence. Words also contract semantic relations syntagmatically, with words occupying other slots in a sentence. Such relations are described in terms of collocation, the mutual expectancy of words, or the ability of a word to predict the likelihood of another word occurring. The verb *flex* in English allows only a limited number of possible words as object in the sentence, primarily *muscles* or parts of the body such as *legs* or *arms*. The adjective *maiden* predicts a limited number of nouns, primarily *voyage* or *flight* and *speech*.

5.1.3 Semantic field

What the existence of these meaning relations shows is that the vocabulary of a language is not an unstructured collection of words. There is some evidence from word association experiments in psychology that these meaning relations are relevant for the way in which we store words in our 'mental lexicon' (Aitchison 1994). Lexicologists also use them to propose descriptions of vocabulary structure. One of the concepts used is that of the semantic or lexical 'field'. The vocabulary is said to be organized into a number of, partially overlapping, semantic fields. A semantic field contains words that belong to a defined area of meaning (e.g. education). The field then becomes the context within which to establish meaning relations.

There is no agreement among lexicologists on a method for establishing semantic fields. One method suggests that the words in a field share a common 'semantic component'. The term comes from an approach to the analysis of word meaning called 'componential analysis', which seeks to express the meaning of a word in terms of its semantic components. The meaning of *mare* could be said to be composed of the components 'equine', 'adult', 'female'. Besides possibly helping to establish semantic fields, componential analysis could also be a way of establishing, or at least confirming sense relations.

Having introduced the topics that this chapter is concerned with, we will look at each of them in more detail, beginning with the sense relations.

5.2 Synonymy

The term 'synonymy' comes from a Greek word (*sunonumon*) meaning 'having the same name'. It is used in modern semantics to refer to a relationship of 'sameness of meaning' that may hold between two words. Synonymy is a widespread relation in the vocabulary of English, for which good evidence is provided by the many synonym dictionaries and thesauruses (e.g. the Concise Oxford Thesaurus, Collins Thesaurus). Here is a list of examples of synonym pairs in modern English:

beseech	implore
glitter	sparkle
havoc	devastation
intricate	involved
lazy	indolent

native	indigenous
near	close
plentiful	abundant
substitute	surrogate
treble	triple.

These have been taken from the synonym essays in the *Longman Dictionary of the English Language* (LDEL) (1991), which attempt to explain the sometimes very subtle differences in meaning between words that are closely related in meaning. For example, *beseech* and *implore* occur in a synonym essay under *beg*:

> **Beg, entreat, beseech, implore, supplicate** and **importune** all signify the making of an appeal which is likely to be refused or demurred at. A person **begs** for what he/she cannot claim as a right; **beg** suggests earnestness, insistence, and sometimes self-abasement. By **entreating** someone, one hopes to persuade him/her by earnest pleading and reasoning. **Beseech** and **implore** convey eager anxiety which seeks to inspire sympathy or pity. **Implore** may be stronger than **beseech**, with a suggestion of tearfulness or evident anguish. **Supplicate** adds to **entreat** a humble, prayerful attitude < *invite, entreat, supplicate them to accompany you* – Lord Chesterfield >. **Importune** denotes persistence with one's requests to the point of annoyance or even harassment. (LDEL 1991: 141)

Such an attempt implies that even between identifiable 'synonyms' there is some, however small, difference in meaning. If we take such a position, there is, arguably, no such thing as true synonymy.

5.2.1 Strict and loose synonymy

Many linguists do take this position and make a distinction between 'strict' or 'absolute' (Cruse 1986) synonymy and 'loose' synonymy. In the strict sense, two words that are synonyms would have to be interchangeable in all their possible contexts of use: a free choice would exist for a speaker or writer of either one or the other word in any given context. The choice would have no effect on the meaning, style or connotation of what was being said or written. Linguists argue that such strict synonymy does not exist, or that, if it does, it exists only as semantic change is taking place.

Strict synonymy is uneconomical; it creates unnecessary redundancy in a language. To have a completely free choice between two words for a particular context is a luxury that we can well do without. Indeed, it would appear that where, historically, two words have been in danger of becoming strict synonyms, one of them has either changed its meaning in some way or fallen out of use. For example, when the word *sky* was borrowed from Old Norse into English it came into competition with the native English word *heaven*: both words denoted both the physical firmament and the spiritual realm of God and the angels. In due course, *sky* came to denote just the physical, and *heaven* just the spiritual; though each is still sometimes used in the context where the other would normally be expected. Similarly, when *spirit* was borrowed from French (ultimately from Latin), it was in competition with the native English *ghost* (compare: *Holy Ghost, Holy Spirit*): *spirit* has taken over as the term with the more general meaning, and *ghost* is more or less restricted to 'disembodied spirit' meanings. Consider also the following archaic or obsolete words, which have fallen out of use and been replaced by the items in brackets:

culver (pigeon)
divers (various)
dorp (village)
erst (formerly)
fain (willing)
levin (lightning)
trig (neat)
warrener (gamekeeper)
wight (human being)
yare (readily)

When we speak of synonymy, then, we mean varying degrees of 'loose' synonymy, where we identify not only a significant overlap in meaning between two words, but also some contexts at least where they cannot substitute for each other. Take the synonyms *find* and *discover*: they are substitutable in the context *Lydia found/discovered the ball behind the garden shed*; but not in the context *Marie Curie discovered radium in 1898* or in the context *Franz found it easy to compose sonatas*. As is evident in this case, synonyms may be substitutable where their meaning overlaps, but where a meaning falls outside of the shared area (*discover* = 'be the first one to come across something', *find* = 'experience something in some way') one cannot be used instead of the other. Synonyms may overlap in meaning to a greater or lesser degree, though it is not clear how this might be measured, nor whether there is a limit at which the notion of synonymy becomes meaningless.

5.2.2 Distinguishing synonyms

The question that we wish to answer now is: can we make any generalizations about the different kinds of contexts in which the meanings of synonyms may differ? The answer is that we can make some generalizations, but they do not cover all the cases, as the need for the synonym essays in the LDEL demonstrates.

Some synonym pairs differ in that they belong to different dialects of English. The dialects in question may be one of the national standards, e.g. British, American or Australian English; or they may be a regional dialect within a country or area, e.g. Tyneside, West Midlands, South-West dialects of British English. Here are some examples of synonym pairs in British and American English:

bonnet (car)	hood
caravan	trailer
drawing pin	thumbtack
farm	ranch
lawyer	attorney
lift	elevator
pavement	sidewalk
refuse/rubbish	garbage
tap	faucet
windscreen	windshield.

Now here are some synonym pairs from standard British and northern British English:

anyway	anyroad
armpit	oxter
brew (tea)	mash
child	bairn
frightening	fleysome
money	brass
nothing	nowt
passageway	ginnel/snicket
sandwich	butty
splinter	skelf.

A second general way in which synonyms may be distinguished relates to the style or formality of the context in which a word may be used. One of a pair of synonyms may be used in a more formal context than the other; or one of the pair may belong to slang or colloquial English, while the other is in more general use. Here are some examples of synonym pairs, where one of the pair is usually used in an informal or less formal context and the other in a more formal context:

archer	toxophilite
argument	disputation
beauty	pulchritude
cross	traverse
die	decease
give up	renounce
letter	missive
praise	eulogy
warning	caveat
western	occidental.

Now here are some synonym pairs from standard English and from English slang:

astonished	gobsmacked
crash	prang

destroy	zap
drunk	sloshed, etc.
face	phizog
heart	ticker
insane	barmy, etc.
money	rhino, spondulix, etc.
prison	clink
steal	nick, etc.

For some ordinary language words, such as *drunk, insane* or *stupid, money,* slang synonyms proliferate.

A third way in which synonym pairs may be distinguished is where connotations differ. Two words may largely share a denotation, in referring to a particular entity, but they may have divergent associative or emotive meanings. Take the words *push* and *shove*: their denotation largely overlaps – forceful propulsion forward; but *shove* connotes roughness or haste, which *push* does not. Here are some further pairs of synonyms that differ in their connotations (in brackets):

ambiguous	equivocal (deliberately)
famous	notorious (disreputably)
hate	loathe (with repugnance or disgust)
misuse	abuse (of privilege or power)
new	novel (strikingly)
obtain	procure (with effort)
persuade	inveigle (with ingenuity or deceit)
proud	haughty (with disdain)
recollection	reminiscence (with pleasure)
simulate	feign (with craftiness).

Arguably, both members of each pair of synonyms belong to the same dialect (the standard) and to the same level of formality. It is the connotation of the second member of each pair that distinguishes them.

5.2.3 Why so many synonyms?

English is a language particularly rich in pairs of synonyms. The primary reason for this has to do with the history of the language and especially with the wholesale borrowing from other languages, especially French and Latin. Chapter 2 traced this history. We can now see the consequences for the meaning relation of synonymy. In the list below, the words on the left have their origin in Old English, those on the right were borrowed from French (F) or Latin (L):

ask for	request (F)
din	commotion (L)
drive back	repulse (L)

drop	globule (L)
glove	gauntlet (F)
need	require (F)
pock (mark)	pistule (L)
rope	cable (F)
slake	satisfy (F)
smother	suffocate (L).

You will notice that the words from Old English are generally shorter than their French or Latin synonyms. They also tend to belong to the ordinary, colloquial language, whereas their Latinate synonyms belong to a more formal context.

Words borrowed directly from Latin may sometimes be more formal or technical than a synonym that entered English as a consequence of the Norman French invasion. Here are some examples of this case, with the French-derived word on the left and the Latin-derived word on the right:

commencement	inception
devise	excogitate
generous	munificent
imprison	incarcerate
mount	ascend
pardon	amnesty
urgency	exigency.

It is not always the case that the Latin-derived word will be more formal and less familiar. In the course of history, some words derived directly from Latin have found their place in the common language, but the clear tendency is for words derived from Latin, especially where these were borrowed into Latin from Greek, to belong to formal and often technical styles.

EXERCISE 5/1

Write a synonym essay in the style of the LDEL for the following set of synonyms:

plentiful, plenteous, ample, abundant, copious.

They all suggest 'more than enough but not too much'.

EXERCISE 5/2

What distinguishes each of the following pairs of synonyms – dialect, formality, or connotation?

1. astonished – flabbergasted

2. chat – gossip
3. earwig – clipshears
4. give – donate
5. hate – loathe
6. ice lolly – icey pole
7. insect – creepy-crawlie
8. much – mickle
9. slippery – slippy
10. throw – hurl

5.3 Antonymy

Oppositeness is perhaps not such a pervasive meaning relation in the vocabulary of English as synonymy, but it has an important role in structuring the vocabulary of English. This is especially so in the adjective word class, where a good many words occur in antonymous pairs, e.g. *long-short, wide-narrow, new-old, rough-smooth, light-dark, straight-crooked, deep-shallow, fast-slow*. While antonymy is typically found among adjectives it is not restricted to this word class: *bring-take* (verbs), *death-life* (nouns), *noisily-quietly* (adverbs), *above-below* (prepositions), *after-before* (conjunctions or prepositions).

Besides having morphologically unrelated antonyms, as in the examples above, English can also derive antonyms by means of prefixes and suffixes. Negative prefixes such as *dis-*, *un-* or *in-* may derive an antonym from the positive root, e.g. *dishonest, unsympathetic, infertile*. Compare also: *encourage-discourage* but *entangle-disentangle, increase-decrease, include-exclude*. Similarly, the suffixes *-ful, -less* may derive pairs of antonyms, e.g. *useful-useless, thoughtful-thoughtless*; but this is by no means always the case, e.g. *hopeful* and *hopeless* are not antonyms, *grateful* has no counterpart **grateless*, *selfless* has no counterpart **selfful*.

5.3.1 Co-occurrence of antonyms

It is often the case that antonyms occur together, either within the same sentence or in adjacent sentences (Fellbaum 1995). One reason is that certain expressions are structured in this way, e.g. 'a matter of life and death', 'from start to finish', 'the long and the short of it', 'neither friend nor foe', 'wanted dead or alive'. A second reason is that antonyms may be used redundantly to emphasize a point, e.g. 'It was a remark made in private, not in public', or to make a rhetorical flourish, e.g. 'Is this the beginning of the end or the end of the beginning?' Another context in which antonyms are typically employed is where reference is to a change of state, e.g. 'The museum opens at nine and closes at four'.

We generally think of antonymy as a relation holding between words belonging to the same word class, but since antonymy is a semantic relation, it may hold between words that belong to different word classes. For example, in 'Lighten our darkness, we pray', a verb and a noun form an antonym pair. In 'She remembered to shut the door but left the window open', a verb and an adjective are in a relation of antonymy. Clearly, oppositeness influences our thinking and communicating to a significant extent, as the widespread use of antonymy demonstrates.

5.3.2 Types of antonym

Unlike synonymy, antonymy covers a number of different types of oppositeness of meaning. Three types are commonly identified: gradable antonyms, contradictory or complementary antonyms, and converses. Antonym pairs of these types express oppositeness in rather different ways, though it is not clear that we as speakers are necessarily aware of these differences or that they play a part in how we store antonyms in our mental lexicon.

Gradable antonyms include pairs like the following:

beautiful	ugly
expensive	cheap
fast	slow
hot	cold
increase	decrease
long	short
love	hate
rich	poor
sweet	sour
wide	narrow

These pairs are called gradable antonyms because they do not represent an either/or relation but rather a more/less relation. The words can be viewed as terms at the end-points of a continuum or gradient. The more/less relation is evident in a number of ways: the terms allow comparison, e.g. 'My arm is longer/shorter than yours', 'I love a good book more than a good meal'; the adjectives can be modified by 'intensifying' adverbs, e.g. *very long, extremely hot, extraordinarily beautiful*. The terms do not represent absolute values; for the adjectives the value depends on the noun being described; the length of arms is on a different scale from the length of, say, roads. In such pairs of adjectives, one is usually a marked term, the other unmarked. This manifests itself, for example, in questions such as 'How long is the street?' To ask 'How short is the street?' already assumes that the street has been identified as short. The use of *long* does not make an assumption either way. Also, in giving dimensions, you would use the 'larger' term, e.g. 'The street is 400 metres *long*' (not *short*).

The following are examples of contradictory or complementary antonyms:

asleep	awake
dead	alive

on	off
permit	forbid
remember	forget
shut	open
true	false
win	lose.

These pairs of antonyms are in an either/or relation of oppositeness. An animate being can be described as either *dead* or *alive*, but not as some grade of these or as being more one than the other. The assertion of one implies the denial of the other member of the pair: if you *permit* some behaviour, then it is not *forbidden*; if you *lose* a contest, then you have not *won* it; if a switch is *on*, then it is not *off*.

The following are examples of converse antonyms:

above	below
before	after
behind	in front of
buy	sell
give	receive
husband	wife
parent	child
speak	listen.

For each pair of antonyms, one expresses the converse meaning of the other. In the case of sentences with *buy* and *sell*, for example, the same transaction is expressed from different (converse) perspectives:

Lydia bought the car from Kirsten.
Kirsten sold the car to Lydia.

Similarly with nouns such as *husband* and *wife*, a sentence may express the relationship in one of two, converse, ways:

Margaret is Malcolm's wife.
Malcolm is Margaret's husband.

And the same is also true for prepositions like *above* and *below*.

The spaghetti is on the shelf above the rice.
The rice is on the shelf below the spaghetti.

5.3.3 How pervasive is antonymy?

If you look at any dictionary of synonyms and antonyms, you will find that far more synonyms are given than antonyms. Sameness of meaning seems to be a more pervasive semantic relation than oppositeness of meaning. Why should this be so?

One reason must be the extraordinary synonym richness of English arising from the blending of words from different language sources in its vocabulary. A converse reason is that the number of words and their related concepts that allow an opposite is limited, whereas there is no such theoretical limitation on the relation of synonymy.

As we noted earlier, the largest group of antonyms are to be found in the adjective word class, among the 'gradable' adjectives (deep-shallow, near-far, clean-dirty). Some adjective antonym pairs belong to the complementary type (dead-alive, open-shut, singular-plural). Many adjectives, however, are not gradable, e.g. those referring to material (wooden, plastic, velvet), provenance (African, European, Cameroonian), shape (round, square, oval).

Other word classes contain antonym pairs, but to a lesser extent, and only of the complementary and converse types. Gradable antonyms are found only in the adjective class, or among adverbs derived from adjectives (slowly-quickly, frequently-rarely, closely-distantly). The noun class contains some complementary antonym pairs (sloth-diligence, joy-sadness, sleep-insomnia) and some converse antonym pairs (parent-child, teacher-student, employer-employee). Similarly, the verb class contains some complementary antonyms (go-stay, float-sink, gather-scatter), as well as some converse antonyms (send-receive, buy-sell, own-belong to). We have also noted some antonym pairs among prepositions/adverb particles (on-off – complementary, above-below – converse). But in all word classes other than adjectives, the incidence of antonym pairs is restricted.

EXERCISE 5/3

For each of the following words: (a) say whether it has an antonym and give it if it does; (b) say what kind of antonymy is involved (gradable, complementary, converse).

emigrate, equine, freedom, frothy, new, proud, simple, speak, straight, triangular

---

5.4 Hyponymy and meronymy

This section deals with a pair of sense relations that relate words hierarchically. The underlying observation is that some words have a more general meaning, while others have a more specific meaning, while referring to the same entity. For example, *tree* and *oak* may be used to refer to the same object, but *oak* is a more specific designation of the object than is *tree*. Indeed, *tree* may be used to refer to objects that are not oaks, but which share with them the essential features of 'treeness' (i.e. large plants, with trunk, branches, leaves, etc.). Similarly, a pain in the *foot* and a pain in the *toe* may refer to the same phenomenon; the second is merely a more specific way of designating the location of the pain.

Both *tree* and *oak*, and *foot* and *toe* are related to each other by a hierachical relation of generality/specificity. However, the two pairs of words illustrate different types of hierarchical relation. In the case of *tree* and *oak*, the relation is a 'kind of' relation: an oak is a kind of tree. This is the relation of hyponymy. In the case of *foot* and *toe*, the relation is a 'part of' relation: a toe is part of a foot. This is the relation of meronymy (Cruse 1986). You can probably begin to appreciate the extent to which these hierarchical relations structure the vocabulary, hyponymy more so than meronymy. These relations, and especially hyponymy, reflect the taxonomies, or classification systems, of the natural sciences, or indeed those that we make informally in talking about the world that we live in and experience. Let us look in a little more detail at each of these relations.

5.4.1 Hyponymy – the 'kind of' relation

The relation of hyponymy serves to structure large parts of a language's vocabulary. The organization of a work like *Roget's Thesaurus* (e.g. Kirkpatrick 1995) suggests that it is perhaps an all-pervasive structuring relation. It is most evident in the taxonomies of natural phenomena (see Godman and Payne 1979, McArthur 1981), e.g.

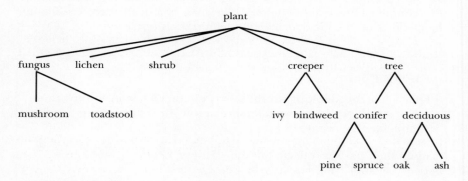

This is not by any means a complete taxonomy, or a very accurate one; it is merely to illustrate the hyponymy relation. The term at the top of the hierarchy (plant) has the most general meaning, and it can be used to refer to all the objects denoted by terms below it. It is a 'superordinate' term. Those immediately below it, the directly 'subordinate' terms (fungus, lichen, shrub, etc.), are its 'hyponyms'. So, *tree* is a hyponym of *plant*, but is in turn a superordinate to its hyponyms *conifer, deciduous; conifer* is in turn a superordinate to its hyponyms *pine, spruce*, etc. Reading up from the bottom of the hierarchy, *pine* is a 'kind of' *conifer*, which is a kind of *tree*, which is a kind of *plant*.

Hyponymy relations are not restricted to the classification systems of natural phenomena. They are found also, for example, in taxonomies of human artefacts, e.g.

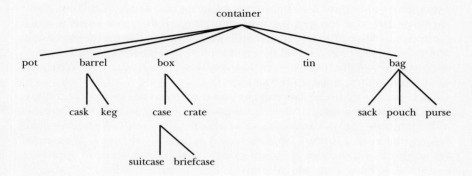

Again, the hierarchy is neither complete nor entirely accurate. For one thing, the term *barrel* probably needs to occur as a hyponym of itself; in other words, *barrel* denotes a class of objects that includes *casks*, *kegs* and *barrels*. *Barrel* has both a more general and a more specific meaning. What this begins to illustrate is that hyponymy hierarchies are not necessarily either complete or neatly arranged. After all, our vocabulary presumably contains the words that we, as members of a particular culture or speech community, need in order to communicate with each other about our environment and our experience. In many instances, we do need words of varying degrees of generality, so that we can refer to classes and sub-classes of entities; but that does not mean that they will always form a neat system of terms. We will explore this point further in 5.4.3 below.

5.4.2 Meronymy – the 'part of' relation

Just as the concern of scientists to classify natural phenomena is reflected in the semantic relation of hyponymy, so too their concern to analyse phenomena into their parts is reflected in the semantic relation of meronymy. The 'part of' relation can similarly be represented by a hierarchy of superordinate and subordinate (meronym) terms, e.g.

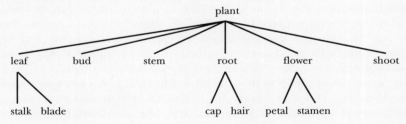

Reading from the bottom of the hierarchy, *petal* and *stamen* are parts (meronyms) of *flower*; *flower*, *root*, *stem*, etc. are parts (meronyms) of *plant*.

The superordinate term is not merely a more general way of talking about its meronyms, as in the hyponymy relation, though there is a sense in which the use of a superordinate term includes reference to the meronyms. *Flower* refers to the entity in its totality, including its petals, stamen, stalk, and so on; but these are not more specific kinds of flower, but rather different parts of it that together make up the whole.

Such part/whole relations exist between many words in the vocabulary. Most human artefacts are made up of parts, which we usually want to label with their own terms. A *knife* consists of a *blade* and a *handle*. A *fountain pen* is made up of a *cap*, a *barrel*, a *nib*, a *reservoir* (for the ink); the *cap* is made up of the *cap* itself and the *clip*. Most obviously, the meronym relation applies to entities that have concrete reference. But we also divide more abstract entities into their parts, e.g.

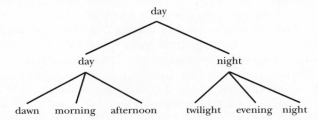

The terms *day* and *night* occur twice in this hierarchy because *day* refers both to the period of twenty-four hours and to the part of that period which enjoys daylight; *night* is in contrast with this second meaning of *day* and also refers to the darkest part of it.

5.4.3 Lexical gaps

When you begin to apply the notions of hyponymy and meronymy to parts of the vocabulary of a language, you soon realize that, as ordinary language users, we do not neatly classify and analyse things in the systematic way that scholars and scientists attempt to do. Consider the parts of the human *finger*: the finger has three joints, but we have a common language term for only one of them, the *knuckle* (see Oxford-Duden 1981: 44). This suggests that there are 'lexical gaps' for the other two potential meronyms, but we presumably so rarely need to refer to them that a periphrastic expression will usually suffice, e.g. *the middle joint* or *the joint nearest the nail*.

That was an example from meronymy. Let us now take a more extensive example, using the hyponymy relation, to illustrate the unsystematic nature of hierarchical organization in vocabulary. The superordinate term is *vehicle*, and so we will look at different kinds of vehicle. As a preliminary, we might propose the following hyponyms of *vehicle*:

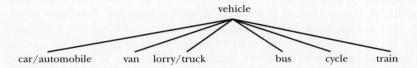

Further hyponyms might include various kinds of *carriage* and *cart*. But a more rational hierarchy might wish to insert an intermediate level of generality, which would distinguish *engine-powered, pedal-powered, horse-drawn, hand-operated/pushed* vehicles. However, these terms are not of quite the same kind as *vehicle, car, van*, etc.: they seem created for the purpose. Moreover, these distinctions would separate pedal cycles from motorcycles, which otherwise could be related thus:

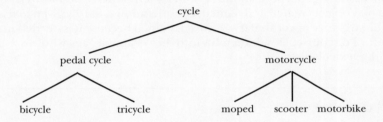

This partial hierarchy is not without its problems either: the terms *motorcycle* and *motorbike* are virtual synonyms and could be interchangeable, and it is arguable whether *scooter* is a kind of *motorcycle, moped* occupies an intermediate position between *pedal cycle* and *motorcycle*, being both pedal-driven and engine-powered. If we attempt to propose hyponyms for *lorry*, we might want to make an initial distinction between *articulated* and *non-articulated* lorries, but English does not have a proper term for lorries that are not articulated. We would then have to find a place in the hierarchy for: *tipper truck, pickup truck, flat truck*, etc. Now consider how the hierarchy might be expanded under *bus*:

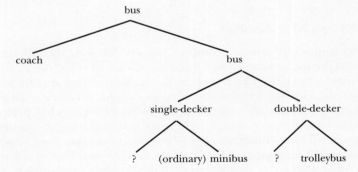

The term *bus* is both the overall term for this kind of vehicle and more specifically differentiates an urban mass passenger vehicle from one used for inter-city travel (coach). A *minibus* is a small *single-decker*, but there seems to be no term for an ordinary-sized *single-decker* as a co-hyponym. Similarly, *trolleybus* is a kind of *double-decker*, though distinguished not by size (as *minibus*) but by method of power. Again, though, there is no co-hyponym for an ordinary *double-decker*. And where would we fit *tram* into this hierarchy?

What this discussion is intended to demonstrate is that, while the hierarchical semantic relations of hyponymy and meronymy are undoubtedly important in the structuring of vocabulary, they do not operate in an altogether systematic and unambiguous way. There are many lexical gaps that are shown up when we begin to build words into hyponymy and meronymy trees, and co-hyponyms may not always be distinguished on the same basis (size, purpose, mode of power, etc.). When a new word is coined, or a new object created and named, consideration is hardly given to its place in the structure of vocabulary. A word is coined because it is needed in some mode of discourse. How it then fits into the vocabulary as a whole is a matter for the lexicologists.

EXERCISE 5/4

Propose a hyponymy tree with *crockery* as the most superordinate term. Can you identify any lexical gaps or where you need to use the same term on more than one level?

EXERCISE 5/5

Propose a meronymy tree for *bicycle*. Can you account for all the parts?

5.5 Analysing meaning

Meanings of words are complex matters. We have already suggested (5.1) that the meaning of a word involves, at least, its reference to an entity in the world of experience, as well as the sense relations it contracts with other words in the vocabulary, and the collocational relations (5.6) that may hold between it and other co-occurring words. From another perspective, some semanticists and lexicologists have suggested that meanings of words can be analysed into a finite number of features or components, which are universal to all languages, and from which the meanings of all words can be composed by new, unique combinations. Such an approach is called 'componential analysis' (Nida 1975, Leech 1981).

5.5.1 Components of meaning

Semantic components are typically represented as binary features, e.g. [+/−ANIMATE]. This means that the meaning of a word may be composed of the component [+ANIMATE] or of the component [−ANIMATE]. For example, the meaning of *vixen* would include the [+ANIMATE] component, while the meaning of *apple* would include [−ANIMATE]. The [+/−ANIMATE] component is one that serves to make a fundamental distinction between one set of words and another in the vocabulary of English, but at a rather high level of generality. Components of a more specific nature are taken to imply or subsume those that are more general; so [+/−FRUIT], for example, would subsume [−ANIMATE], and [+/−MAMMAL] would subsume [+ANIMATE].

Let us attempt a componential analysis of the meaning of *vixen*. A vixen is a female fox and so belongs to the class of mammals: the component [+MAMMAL] implies the components [+ANIMATE], [+ANIMAL]. We need a component to indicate that *vixen* is the female, in contrast to the *dog fox*; this component is usually marked as [−MALE]. We also need a component to indicate that *vixen* usually refers to a fully grown, adult fox, in contrast to a *fox cub*; this is usually marked as [+ADULT]. So far, our components – [+MAMMAL], [−MALE], [+ADULT] – could apply to a large number of words referring to adult female mammals (e.g. *bitch, mare, cow, sow, doe*). We need a component that will distinguish *vixen* from all of these. We could suggest [+VULPINE], from the Latin genus name *Vulpes*, in the same way that [+CANINE] is used for *dog*, [+BOVINE] for *cow*, [+EQUINE] for *horse*, etc. These components all imply the component [+MAMMAL], which now need not be indicated in their semantic description. What exactly the minus values for these components ([−VULPINE], [−EQUINE]) indicate is not clear, except 'any mammal that is not a fox', which is redundant if all other mammals also have positively valued unique components.

Within a genus, however, these components can usefully distinguish the meanings of the relevant set of lexemes, e.g.

	VULPINE	ADULT	MALE
fox	+	+/−	+/−
(dog) fox	+	+	+
vixen	+	+	−
fox cub	+	−	+/−

The '+/−' indicates that either may apply: *fox* as the general term includes both males and females, young and adult; *fox cub* is not differentiated for gender. Each lexeme has a unique set of components. They all share a plus value for [VULPINE], which is thus a 'common' component. The others serve to distinguish the meanings, and are therefore 'diagnostic' components. From this analysis, *fox*, with its '+/−' values under [ADULT] and [MALE], emerges as the superordinate term in a hyponymy hierarchy.

One of the early applications of componential analysis was by ethnographers in the study of kinship systems. Using the components [MALE], [ASCENDING GENERATION], [DESCENDING GENERATION], [LINEAL DESCENT], we can account for the following kinship terms in English:

	MALE	ASCEND	DESCEND	LINEAL
father	+	+	−	+
mother	−	+	−	+
uncle	+	+	−	−
aunt	−	+	−	−
brother	+	−	−	+
sister	−	−	−	+
cousin	+/−	−	−	−
son	+	−	+	+
daughter	−	−	+	+
nephew	+	−	+	−
niece	−	−	+	−

The components [ASCENDING GENERATION] and [DESCENDING GENERATION] account for a three-way meaning distinction between 'same generation as self' ([−ASCEND], [−DESCEND]), 'higher generation than self' ([+ASCEND], [−DESCEND]), and 'lower generation than self' ([−ASCEND], [+DESCEND]). The combination [+ASCEND]/[+DESCEND] is impossible: someone cannot be, for example, both your father and your son, or both your aunt and your niece. Now let us add the terms *grandfather, grandmother, grandson, granddaughter* to the list; we need a component that means 'two generations removed from self'. Such a component could be more easily and economically accommodated if we were to abandon the requirement for components to be binary. A single [GENERATION] component would encompass [ASCEND] and [DESCEND] as well: it would have values such as '0' for 'same generation', '+1' for 'one generation above self', '+2' for 'two generations above self' (i.e. grandparents), '−1' for 'one generation below self', and so on.

Arguably, multivalued components could usefully be employed for analysing the meaning of other lexemes. In the field of vehicle words, a component such as [MEDIUM] would have the values 'land' (for land-based vehicles), 'water' (for ships and boats), and 'air' (for aircraft). A component [MODE OF PROPULSION] would, likewise, be multivalued: e.g. 'engine', 'horse', 'wind', 'human'. As this example suggests, componential analysis may provide a useful tool for differentiating the meanings of lexemes within a semantic field (see Lehrer 1974).

The identification of components may contribute to establishing the essential meaning differences between semantically related lexemes. Much of Lehrer's (1974) discussion is concerned with cooking terms. Consider the following cooking verbs: cook, boil, bake, fry, braise, stew, grill, poach.

Components will need to be derived from considerations related to: whether liquid is used, and if so, whether water or fat/oil; whether immersion in liquid is required; whether cooking occurs in an oven or on a hob; whether a covered container is required; and so on.

EXERCISE 5/6

Construct a matrix with binary components only for the cooking verbs above, and then adapt it to one that may use multivalued components. Is one more revealing than the other?

There is no sure way of establishing what the universal set of semantic components might be: [ADULT] and [MALE] seem likely candidates, but [VULPINE] seems rather less obvious. Componential analysis also appears rather Anglocentric, with semantic components labelled in English, and reflecting Anglo-American culture and views of the world. Only the analysis of considerable numbers of lexemes in many different languages will reveal what such a set of components might plausibly look like. And it may well be the case that the meanings of many lexemes, even in English, cannot be exhaustively described by means of semantic components, especially those lexemes that have a more abstract reference (e.g. naive, aware, wise, foolish, sophisticated, etc.). And it is unlikely that very many components will turn out to be universal. Perhaps componential analysis has limited but powerful application to certain areas of semantic description.

5.5.2 *Semantic primitives*

An alternative approach to the analysis of meaning searches for the words in a language whose meaning is so basic that it cannot be further analysed and by means of which the meanings of more semantically complex words can be expressed (Wierzbicka 1995, 1996). Such an approach recognizes a basic set of meanings that is common to all people as communicating human beings, whatever particular language they may speak. Such meanings relate to innate human concepts. Anna Wierzbicka and her colleagues at the Australian National University in Canberra have so far identified some fifty or so 'semantic primitives', which have been found in a diverse range of languages from a number of different language families (Goddard and Wierzbicka, eds, 1994).

Semantic primitives are concepts that are indefinable, which find expression in words or bound morphemes in all languages. Words expressing such concepts in English include: *someone, something, this, do, happen, want, say, think, know, I, you, big* and *small, good* and *bad, can, not, where* and *when, because, if.* When dictionaries attempt to define such words, they usually either use far more complex language or resort to circularity. For example, *Collins*

English Dictionary (1986) defines *happen* as 'to come about or take place; occur'; and then it defines occur as 'to happen; take place; come about' – a circularity of definition. The same dictionary defines *good* as 'having admirable, pleasing, superior, or positive qualities; not negative, bad or mediocre' – a rather prolix definition for so simple a word. Semantic primitives, because they are basic and innate, cannot be further decomposed or analysed; they are not capable of definition.

The full list of semantic primitives, at the present state of research, as expressed in English, is given in Wierzbicka (1996: 35–6, 73–4) as:

'substantives'	I, YOU, SOMEONE, SOMETHING, PEOPLE
'determiners'	THIS, THE SAME, OTHER, SOME
'quantifiers'	ONE, TWO, MANY (MUCH), ALL
'augmentor'	MORE
'mental predicates'	THINK, KNOW, WANT, FEEL, SEE, HEAR
'non-mental predicates'	SAY, DO, HAPPEN, MOVE, THERE IS, (BE) ALIVE
'evaluators'	GOOD, BAD
'descriptors'	BIG, SMALL
'space'	WHERE, UNDER, ABOVE, FAR, NEAR, SIDE, INSIDE, HERE
'time'	WHEN, BEFORE, AFTER, A LONG TIME, A SHORT TIME, NOW
'partonomy and taxonomy'	PART (OF), KIND (OF)
'metapredicates'	NOT, CAN, VERY
'interclausal linkers'	IF, BECAUSE, LIKE
'imagination and possibility'	IF ... WOULD, MAYBE
'words'	WORD

This list of 55 semantic primitives combines two lists from Wierzbicka (1996), one of 37 'old' primitives, which are deemed well-established, and a second of eighteen 'new' primitives, whose status is less certain, because they have yet to be tested across a wide range of languages.

Semantic primitives can be used to define words with more complex meanings. Wierzbicka (1995: 150) suggests the following analysis of the meaning of *order* in the structure 'I order you to do it':

I say: I want you to do it.
I say this because I want you to do it.
I think you have to do it because I say this.

She contrasts this with the analysis of the meaning of *ask* in the structure 'I ask you to do it':

> I say: I want you to do it.
> I say this because I want you to do it.
> I don't think that you have to do it because I say this.

Wierzbicka (1996: 179) suggests the following analysis of the meaning of *disappointment*:

> X feels something
> sometimes a person thinks something like this:
> > something good will happen
> > I want this
> after this, this person thinks something like this:
> > I know now: this good thing will not happen
> because of this, this person feels something bad
> X feels something like this.

These do not look like conventional definitions, such as you find in most dictionaries, but they are certainly relatable to dictionary definitions. For example, *disappoint(ment)* is defined in the LDEL (1991) as: 'fail(ure) to meet the expectation or hope of; also sadden by so doing'. Such analyses are also arguably more revealing than the reductive analyses of componential analysis, besides being founded on a more secure empirical basis.

5.5.3 Semantic fields

In semantic (or lexical) field analysis, words are grouped together into 'fields' on the basis of an element of shared meaning. Such a field might comprise words referring to drinking vessels, or verbs of communication (*speak, order, warn, promise*, etc.). There is no set of agreed criteria for establishing semantic fields, though a 'common component' of meaning (see 5.5.1) might be one.

One of the arguments for a semantic field description of vocabulary, as against the description of words in isolation, as in the alphabetical arrangement of conventional dictionaries, is that it makes for a more revealing account of word meaning if a word is considered within the context of the semantic space it occupies with other semantically related words. In such a description, the sense relations play an important part in relating the meanings of words in the same semantic field.

An early example of a semantic field arrangement of English vocabulary is *Roget's Thesaurus* (originally 1852, latest edition Kirkpatrick 1995). The *Thesaurus* has a hierarchical organization, akin to the relation of hyponymy; and entries are arranged in two columns on the page, using the relation of antonymy; within the articles, the relation of (loose) synonymy groups words together. Roget divides the vocabulary initially into six broad 'classes': abstract relations, space, matter, intellect, volition, affections. Each of these classes is then sub-divided into 'sections'; e.g. affections has the sections: generally, personal, sympathetic, moral, religious. A further two sub-divisions take place to reach the articles (or semantic fields); moral affections, for example, are sub-divided into: obligations, sentiments, conditions, practice, institutions; and the obligations category, for example, has the articles: right/wrong, dueness/undueness, duty/dereliction and exemption. An article contains lists of words, organized by word class, that would fall under the heading of the article, 'dereliction of duty' for example.

As an attempt to organize the vocabulary of English into semantic fields (a term not used by Roget, incidentally), *Roget's Thesaurus* is a remarkable achievement. But the articles contain only lists of words and expressions. There is no attempt to differentiate the meanings of the words listed. That was not Roget's intention: he wanted to provide for users of the language a practical guide to the available vocabulary to express given ideas. The user of the *Thesaurus* would have a particular idea that they wanted to express, and the *Thesaurus* would tell them the words that were available in English to express that idea. In order to provide such a guide, Roget performed a semantic field analysis of English vocabulary, though his categories were based on a 'philosophical arrangement' (Editor's Preface to the 1879 edition).

A more recent attempt at a semantic field analysis of English is found in Tom McArthur's (1981) *Longman Lexicon of Contemporary English.* McArthur has taken around 15,000 words from the *Longman Dictionary of Contemporary English* (LDOCE) (1978) and arranged them into fourteen semantic fields 'of a pragmatic, everyday nature' (Preface, p. vi), e.g. Life and Living Things; People and the Family; Food, Drink and Farming; Thought and Communication, Language and Grammar; Movement, Location, Travel and Transport. The broad semantic fields are sub-divided; so the Movement field has sub-divisions of: Moving, Coming and Going; Putting and Taking, Pulling and Pushing; Travel and Visiting; Vehicles and Transport on Land; Places; Shipping, Aircraft; Location and Direction. These sub-divisions are further decomposed into smaller groups of related words; so Travel and Visiting has a group of nine verbs of 'visiting', a group of ten verbs of 'meeting people and things', a group of thirteen nouns of 'visiting and inviting', and so on. Each word has the appropriate dictionary information from the LDOCE (1978), including definitions, grammatical coding and illustrative examples. The user is thus enabled to see how words that are semantically related differ from each other in meaning, often in quite subtle ways.

Arguably, the *Longman Lexicon* is a more interesting and more revealing account of English vocabulary than that found in ordinary alphabetical dictionaries. The semantic field arrangement brings together words that share the same semantic space; it is a record of the vocabulary resources available for an area of meaning; and it enables a user of the language, whether a foreign learner or a native speaker, to appreciate often elusive

DRINKING VESSELS

Hot

Cold

Glass

Metal

China

Plastic

Alcoholic

Non-alcoholic

Material

Glass

Metal

China

Plastic

Drinks

Hot/Cold

Cold

Alcoholic — Beer / Wine / Spirits.

Non-alcoholic

meaning differences between words. But the *Lexicon* contains only 15,000 words; and it has not been updated with successive editions of the LDOCE (1987, 1995).

Another, but more specialized, semantic field dictionary, aimed like the *Lexicon* at foreign learners, though predating it, is Godman and Payne (1979). It arranges some 10,000 terms from the vocabulary of science into 125 sets according to subject matter (e.g. Crystal Structure, Plant Tissue, Chromatography, Metabolism, Magnetism). A semantic field arrangement also underlies the *Longman Language Activator* (1993), a 'production' dictionary to enable learners of English find an appropriate word for a given context. It is arranged around some 1000 'Key Words', which represent labels for semantic fields, such as: clothes, give, nervous, typical.

Semantic field analysis has, thus, been used to structure descriptions of the vocabulary in dictionaries, though there is, as yet, no general-purpose dictionary that uses the semantic field as its organizing principle. It is, perhaps, an area of lexicology that needs further investigation and elaboration before lexicographers feel confident in applying it more generally to dictionary structure.

EXERCISE 5/7

Suggest the words that might be included in a semantic field of 'drinking vessels'. Can they be organized within the field in some way? Are any of the sense relations relevant?

5.6 Collocation

The meaning relations that we have considered so far in this chapter have been of a substitutionary or paradigmatic nature. They have been concerned with words as alternative items in some context. Collocation refers to a structural or syntagmatic relation, to meaning relations that a word contracts with other words occurring in the same sentence or text. It is concerned with meaning arising from co-occurrence, more specifically to meaning arising from predictable co-occurrence.

5.6.1 A structural relation

Take the noun *kettle*, referring to a device for heating water. If the word *kettle* occurs in a sentence, there is a strong likelihood that the (verb) word *boil* will also occur, e.g.

I'll just boil a kettle.
Is the kettle boiling yet?

The co-occurrence of *kettle* and *boil* has a degree of predictability, and they each thus contribute to the meaning of the other. Part of the meaning of *kettle* is that it co-occurs predictably with *boil*, and part of the meaning of *boil* is that it co-occurs predictably with *kettle*, though the collocation in this direction is less predictable than from *kettle* to *boil*. The number of verbs that regularly co-occur with *kettle* is less than the number of nouns that regularly co-occur with *boil*.

Collocation most clearly occurs between words in specified syntactic relations, e.g. Subject + Verb (kettle + boil), or Verb + Object (boil + kettle), or Adjective + Noun (red + wine). This type of collocation is extensively illustrated in *The BBI Combinatory Dictionary of English* (Benson *et al.* 1986a, and its updated version, Benson *et al.* 1997). However, collocation as a meaning relation of predictable co-occurrence may be found across sentence boundaries (Halliday and Hasan 1976), e.g.

Would you mind filling the kettle and switching it on?
I need boiling water for the vegetables.

Here, *fill* and *switch on* collocate directly with *kettle* in a Verb + Object structure; but arguably *boil*, while collocating directly with *water* in an Adjective + Noun structure, also collocates across the sentence boundary with *kettle*, though less directly.

The kind of collocation that we have been discussing and illustrating is sometimes more explicitly referred to as 'lexical collocation'. This is to differentiate it from 'grammatical collocation', which is a grammatical rather than a semantic relation. In the narrowest sense, grammatical collocation refers to the specific preposition that must occur after a particular verb, noun or adjective: rely + on, fear + of, fond + of. More widely, it refers to any kind of syntactic element that must accompany a particular word (usually verb, noun or adjective in English), e.g. infinitive clause after *promise* or *attempt*, 'that' clause after *afraid*, and so on (see Benson *et al.* 1986a: ix–xxiii).

5.6.2 A relation of mutual expectancy

Lexical collocation has been called a relation of mutual expectancy or habitual association (McArthur (ed.) 1992). The occurrence of one word predicts the greater than chance likelihood that another word will occur in the context, either in some syntactic construction or across a syntactic boundary. Notice that this expresses the collocation relation in statistical terms: 'greater than chance likelihood of co-occurrence'. From this we might then conclude that the mutual expectancy of two words could be stronger or weaker, depending on both the direction of expectancy and the number of alternative predictable words.

We noted earlier, with *kettle* and *boil*, that the direction of the collocation relation affected the strength of the predictability: the collocation from *kettle* to *boil* is stronger than that from *boil* to *kettle*. Similarly, the collocation fundamental + change, issue.

spend + time/money

severe + trauma

+ unite + party/notion etc.

behave + well/badly/oneself et.

boost + income/confidence

from *rancid* to *butter* is stronger than vice-versa, because the number of nouns that are predicted by *rancid* is very restricted, perhaps *bacon* in addition to *butter*, and maybe one or two more. The number of adjectives that may occur with *butter*, on the other hand, is much larger.

The same point can be made by comparing the verbs *wreak* and *settle* and the range of nouns that may occur as the syntactic object of each of them. *Wreak* occurs predominantly with two nouns: *havoc* and *revenge/vengeance*. *Settle* occurs with a whole range of nouns: *dispute, argument, claim, stomach, nerves, child/baby,* and so on. *Wreak* thus has a stronger collocational relation with its object nouns than does *settle*.

EXERCISE 5/8

Give what you think are the typical collocations for the words in the following structures. For example, '*false* (Adj) + N' asks for the typical nouns that are modified by the adjective *false*: teeth, eye, passport, number plates, ceiling, etc.

> fundamental (Adj) + N
> spend (V) + Object N
> Adj + trauma (N)
> N + unite (V) + Prep
> behave (V) + Adv
> boost (V) + N

5.6.3 Discovering collocations

The few examples that we have used so far to illustrate collocations have tapped our intuitions about English words. While it is possible to come up with a reasonable amount of widely accepted data by this method, it is not a reliable method for investigating a statistical probability, which implies a degree of accuracy. However, until relatively recently, the intuitive method was the only one possible for lexicologists interested in collocation, and it is the method that is reflected in the content of most dictionaries. To achieve a measure of statistical accuracy, however, an empirical study, based on a corpus of texts, is required. The corpus will have to be quite large in order to provide reliable results, and in order to capture words that appear relatively infrequently. Today, corpora of a hundred million words and more are available on computer (see Chapter 7), and programs (e.g. TACT, MonoConc) have been written that can calculate the collocation relations for any word and their relative strengths (see also, *Collins COBUILD English Collocations on CD-ROM*). Here are the results for the word *die/died*, taken from a small (90,000 word) corpus of obituary texts:

Word: die/died

left 2	left 1	right 1	right 2
7 who	8 has	6 aged	5 week
	5 who	5 last	3 the
		5 on	2 78
		2 in	

To the left of the word *die/died*, the relative pronoun *who* occurs 12 times. To the right, the most frequently occurring item is *aged*, then *last* (1) + *week* (2). These collocations betray the type of text from which the data is derived. In an obituary, a typical opening sentence might be: *X, who died last week* ... or *X, who has died aged* ... But the data serve to illustrate the kind of information about collocation that can now be retrieved quite easily using a computer corpus. Here is a further example, for the (adjective) word *political*, from the same corpus:

Word: political

left 2	left 1	right 1	right 2
4 of	4 his	3 career	3 the
2 the	3 a	2 life	3 to
	3 of	2 courage	3 in
	2 into	2 in	
	2 great		

The nouns, indicated at 'right 1', with which *political* collocates in this corpus, are shown as: *career*, *life* and *courage*. The last of these is a little unusual, except perhaps in the context of an obituary, where it is customary to highlight the deceased's strong points.

5.7 Summary

In this chapter, we have considered the relations of meaning that words contract with other words in the vocabulary of a language. In the main we have concentrated on the paradigmatic 'sense relations': synonymy, antonymy, hyponymy and meronymy. The first two refer to relations of 'sameness' and 'oppositeness' of meaning. The second two refer to hierarchical relations between words: the 'kind of' relation of hyponymy, and the 'part of' relation of meronymy.

Before attending to the syntagmatic meaning relation of collocation, we looked at some ways of analysing the meaning relations between words. Componential analysis goes some way to explicating semantic relations, but seems to be limited in its application. Using semantic primes, the irreducible, undefinable universal semantic concepts, seems a more promising way forward. And the arrangement of words into semantic fields enables meaning relations between words sharing the same semantic space to be more adequately ascertained.

Finally, we examined collocation, to see how words may predict the presence of others in a context, because of a meaning relation of mutual expectancy. We saw that collocation rests on a statistical basis, and we explored how reliable data for collocational relations may be obtained from text corpora.

6 Words in Use

In this chapter we shall consider the vocabulary of English as a package of sub-sets of words that are used in particular contexts. These contexts may be geographical, social, occupational, and so on.

6.1 Vocabularies

When we pick up an English dictionary, we imagine that we hold in our hands a representative collection of the words that exist in the English language, the vocabulary of an educated speaker of the language. All the words are, as it were, in one bag; all of a type; just as they are printed in an alphabetical list between the covers of a single book. When we open the dictionary and look more carefully at the entries, we see that quite a number of them are marked with labels of one kind or another, e.g. *botanical, baseball, slang, American English*. These labels indicate that the word is restricted in its use, and taken together, these labels indicate that there are a number of sets of words in English with a restricted use. It is these sets that we want to explore in this chapter.

6.1.1 Core and specialist vocabulary

In the 'General Explanations' at the beginning of the first (1933) edition of the *Oxford English Dictionary* (*OED*), the editors discuss the nature of the English vocabulary that the dictionary intends to chart and describe, offering a diagram to explain how they see the vocabulary of English (see Figure 6.1).

The editors explain the chart in the following terms:

> The centre is occupied by the 'common' words, in which literary and colloquial usage meet. 'Scientific' and 'foreign' words enter the common language mainly through literature; 'slang' words ascend through colloquial use; the 'technical' terms of crafts and processes, and the 'dialect' words, blend with the common language both in speech and literature. Slang also touches on one side the technical terminology of trades and occupations, as in 'nautical slang', 'Public School slang', 'the slang of the Stock Exchange', and on another passes into true dialect. Dialects similarly pass into

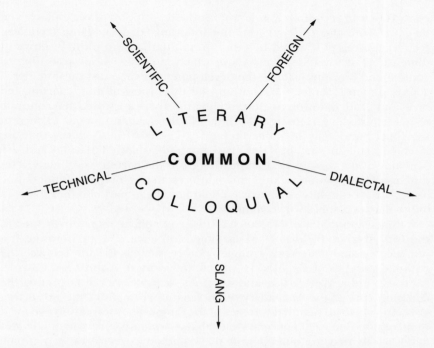

Figure 6.1 The vocabulary of English according to the *OED* (*OED* 1933), by permission of Oxford University Press

foreign languages. Scientific terminology passes on one side into purely foreign words, on another it blends with the technical vocabulary of art and manufactures. It is not possible to fix the point at which the 'English Language' stops, along any of these diverging lines.

The *OED*'s account of the vocabulary of English recognizes a fundamental distinction between words that belong to the common core of the language, and those that belong to particular specialist sub-sets. In fact, this distinction may apply not only between words, but also between the senses of a single word. While some senses may belong to the common core, one or more senses may be part of a specialist vocabulary. For example, *comeback* has the technical sense in Australian sheep farming of 'a sheep that is three-quarters merino and one-quarter crossbred' (*Collins English Dictionary* (*CED*) 1986: 315), *proof* has specialist senses in law, maths/logic, printing and engraving (see *CED* 1986: 1225).

6.1.2 *Dimensions of variation*

We have established that a distinction exists between those words, or senses of words, that belong to a 'common core' vocabulary and those that are restricted in their contexts of use. We now need to determine what types of context we can recognize as relevant for the description of vocabulary. The diagram from the *OED* suggests the following: dialect, slang, technical, scientific, foreign. It would be more useful, perhaps, to think in terms of dimensions of variation: the ways in which language varies according to context and how this leads to the development of specialist vocabularies.

One dimension of variation would be the historical one, charting the birth and death of words. At any point in time, there are words that continue to be recorded, even though they are 'obsolete', i.e. no longer in current use, but found only in older literature. There are also words that are 'archaic', still in use, but they have an old-fashioned flavour and are probably in the process of disappearing from the current vocabulary. This dimension of variation is not of much interest to us, since it does not define a specialist vocabulary. Such words could have been part of either the core vocabulary or a specialist vocabulary.

A dimension that is of relevance is the geographical one, represented in the *OED* diagram by 'dialect'. This dimension encompasses, however, not just the regional dialects of a single country, such as Britain, but also the national varieties of English, as spoken and written in the USA, Canada, Australia, India, West Africa, and so on. As such, we are reinterpreting the common core as the vocabulary of 'international English', the words that are common to all national varieties of the language. Alternatively, we need to recognize that each national variety has a common core, which includes many words that are shared with the common cores of other national varieties, but also some words that are restricted to that particular national variety. For example, the word *book* belongs to the common core of all national varieties, but while *faucet* belongs to the common core of American English, *tap* is the equivalent word in British English and other Commonwealth varieties, except that Canadian English has both terms (de Wolf 1996).

A second relevant dimension is that of occupation, which includes *OED*'s 'technical' and 'scientific'. The term 'occupation' is interpreted broadly to include any pursuit, whether as part of daily work or a leisure interest, which develops its own specialized vocabulary. It encompasses scientific, religious, legal, political, and journalistic language (Crystal 1995), as well as the vocabulary associated with particular jobs and professions, sports and hobbies. Such specialist vocabulary is referred to, often disparagingly, as 'jargon'.

The language associated with identifiable social and cultural groups in society constitutes a third relevant dimension. This dimension is probably included under the *OED*'s 'slang' label. An example might be the vocabulary peculiar to youth culture, or to the criminal underworld, or to the CB (Citizen's Band) Radio fraternity, or to Internet surfers. There is perhaps some overlap with the occupational dimension, but the emphasis here is on a shared sub-culture rather than on an 'occupation'.

Fourthly, we can identify a dimension of variation related to the formality of the context, which influences the style of language that a speaker or writer uses. Certainly there are differences of vocabulary between 'formal' and 'informal' discourse. Compare:

Patrons are kindly requested to deposit their outer garments at the wardrobe.
Please leave your coats in the cloakroom.

Whether this leads to our being able to establish a specialist 'formal' (or 'informal') vocabulary is another question, which we shall need to explore. At the informal end of the spectrum, it shades into colloquialism, slang and taboo words, where we can more readily identify special sets of terms.

Some linguists would also recognize a dimension of variation that relates to the medium in which a particular message is communicated, with a basic distinction between the spoken medium and the written medium. Arguably, there are no specialist vocabularies of speech and writing, though there may be some words that we associate more readily with either the spoken or the written medium. To a large extent, though, this corresponds with the formal/informal dimension, except that we speak of informal and formal writing, or indeed speech. The broadcast media have made an interesting and complicating contribution to this dimension, with their use of much scripted or semi-scripted speech; and more recently, 'speaking' on the computer internet by means of electronic mail has added a further aspect to consider. But the vocabulary differences are perhaps less significant than other, especially grammatical, differences; and so we will consider this dimension to be subsumed under that of formality for lexical purposes.

One further topic, however, that we need to consider as we look at specialist vocabularies concerns the use of 'restricted languages', such as that which airline pilots speak when communicating with airport controls.

We have set the agenda for the chapter. Let us now proceed to a more detailed discussion of the points that we have raised.

6.2 National and regional vocabularies

McArthur (1987) accompanies his article discussing 'English languages' with a diagram called 'The circle of World English' (reproduced in McArthur 1992) (see Figure 6.2). The central circle implies a 'world' or 'international' English, which English speakers with differing national Englishes use with each other when they meet at conferences, business meetings, or on holiday. Crystal (1995) disputes whether such a variety yet exists. As far as vocabulary is concerned, it would not be clear, for example, whether *car* or *automobile* would be the preferred term. Nevertheless, Crystal agrees that when we meet English speakers from different national backgrounds, we take care not to use words that we perceive as peculiar to our variety; at the least, we check that our interlocutor has understood a word that we are not sure that they know.

The languages inside the segments of the larger circle in McArthur's diagram are the national and regional standards of English. Outside the

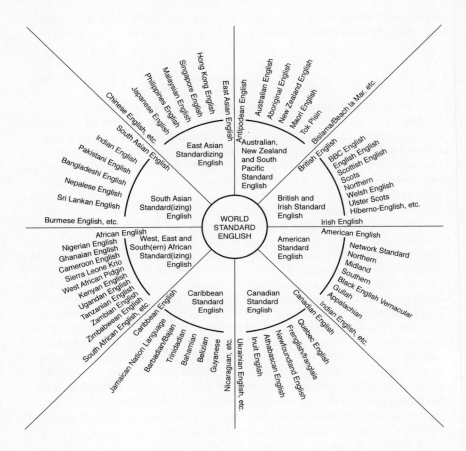

Figure 6.2 The circle of World English (McArthur 1987), by permission of Tom McArthur

circle are the regional varieties (languages and dialects) of these standards. This represents one method of diagramming the geographical varieties of English and their relationships; see McArthur (1992) for a discussion of alternative methods. In this book we shall be concerned mainly with the varieties listed within the larger circle; space precludes a more wide-ranging consideration. And we are concerned only with vocabulary, not with grammar or pronunciation.

6.2.1 British and American English (BrE and AmE)

The British and American varieties of English account for around 70 per cent of mother-tongue English speakers, with Americans outnumbering British by four to one (Crystal 1995). They are also the major players in the

English-language teaching market (EFL and ESL). Although BrE speakers do not often like to think so, AmE is the dominant variety in the world today, as a consequence of the political, cultural and economic dominance of the USA. Because of the influence especially of American films and television series, as well as the pop music industry, many words that were formerly restricted to AmE are now well understood in BrE and in many cases also part of many, especially younger, speakers' active vocabulary.

We need to account for the fact that some words are specific to either the American or the British variety and not used in World English, some are variety-specific but are used in World English, some have a sense which is variety-specific, and so on. Benson *et al.* (1986b) identify ten groups of lexical differences. The first five of these groups are:

I   Words that reflect cultural differences, with no equivalent in the other variety, e.g. *Ivy League, Groundhog Day* for AmE; *Honours Degree, Value Added Tax* for BrE.
II Words that are variety-specific but which have an equivalent in the other variety, e.g. AmE *baggage room* = BrE *left-luggage office*, AmE *potato chip* = BrE *crisp*.
III Words that have at least one sense used in World English (WE), with an additional sense or senses specific to either or both varieties. For example, *caravan* has the WE sense of 'a company of traders or other travellers journeying together, often with a train of camels, through the desert' (*CED* 1986), but it has the specific sense in BrE of 'a large enclosed vehicle capable of being pulled by a car or lorry and equipped to be lived in' (*CED* 1986), which is equivalent to AmE *trailer*. A further example is *homely*, which has the WE sense 'characteristic of or suited to the ordinary home; unpretentious', and with a BrE sense '(of a person) warm and domesticated in manner or appearance' but an AmE sense '(of a person) plain or ugly' (*CED* 1986).
IV Words that have a single sense in World English and have an equivalent word in either AmE or BrE. An example is *ball-point pen*, with BrE equivalent *biro*; or *undertaker*, with AmE equivalent *mortician*. WE *filling station* has AmE equivalent *gas station* and BrE equivalent *petrol station*.
V   Words that have no World English meaning, but that have different specific meanings in the two varieties. For example, *flyover* has AmE meaning 'a ceremonial flight of aircraft over a given area', equivalent to BrE *flypast*. In BrE, *flyover* has the meaning 'an intersection of two roads at which one is carried over the other by a bridge' (*CED* 1986), equivalent to AmE *overpass*. In AmE *public school* is a free school financed by the state, whereas in BrE it is a fee-paying private educational establishment.

Crystal (1995) adapts Benson *et al.*'s (1986b) scheme to give a fourfold division in terms of the crossover potential of equivalent words between the AmE and BrE varieties:

1. no crossover potential from either side, e.g. (AmE words on the left, BrE on the right):

candy	sweets
cot	camp bed
diaper	nappy
freeway	motorway
grab bag	lucky dip
kerosene	paraffin
wrench	spanner
zip code	post code

2. crossover potential from AmE to BrE, but not from BrE to AmE; so the AmE word is in World English, e.g.

can	tin
crepe	pancake
eraser	rubber
French fries	chips
intermission	interval
leash	lead
stroller	pushchair
zero	nought

3. crossover potential from BrE to AmE, but not from AmE to BrE; so the BrE word is in World English, e.g.

ash can	dustbin
bathtub	bath
casket	coffin
drapes	curtains
fall	autumn
faucet	tap
line	queue
pantyhose	tights

4. crossover potential both from AmE to BrE and from BrE to AmE; so both words are in World English, e.g.

administration	government
antenna	aerial
baggage	luggage
dry goods	drapery
nightgown	nightdress
mail	post
sweater	jumper

All the above examples are taken from Crystal (1995: 309). They only begin to illustrate the vast differences in vocabulary between AmE and BrE, differences that have come about as the two nations have developed their own identities and pursued their own goals since the first settlers emigrated to America in the seventeenth century. Benson *et al.* (1986b) contains many more examples, including idioms, which may or may not have equivalents in the other language, e.g. AmE *shoot the breeze* = 'chat informally' (no BrE equivalent idiom), BrE *fall off the back of a lorry* = 'be stolen' (no AmE equivalent idiom).

The vocabulary of Canadian English is not the same as that of American English. While there has been steady cross-border contact with the USA, Canada has also experienced a continuous flow of immigration from Britain. Other factors include the bilingual influence of French in Quebec and contact with the Native American languages of Canada. Words for vehicles and their parts are usually AmE: *truck, hood, fender, trunk, station wagon.* Some BrE and AmE words co-exist, and may be more commonly used in some regions than others, e.g. AmE *fry pan* and BrE *frying pan*, AmE *silverware* and BrE *cutlery* (de Wolf 1996). Words from French include *bateau* (flat-bottomed river boat), *brulé* (area of forest destroyed by fire), *habitant* (a French Canadian, especially a farmer) (*CED* 1986: xxiii). Words from Native American languages include: *bogan* (a sluggish sidestream) from Algonquian, *mowitch* (deer) from Chinook, and *hooch* (alcoholic drink) from Tlingit, which has now passed into World English.

6.2.2 Antipodean English

The first immigrants to Australia, at the end of the eighteenth century, were deported convicts from overcrowded British jails. Australia continued to be used as a penal colony well into the nineteenth century, although free emigrants from Britain also chose to make a new life on the other side of the world. Australian English has some ten thousand distinctive words, drawn from a variety of sources.

The convict language of the first settlers, drawn from a number of British English dialects, not to mention underworld slang, furnished Australian English with a number of its special words, e.g. *cobber* (friend), *dinkum* (genuine), *larrikin* (hooligan), *shake* (in the sense of 'steal'). As settlers spread out from the first point of arrival, they encountered new flora, fauna and geographical features in this vast country. Names were partly borrowed from the aboriginal languages, partly coined from English, e.g. *dingo, brolga* (bird), *morwong* (fish), *billabong* (stagnant pool in a stream), *dillybag, outback, backblocks.*

As the distinctive Australian sheep and cattle farming developed (on *stations*), so a distinctive vocabulary developed, e.g. *stockman, squatter* (sheep or cattle farmer), *rouseabout* (unskilled labourer), *sundowner* (tramp, seeking shelter at sundown). When the gold rush started in the mid-nineteenth century, this produced its own crop of new words, e.g. *fossick* (search for gold in abandoned workings), *mullock* (waste material from a mine), *nuggety* (thickset or stocky).

Immigration to New Zealand took a different course from that to Australia. Although some settlement began in the late eighteenth century, it was not until after the Treaty of Waitangi with Maori chiefs in 1840 that a larger influx of settlers from Britain began to arrive. While NZ English (NZE) shares a number of words with Australian English (*sheep station, bowser* (= BrE petrol pump), *domain* (= BrE public park)), it also has two particular sets of words that contribute to a dictinctive NZE vocabulary.

One set comprises words borrowed from native Maori dialects. Some of these words relate to geographical features, flora and fauna; e.g. *kowhai* and *totara* (trees), *kumara* (sweet potato), *takahe* (bird), *katipo* (spider), *tuatara* (lizard). Others relate to Maori culture, such as *ariki* (chief), *haka* (war dance), *pa* (village), *tangi* (ceremonial funeral), *tohunga* (Maori learned in traditional lore), *wahine* (woman or wife), *waka* (canoe). Others are more general words, taken over from Maori, such as *pakeha* (white person), *aroha* (affection, sympathy), *kuri* (dog, unpleasant person), *taihoa* (wait!).

The other set of distinctive New Zealand words comes from the adaptation and extension of BrE words to the culture of New Zealand as it has developed over the years. The NZ word for a holiday or beach cottage is *bach*, which is a clipped form of bachelor (McArthur (ed.) 1992). You might carry your picnic in a *chilly bin* (BrE cool box). Mail for rural areas is addressed to a *private bag* (i.e. P.O. Box) number. What in BrE is a council house is a *state house* in NZE. A university graduation is a *capping ceremony*.

It is estimated that NZE has some three to four thousand distinctive words or senses of words. Many of them can be found in the *New Zealand Pocket Oxford Dictionary* (Burchfield, ed., 1986).

6.2.3 African English

Immigration to the African continent from Britain took place in the early nineteenth century, with several thousand settlers arriving in the eastern Cape from south-east England. This area had already been colonized by the Dutch in the mid-seventeenth century. Today around 10 per cent of the population of South Africa speaks English as a first language, with a substantial additional proportion using English as a second language. South African English (SAE) is a distinct regional variety, with a distinctive vocabulary drawn in part from Afrikaans (the South African variety of Dutch), in part from native African languages (such as Khoisan, Tswana, Xhosa, Zulu), and in part from developments and adaptations of English words. The *Dictionary of South African English* (Branford and Branford, eds, 1991) contains over five thousand items considered unique to this variety.

Some of the words from Afrikaans have made their way into World English, e.g. *aardvark, apartheid, eland, trek, veld*. Others remain restricted to the SAE variety, such as *bakkie* (basin, container), *kloof* (ravine or mountain pass), *lekker* (nice, enjoyable), *platteland* (area outside cities and main towns), *verkrampte* (conservative, narrow-minded), *voorkamer* (front room). Words from African languages that have entered South African English include: *gogga* (insect) from Hottentot, *indaba* (matter of concern or for discussion) from Zulu, *muti* (medicine) from Zulu, *sangoma* (witch doctor) from Zulu, *tsotsi* (violent young criminal) from, it is thought, a Bantu language. Words from English that are peculiar to South Africa include: *bioscope* (BrE cinema), *bottle store* (BrE off-licence, AmE liquor store), *camp* (paddock), *matchbox* (small standardized dwelling), *robot* (BrE traffic lights).

Two other major varieties of English are found in Africa: West African English (WAfrE), and East African English (EAfrE). English is an official language in the West African states of Nigeria, Ghana, Sierra Leone, Gambia, Cameroon and Liberia; and it is a 'second' language in the other eight states that comprise West Africa (McArthur (ed.) 1992, Todd and Hancock 1990). Peculiar to WAfrE vocabulary are: loans from local languages, e.g. *buka*, 'food stand' (from Hausa), *danfo*, 'minibus' (from Yoruba); loan translations, e.g. *bush meat*, 'game meat', *father* and *mother* for father's and mother's relatives; and local English words or local meanings for English words. Collins (1992) includes: *bush* (adjective), 'ignorant, stupid', *chop* (verb), 'eat', *coaster*, 'European resident on the coast', *day-clean* (noun), 'the time after first dawn when the sun begins to shine', and *linguist*, 'the spokesman for a chief'. (See also Awonusi 1990, Gyasi 1991, Bamiro 1994, Ahulu 1995.)

EAfrE describes the form of English used by educated East Africans in Kenya, Malawi, Tanzania, Uganda, Zambia and Zimbabwe. It is used as a medium of communication in politics, business, the media and popular culture (McArthur (ed.) 1992). The lingua franca in this region of Africa is Swahili, an official language in Kenya and Tanzania; so English is an additional language for most speakers. Like WAfrE, EAfrE borrows from local languages, including Swahili, e.g. *duka*, 'shop', *shamba*, 'farm', *ndugu*, 'brother/friend'. It also has loan translations, e.g. *clean heart*, 'pure', *dry* (coffee), 'without milk or sugar'; and it has local English words or meanings of English words, e.g. *duty*, 'work or occupation', *refuse*, 'deny', *tea sieve*, 'tea strainer'. (See also Tripathi 1990, Sure 1992.)

6.2.4 Indian English

English has been spoken in the Indian subcontinent since the East India Company established trading 'factories' in the seventeenth century. It is now the associate official language of India, along with Hindi; and it is estimated that around 30 million people in India (4 per cent of the population) use English regularly (McArthur (ed.) 1992). Indian English has developed as a distinctive variety, including many unique vocabulary items.

A sizeable number of words has been borrowed into Indian English (IndE) from local languages, as well as from Portuguese. Directly from Portuguese are *ayah*, *caste* and *peon*; from local languages via Portuguese, *bamboo*, *betel*, *curry* and *mango*. Directly from local languages into Indian English are: *anna*, *chit(ty)*, *pukka*, *pundit*, *sahib*, etc. Among words borrowed from Arabic and Persian via local languages are: *mogul*, *sepoy*, *shroff* (banker), *vakeel* (lawyer). Loan translations include: *dining-leaf,* 'a banana leaf used to serve food' and *cousin sister,* 'a female cousin'.

Indian English vocabulary also has items (compounds) that are composed from one element of English origin and one element from a local language: *grameen bank,* 'village bank', *policewala,* 'policeman', *tiffin box,* 'lunch-box'. Some English words have also developed new senses or been adapted to new forms, e.g. *batch,* 'group of people' as in *batch-mate,* 'class-mate', *drumstick,* 'green vegetable', *condole,* 'offer condolences', *head-bath,* 'washing one's hair', *prepone,* 'opposite of postpone'.

Indian English is not the only variety of the subcontinent, though many of its features are shared with Pakistani English (Baumgardner 1990), Lankan English (spoken in Sri Lanka) and the variety of English spoken in Bangladesh.

6.2.5 *Other Englishes*

What has been discussed so far should give a good flavour of the variety that occurs in the regional forms of English. We do not have space to mention other Englishes, such as those spoken in the Far East (Hong Kong, Malaysia, Singapore), or in the Caribbean (including creole varieties). Nor do we have space to reflect on the rich diversity of regional dialects, e.g. in Britain and America, which have been investigated by extensive projects such as the Survey of English Dialects (Orton *et al.,* eds, 1962–71) or the *Dictionary of American Regional English* (Cassidy, ed., 1985).

EXERCISE 6/1

Can you think of a local (dialect) word in the area where you live, or where you come from, for any of the following? They all have variants in British English dialects.

gym shoe, bread roll, sandwich, attic, broom, beautiful, left-handed, excellent, tired out, lavatory, nothing.

6.3 Jargon

We are using the term 'jargon' to refer to specialist vocabularies associated with 'occupations' that people engage in, either as a mode of employment or as a leisure pursuit or for some other purpose. We all have access to a number of jargons, which we understand 'passively' and may use more or less 'actively', as a consequence of the routines of daily life that we engage in. Our daily work, whether in paid employment, in the home, or with a voluntary agency, engenders its own vocabulary. Our leisure time interests, whether sports or hobbies or some other activity, have their own vocabulary. If we are involved in religious observance, that too has its jargon.

The term 'jargon' often has a pejorative connotation. We use it in this way when a professional (e.g. doctor or lawyer) uses their specialized vocabulary in inappropriate contexts, either to display their knowledge or to obscure what they have to say. Jargon is impenetrable to the outsider, often deliberately so; only those inside the particular occupational group have access to its specialist vocabulary. You can become a member of the group only by learning the vocabulary, the jargon, and by using it appropriately. In part, that is what a professional training or an apprenticeship does: it familiarizes you with the jargon and then tests that you have acquired it sufficiently to be allowed to call yourself a member of the group (lawyer, electrician, or whatever).

In this section, we will take examples from the jargons of professional occupations and of leisure pursuits, and we will consider particularly religious jargon and that of the modern ecology movement.

6.3.1 Occupational jargons

Medicine and allied professions have created a jargon that is based on Latin and Greek, especially in the formation of neo-classical compounds (see Chapter 4). There are, for example, a number of *-ology* words – *angiology, enterology, haematology, psychology* – relating to the 'study of' various parts of human beings that may become diseased. Similarly, there are a number of *-iatry* or *-iatrics* words, relating to the 'treatment' of diseases or conditions: *geriatrics, paediatrics, podiatry, psychiatry*. A group of words with *-gram* or *-graph* relates to the measuring and recording of bodily functions or conditions: *angiogram, audiogram, cardiogram, electrocardiograph, encephelograph, mammograph*. A further group, with *-ectomy*, relates to the surgical removal of a part of the body: *hysterectomy, lobectomy, mastectomy, pneumonectomy*. Medical jargon has a pattern to it; becoming familiar with it involves recognizing the patterns and learning the meanings of the Latin and Greek roots that form these neo-classical compounds.

Psychology and psychiatry, whose jargon has been derogatorily referred to as 'psychobabble', has a vocabulary composed partly of neo-classical compounds (*hedonics*), but also of words borrowed directly from Latin and Greek (*ego, id, eros, thanatos* in Freudian psychiatry; *persona, animus, horme* in Jungian), as well as ordinary English words either forming novel compounds or invested with a technical sense, e.g. *wish fulfilment, death wish* (Freud), *shadow, collective unconscious* (Jung).

The jargon of computing is largely of this last type: novel compounds formed from established English words, or new meanings for ordinary words. Among the compounds, consider: *central processing unit, disk drive, read only memory* (ROM), *touch sensitive screen, virtual reality, word processor*. Words with new meanings include: *chip, file, icon, monitor, keyboard, printer, scroll, setup, terminal, window*. What makes computer jargon especially difficult to understand is the extensive use of abbreviations and acronyms: ASCII, BIT, CPU, DOS, SQL, SSADM, WYSIWYG. (See Lynch 1991.)

Traditional industries also have their jargon. As an example we will take the mining industry. Here there is no erudite vocabulary from classical sources, but rather ordinary vocabulary extended in meaning or words taken from dialect for the purpose. Common core words used with a specialist mining sense include: *pack* ('a roof support, especially one made of rubble'), *pulp* ('pulverized ore'), *sump* ('a depression at the bottom of a shaft where water collects before it is pumped away'), *whim* ('a horse-drawn winch for drawing up ore or water'). Words with a local or dialect origin include: *swag* ('a depression filled with water due to mining subsidence'), *vug* ('a small cavity in a rock or vein' – from Cornish). Other words not in common core English are found in mining jargon, some borrowed from other languages: *culm* ('coal-mine waste'), *kibble* ('a bucket used for hoisting' – from German), *stull* ('a timber prop or platform' – from German), *winze* ('a steeply inclined shaft, as for ventilation between levels' – Dutch). A further type of jargon arises from word-formation processes producing novel lexemes: *millrun* ('the process of milling an ore or rock in order to determine the content or quality of the mineral'), *mucker* ('a person who shifts broken rock or waste'), *poppet head* ('a framework above a mine shaft that supports the winding mechanism'). (Definitions taken from *Collins Electronic Dictionary* 1992.)

Some occupational jargons begin to filter into the core vocabulary, because the professional areas concerned impinge more extensively on the lives of lay people and are mediated by newspapers and other journalism. This is the case, for example, with some medical jargon (*carcinoma, cardiac arrest*) and with financial jargon (*'bull'* and *'bear' markets, inflation, money supply*). The increasing use of word processors has brought printing jargon into everyday use: we now know about *fonts, point sizes, run-on text, justification, widows* and *orphans*. There still remains, however, much printing jargon exclusive to the printing profession, both formal (*mackle, quoin, shank, slug*) and informal (*screamer* (= 'exclamation mark'), *idiot tape*).

6.3.2 Sports jargons

It is not just our daily work that generates its own specialist vocabulary; our leisure time pursuits do also. This is the case with hobbies and cultural pursuits (music, theatre, cinema). Perhaps nowhere is this more evident than in the various sports that we may be involved in, either as players, or more often as spectators. Cricket fans across the Commonwealth will be familiar with a common jargon that is used in the game, nearly all of it involving the extension of the meaning of core vocabulary items or compounding of familiar words. Here is a selection of cricket jargon, arranged under a number of headings:

General
wicket, stumps, bails, bat, crease, boundary, sightscreen
innings, follow-on, declare

over, maiden over
opening batsman, middle order (batsman), tailender, nightwatchman

Field positions
leg side, off side
slip, gully, cover, point, square leg, silly (mid-off), long (on)
wicket keeper

Types of 'out'
bowled, lbw (leg before wicket), stumped, run out, caught and bowled,
played on

Types of 'bowling'
pace, seam, swing, spin
off-break, leg-break, googly, Chinaman, inswinger, outswinger, yorker,
bouncer

Types of batting 'stroke'
on-drive, off-drive, cover drive, sweep, hook, edge, push, glance

Types of score
single, boundary, bye, leg bye, dot ball.

Such an array of specialist vocabulary, probably similarly derived mostly
from core vocabulary, can be duplicated for other sports: football, baseball,
athletics, and so on. There is no resort to neo-classical compounds, as with
many of the professions; the vocabulary does not sound erudite; but for the
outsider it can be equally baffling to hear familar words used with an
unfamiliar sense.

6.3.3 Religious language

A jargon that has been of considerable interest not only to linguists (e.g.
Crystal 1964, Brook 1981) but also to theologians and philosophers (e.g.
Donovan 1976) is religious language (Crystal and Davy 1969, Chapter 6).
We are concerned here with the language of Christianity, which was
brought to Britain initially during the period of Roman occupation during
the first four centuries of the Christian era. The English language had not
yet been established in Britain; the languages of the Roman subjects in
Britain were Celtic. Only after the Romans left in the early fifth century did
the Anglo-Saxon tribes invade and bring with them the language that would
be English. The reintroduction of Christianity to Britain was needed; it was
a two-pronged affair. From the south, a missionary thrust began with
Augustine, who landed in Kent in 597, sent by Gregory I, Bishop of Rome;
and from the north came Irish missionaries. Columba (died 597) established a centre on the island of Iona, from which Scotland was evangelized,
and in the first half of the seventh century Aidan and Cuthbert continued
the work of mission in Scotland and northern England. In due course the
Irish Celtic form of Christianity was absorbed into the Roman form (Bede
731).

Because of the dominance of Rome, much ecclesiastical and theological vocabulary in English is borrowed from Latin. However, some religious words are of Anglo-Saxon origin, having been adapted to a Christian meaning; for example, *holy, ghost* (= 'spirit'), *sin, forgive, gospel* (from *god*, 'God' + *spell*, 'story'), *believe, heaven, worship*. The vast majority of religious terms in English have been borrowed from Latin. Until the first translation into English in the 1380s by John Wycliff and his associates, the Bible used was the Latin Vulgate translated by Jerome in the fourth century. Indeed, it was from the Vulgate that the Wycliffites translated into English, borrowing more than a thousand Latin words in the process (see 2.4.1).

One of the features of ecclesiastical life as established by Augustine and his successors was the religious house (*monastery* – itself a fifteenth-century word), where education and training for the priesthood took place and books were kept and copied. Some words dealing with monastic life were borrowed from Latin during the Old English period – *abbot, altar, cowl, mass, monk, nun, priest* – but many more entered English after the Norman conquest, during the Middle English period, when religious houses were revived and multiplied – *chapel, cloister, compline, convent, eucharist, offertory, office, prior, rule, tonsure.*

Parts of church buildings are mostly derived from Latin during the medieval period: *cathedral, chancel, choir, nave, transept, sanctuary, crypt, tower, buttress.* However, *steeple* is of Old English origin, as is the word *church*, though it is thought to be derived from Greek *kyriakon* ('belonging to the Lord').

Apart from words such as those already noted, like *believe* and *gospel*, the terms relating to Christian belief and theology also have their origin in Latin, if for no other reason than because, as in the case of the Wycliffite translation, early Bible versions into English were based on the Latin Vulgate. It was not until William Tyndale's version in the early sixteenth century that the Greek New Testament and Hebrew Old Testament were used as the basis of the translation. Although we recognize them as 'technical' words of the Christian faith, we are no longer aware of the Latin origins of terms such as: *cross, faith, salvation, eternal, trespass, justify, scripture, confess, admonish, glory, praise, hymn, psalm, revelation, prophet, incarnation, resurrection, advent.*

Since this vocabulary has been in use amongst Christians over such a long period of time, it does not have the sound of an 'alien' jargon. It may seem strange to someone who has not grown up with it from childhood through Sunday school and church attendance. And it is true to say that it is the 'jargon' by which Christians talk about and share their common religious experience and understanding.

6.3.4 'Green' jargon

We will consider one further, very contemporary jargon, the one developed by the 'green', ecology movement, and which modern editions of dictionaries would claim to cover. In the two editions of the Oxford Dictionary of New Words (Tulloch 1991, Knowles and Elliott, eds, 1997), which chart neologisms of the 1980s and 1990s, 'environment' is one of the subject categories that is specially marked. The following items are marked as such: acid rain, additive, Alar, alternative energy/technology, alternative fuel, (environmentally) aware, ecobabble, bio- (e.g. biodegradable, bio-diesel, bio-diversity), beetle bank, blue box (for collecting recyclable items), bottle bank, can bank, carbon tax, cat (= catalyser), CFC (chlorofluorocarbon), crop circle, cruelty-free, deforestation, desertification, dumping (of toxic waste), Earth Summit, eco- (e.g. eco-friendly, eco-tourism), ecology, eco-logical footprint, energy audit, E number, (the) environment, environmentally sensitive/sound, fly-tipping, -free (e.g. meat-free, lead-free, nuclear-free), fundie (= fundamentalist, i.e. a committed 'green'), Gaia, global warming, green, greenhouse (effect, gas), guppie (= green yuppie), heritage, horsiculture, irradiation, landfill site, monergy, mousse, nega- (negawatt, negamile), nimby, nuclear winter, organic, orimulsion, oxygenated (of fuel), ozone, PCB (polychlorinated biphenyl), recycling, red route, set aside (of land), speed bump/hump, sustainable, traffic calming, tree house, tree hugger, twigloo, -unfriendly (e.g. ozone-unfriendly), ungreen, unleaded, Valdez principles, veal crate, Waldsterben, wind farm, wise use, zero-emission vehicle.

Collins Electronic Dictionary (1992) includes some ninety words that are marked 'ecology' or have 'ecology' in their definitions, including: biono-mics, consocies, eurytopic, halosere, lentic, microclimate, paralimnion, plagioclimax, xerarch.

From these lists, it will be clear that *Collins Electronic Dictionary* (1992) concentrates on the more technical vocabulary of ecology and the environ-ment, with the words being mostly neo-classical compounds or based on classical roots. Tulloch (1991) taps the more populist vocabulary of the 'green' movement, which will be more familiar to the ordinary newspaper reader or television viewer, with the use of a variety of means of word formation, including meaning extension (global warming), blending (monergy), acronym (nimby, PCB), derivation (unleaded), borrowing (waldsterben).

EXERCISE 6/2

Write down twenty or so of the main items of specialist vocabulary from one of your leisure pursuits. Where does the vocabulary come from? What word-formation and semantic processes have been used to derive the terms?

Try the words out on someone who doesn't share your pursuit, to see if the words make any sense to them.

6.4 Sub-cultures

Within a society or culture, people who regularly associate with each other because they have some characteristic or interest in common may form a sub-culture that gives rise to its own special vocabulary. This vocabulary then becomes a badge of membership of the sub-culture; you learn and use the appropriate words to prove that you are a member and in order to associate with other members. Such a sub-culture can be found, for example, among young people – adolescents, teenagers. Indeed one such sub-culture has provided the word *Valspeak*: 'a variety of US slang which originated among teenage girls from the San Fernando valley in California and was later taken up more widely by youngsters in the US' (Tulloch 1991: 299). Two sub-cultures that have a long history of lexical innovation are the armed forces and the criminal underworld; both are well represented in Partridge (1984). Of more recent origin are the vocabularies associated with the sub-cultures of Citizens Band Radio users and of Rastafarianism.

6.4.1 Youth culture

Tulloch (1991) has over eighty words marked as associated with 'youth culture' and as having come into the language from that source during the 1980s. Knowles and Elliott (eds, 1997) do not have a separate 'youth culture' category; they include such words in a more general 'popular culture' category. Many of the terms associated with youth culture from the two dictionaries of new words fall into quite distinct lexical categories. One set comprises adjectives to express approval and disapproval, a set that is renewed by each succeeding generation of young people. This set includes, for approval: ace, awesome, bad, brilliant, crucial, fresh, kicking, mad, neato, phat, rad, safe, sorted, stonking, storming, tubular, wicked. And for disapproval: grody, naff, scuzzy, wack. Related is a set of nouns to refer to people you approve of or who belong to your crowd – crew, dude, homeboy, posse – or those that you despise – anorak, crumblie (older person), crusty, dweeb, geek, headbanger, headcase, nerd, otaku, propeller-head, saddo, scuzz, slapper, sleazebag, wazzock. A small set of verbs expresses inter-personal attitudes or personal reactions: blanked ('ignored, cold-shouldered'), diss ('put someone down'), gobsmacked ('very shocked or surprised'), gutted ('very disappointed, devastated'). It is, of course, also important to have 'street cred', or just 'cred', and to be 'sussed' (in the know); someone who has not made it may be instructed to 'get a life'.

Youth culture also regularly adopts a number of adverbs that are used to emphasize or intensify an adjective, and modern youth culture is no exception. Those noted are: drop-dead (e.g. 'drop-dead gorgeous'), max (as in 'to the max'), mega, mondo, serious (as in 'serious bad'), totally, way, well (as in 'well safe'). A couple of greetings are also noted: yo, cowabunga (originating in the 1950s but more recently popularized by the Teenage Mutant Turtles).

One of the largest sets of words associated with youth culture relates to the different styles of music listened to by young people. Terms noted by Tulloch (1991) and Knowles and Elliott (eds, 1997) include: acid house, acid jazz, ambient, baggy, bhangra, black metal, -core (e.g. hardcore, foxcore, queercore), electro, ethnic, funk, gabba, gangsta, garage, go-go, goth, grunge, handbag, heavy metal (also 'HM' and 'metal'), hip hop, house, indie, jungle, new jack swing, New Wave, ragga, rai, rap, Romo, scratch, soca, speed metal, swingbeat, techno, thrash metal, trip hop, zouk. Associated words relating to partying and dancing include: body-popping, breaking (or 'break-dancing'), lig ('gatecrash'), mosh ('dance violently and recklessly), orbital (a party near the M25 London orbital road), rage ('to party'), rootsy (of music, 'down-to-earth'), slam dancing, stage diving, warehouse (party). After all this a young person may just 'spazz out' (lose physical or emotional control), especially if they are 'loved-up' (intoxicated by the drug ecstasy).

Words or senses of words adopted by a youth culture tend to be ephemeral; they disppear with that generation's progression to full adulthood. Such words or senses therefore rarely appear in general dictionaries, which usually only record neologisms that have demonstrated some staying power.

6.4.2 Underworld slang

Special vocabulary used by the criminal sub-culture has a long history. It was noted as 'thieves' cant' by eighteenth-century lexicographers, and it has been well documented by Eric Partridge in successive editions of his *A Dictionary of Slang and Unconventional English* (e.g. Partridge 1984). We review briefly here some of the relevant 'slang' words to be found in *Collins Electronic Dictionary* (1992).

As might be expected, quite a large number of words are recorded denoting 'prison', such as: can, chokey, clink, cooler, nick, peter, slammer, stir. A further set refers to being sent to prison or being in prison: bang up, do bird, go down, be inside, do porridge, send up/down. Someone in prison may be a *star* (a first time prisoner) or a *lag*, while a prison warder is a *screw*, before whom, if they are a *div* (stupid person), they may *cheese* (act in a grovelling manner).

The police are referred to by a number of slang terms, including: a bogey, the filth, the fuzz, the pigs. A police informer is a *nark*, who may *grass* (inform) and so *shop* (betray to the police) one of his colleagues, because he has decided to *go straight* (not engage in criminal activity). The head of a *mob* (criminal gang), each of whom will have a *form* (criminal record) unless they are a *cleanskin* (without a criminal record), is *Mr Big*, who may well have a *minder* (bodyguard), since he may be in danger of being *hit* (murdered) in fulfilment of a *contract* (killing). If caught, perhaps as a result of a *stakeout* (police surveillance), and taken down the *nick* (police station), he may produce a *verbal* (confession of guilt).

6.4.3 Rastafarian culture

Rastafarians are a group among the African Caribbean community who regard Haile Selassie, the former emperor of Ethiopia, whose Amharic title was 'Ras Tafari', as an incarnation of God (*Jah*). He will take the faithful from the black diaspora (in the Caribbean, UK and USA) out of *Babylon* (oppressive white society) to the promised land of Ethiopia. The movement began in the 1930s in Jamaica, and its distinctive language, Afro-Lingua (Bones 1986), derives from Jamaican Creole, but with many characteristic features of its own.

Perhaps the word most readily associated with Rastafarianism is *dread*, which derives from the Old Testament word 'dread', meaning 'fear of the Lord', but is the word used to denote a Rastafarian. The typical Rastafarian hairstyle is called *dreadlocks*. The word *dread* is also used as an adjective meaning 'excellent', something deserving Rastafarian approval.

Language is seen as very significant in Rastafarian culture. Bones (1986: 48) expresses it like this:

> According to Rasta doctrine and reasoning, a language must have great significance in terms of its words, sounds and 'powah', which means 'power'. Language must also relate to manifestations: it represents the ideal and the real. Language relates everything that is seen, heard, felt, imagined, known.

Rastafarians have gatherings for reasoning and celebrating Rasta identity, called *grounation*, and *reason hard* is the term used for 'argue'.

Equally, Rastafarian culture is acutely conscious of the positive and negative connotations of words, and so adapts words to change their connotation: *overstand* for 'understand', *crelove* for 'create', *apprecilove* for 'appreciate', *livealek* for 'dialect', *downpression* for 'oppression'. Rastafarians also have a creative use of the pronoun *I*, explained by Bones (1986: 46) as follows:

> We are told that in the context of grammar 'I' is the first-person pronoun and that the latter takes the place of a noun. We also know that other personal pronouns (you, he, she, they) are second- and third-person pronouns. Rastas say that this is a reflection of a class society where the blacks are seen as 'you', 'they' and so forth but never as 'I'. But since 'I' is the first person singular, 'I' is Jah Rastafari, Haile Selassie I, the one and only. Jah is black, so it follows that 'I' is black. Black, Jah and 'I' are now interchangeable terms, each meaning the same as the other. Each Rastaman is a 'Jahman'; equally each 'Jahman' is an 'I-man'. Hence an 'I-man' is also a 'you-man' (or 'human'). Now the 'I-man' is different from the 'you-man' or 'me-man' because he is the first person. So since Rasta is 'I', a plurality of Rastas become 'I-n-I'.

The 'I' then becomes used as a prefix with a positive connotation in the adaptation of words: *Iration* for 'creation', *Iginin* for 'beginning', *I-tal* for 'food fit to eat' (compare 'vital'), *Idrin* for 'brethren' (i.e. black brothers, fellow-Rastas).

Other associations of Rastafarian culture are 'reggae' music and 'rap', the latter with its emphasis on verbal artistry; and drug taking, especially marijuana or 'ganja', known as the *weed of wisdom*, which is smoked in a *chalice* (pipe). (See also the glossary in Sutcliffe 1982.)

6.4.4 CB talk

CB is the abbreviation for Citizen (or Citizen's, or Citizens') Band Radio, used initially by truckers (BrE lorry drivers) in the USA (CB-ers) to communicate with each other and inform each other of potential difficulties on the roads (AmE highways). CB talk, or trucker talk, developed a series of numerical messages (CB-10 codes) for routine operating information, e.g. 10–4, 'message understood', 10–9, 'repeat'. In addition it developed a jargon (also called CB slang), including the following items (mostly from Crystal 1987: 56):

affirmative	'yes'	anklebiters	'children'
bears	'police'	break	'access to a radio channel'
breaker	'CB radio operator'	doughnuts	'tyres'
eyeballs	'headlights'	five-finger discount	'stolen goods'
good buddy	'another CB-er'	grandma lane	'slow lane'
handle	'CB-er's nickname'	mobile mattress	'caravan'
motion lotion	'fuel'	rubber duck	'first vehicle in a convoy'
smokey	'policeman'	super cola	'beer'.

CB talk is an example of what Crystal (1987) calls a 'restricted language'. It was developed partly to facilitate the necessarily abbreviated and almost telegraphic messages passed from radio to radio with variable quality of reception; but it also became a kind of private language, binding truck drivers together in a fraternity. In this sense it fulfils the functions of a jargon.

EXERCISE 6/3

Rhyming slang is thought to have originated as a criminal language in London's Cockney-speaking East End. What do you think are the equivalents of the following rhyming slang terms? In some cases, they have been reduced to the first part of the expression, so the second, rhyming part is put in brackets.

> Apples and pears, bird(lime), butcher's (hook), china (plate), half-inch, jam jar, pig's ear, porky (pie), raspberry (tart), Rosie Lee, tea leaf, tit for (tat), trouble and strife, Uncle Ned, whistle (and flute)

6.5 Style

Whenever we speak and write, we adjust our style to the context and audience of our communication. The note we leave for a friend confirming a social engagement ('See you for lunch at Chris's. Don't be late!') is not in the same style as an essay written for course assessment ('The convoluted structure of the fifth sentence substantially vitiates the flow of information in the text.'). The discussion of the football match in the bar or café is not in the same style as a committee meeting. Part of the distinctiveness of a style is achieved by the choice of vocabulary. A more formal context requires 'formal' vocabulary; an informal context will allow 'colloquial' vocabulary, perhaps 'slang'; a very informal context may even allow the use of 'taboo' vocabulary.

Dictionaries do not mark the vast majority of their words with any style or formality labels, though native speakers and non-native speakers alike know that a choice has to be made according to the formality of the context. Most words are deemed to be 'neutral' in their formality. Dictionaries tend to label words that are towards the extremes of the styles. Few words are marked as 'formal'; somewhat more are marked as 'informal' or 'colloquial' – the two terms are usually interchangeable; quite a number of general 'slang' words will be included; and a dictionary these days will usually also include a number of well-established 'taboo' words. We can thus identify a number of vocabularies in English along the dimension of style or formality.

6.5.1 Formal words

Some texts must by their nature and purpose be formal. Such is the case, for example, with legal texts. A large number of words that we associate with legal texts – hereinafter, hereunder, thereto, wherein, whomsoever – which have an archaic ring to them, are marked in dictionaries as 'formal', and in some instances with the occupational label (see 6.3.1) 'legal' as well (e.g. *Collins Electronic Dictionary* 1992, *Concise Oxford Dictionary* 1996).

Some formal words are the precise technical names for ordinary language words; they are usually derived from the classical languages. *Occident* (from Latin) and *orient* (also from Latin) are the formal terms for 'west' and 'east'; *carnivore* and *herbivore* (from Latin) are formal for 'meat-eater' and 'plant-eater'. A *philatelist* (from Greek) is a 'stamp collector', and a *toxophilite* (also from Greek) is an 'archer'; similarly, *cuneiform* (Latin), 'wedge-shaped', *horticulture* (Latin), 'gardening', *ornithologist* (Greek), 'bird watcher', *troglo-*

dyte (Greek), 'cave dweller'. Words that have been formed by abbreviation may have their unabbreviated form as a formal equivalent: *omnibus* for 'bus', *perambulator* for 'pram', *refrigerator* for 'fridge', *zoological garden* for 'zoo'.

A formal word may be a means of speaking appropriately about bodily functions and other matters that are not normally mentioned in public. The formal word has a distancing or euphemistic effect, such as *demise* or *decease* for 'death', *copulation* for 'sex(ual intercourse)', *defecate* for 'pass a motion'/ 'shit'.

Using a formal word may be merely a way of putting on airs or sounding posh or erudite. When, for example, might you use *ameliorate* instead of 'improve', *duteous* instead of 'dutiful', *explicate* instead of 'explain', *nescience* instead of 'ignorance', *pulchritude* for 'beauty', *reside* for 'live', *residuum* for 'residue'? Perhaps only if you are being ironically formal.

6.5.2 Colloquial and slang words

Towards the other end of the formality spectrum, though not at its extreme, are words marked in dictionaries as 'colloquial' or 'informal', and as 'slang'. The *Concise Oxford Dictionary* (1996), for example, uses the labels 'colloq' and 'slang'; the difference appears to be simply one of informality, with 'slang' words likely to be used in more informal contexts, though the rationale for the lexicographer's dividing line is not always clear. For instance, *bellyache* as a noun, meaning 'stomach pain', is marked as 'colloq', while the verb, meaning 'complain' is marked as 'slang'; *booze*, meaning 'alcoholic drink' is 'colloq', but *booze-up* is 'slang'; *beanfeast* is 'colloq', while *beano* is 'slang' – both meaning 'party, celebration'; *bitch* (verb) is 'colloq', while *beef* is 'slang' – both meaning 'complain'.

The 'colloquial' category includes words that are abbreviated for informal effect: *agin* (against), *bicky* (biscuit), *brill* (brilliant), *brolly* (umbrella), *budgie* (budgerigar), *celeb* (celebrity), *champ* (champion), *choc* (chocolate), *comfy* (comfortable), *demo* (demonstration). Similar items involve coalescence and abbreviation, e.g. *cuppa* (cup of (tea)), *dunno* (don't know). Others involve reduplication, e.g. *arty-farty*, 'pretentiously artistic'; *dilly dally*, 'dawdle'.

Other colloquial words have no obvious motivation for their informality, other than that they are conventionally restricted to informal contexts: *barney*, 'noisy quarrel', *bigwig*, 'important person', *bod*, 'person', *chunter*, 'mutter, grumble', *conk out*, 'break down', *doddle*, 'easy thing', etc.

The words that are marked as 'slang' are in part informal items that have perhaps not yet reached wide enough acceptance to be labelled 'colloq': *ace*, *awesome* – both meaning 'excellent', *bash*, 'party', *bottle*, 'courage', *buzzword*, 'catchword, fashionable jargon word'. Other slang words are on the way to becoming 'taboo' (see next section): *bog* for 'lavatory', *bogey* for 'nasal mucus', *boob* for 'breast', *bum* for 'buttocks'. But the majority of 'slang' words are slang because they are used in contexts that are very informal, between people who know each other well, or for a particular effect: *barmy, belt up, burk, bilge, binge, blub, bonce,* etc.

6.5.3 Taboo words

The Concise Oxford Dictionary (1996) defines *taboo* (borrowed into English from the Tongan language) as: '1   a system or the act of setting a person or thing apart as sacred, prohibited, or accursed. 2   a prohibition or restriction imposed on certain behaviour, word usage, etc., by social custom.' Taboo subjects or words may often be of a religious or cultural nature, the name of God, for example; or men may be prohibited from mentioning certain things associated with women.

In lexicology, the label 'taboo' is usually applied to words that would be extremely offensive if spoken in most contexts. Indeed, many dictionaries no longer use the label 'taboo' for these kinds of word: *Collins Electronic Dictionary* (1992) still does, but the *Longman Dictionary of the English Language* (LDEL) (1991) uses 'vulgar', and the *Concise Oxford Dictionary* (1996) uses 'coarse slang'. This is perhaps a recognition that such words, which would at one time have been almost unmentionable and even excluded from dictionaries, can now be found to a large extent in popular fiction and even in daily newspapers.

Taboo words in English are largely concerned with non-technical words for parts of the human anatomy associated with sex and excretion and for the act of sexual intercourse – some eighteen such terms labelled 'coarse slang' in *The Concise Oxford Dictionary* (1996). The topics that such words refer to were at one time taboo; now they are the subject of almost too much comment, at least in British and American society, but speakers and writers may have no choice between a relatively technical term, e.g. *penis*, and a number of slang alternatives. But as particular members of this group of words appear more frequently in print, their ability to shock diminishes, and they become less 'taboo': *crap* and *piss* might be cases in point. This may account for the disappearance of the 'taboo' label itself from dictionaries.

It is also the case that dictionaries do not agree among themselves on which of the labels 'colloquial/informal', 'slang', and 'coarse slang/vulgar' should apply to particular words. For example, *booze* is 'slang' in LDEL (1991) and 'colloquial' in *The Concise Oxford Dictionary* (1996), while *bugger* as an exclamation is 'coarse slang' in *The Concise Oxford Dictionary* (1996) and only 'slang' in LDEL (1991).

EXERCISE 6/4

Give a 'neutral' term for the following 'formal' words. If you cannot even guess at the meaning, look the word up in a dictionary. They are all marked as 'formal' in *Collins Electronic Dictionary* (1992).

hitherto, incumbent (adjective), inveracity, laudation, lavation, lubricious, manifold, mariner, natation, yesteryear

---

EXERCISE 6/5

Give a 'neutral' term for the following words, which are marked as either 'colloq' or 'slang' in *The Concise Oxford Dictionary Ninth Edition*. You might also like to see which label a dictionary other than *The Concise Oxford Dictionary* uses for these items.

cold feet, floozie, footling, gamp, (play) hookey, lughole, miffed, piddle, slaphead, stroppy, twerp, unfazed, veggie, wag (verb), zilch, zit

---

6.6 Restricted languages

Look at the following texts:

[1] 1 e4 c5 2 Nf3 e6 3 d4 cxd4 4 Nxd4 Nc6 5 Nb5 d6 6 Bf4 e5 7 Be3 Be6?! A dubious move order. If first Nf6 then 8 Nd2 is met by Ng4. 8 Nd2!? Nf6 9 Bg5 d5 10 exd5 Bxd5 11 Bxf6 gxf6 12 Bc4 Highlighting Black's central weakness; the white knights threaten to invade at c7 or d6.

(*Guardian*, 'Weekly' 15.2.98, p. 34)

[2] Noon today: Lows N and P will fill as Low S runs north-east and deepens. Low R will move north-east. High G is stationary.

NW & SW England, Wales: Mostly dull, mild and misty. Drizzle in places. A light to moderate south-west wind. Max temp 10–12C (50–54F). Tonight, misty with drizzle. Min temp 7–8C (45–46F).

Outlook: Windy in the north and north-west of the UK with showers. Elsewhere it will be dry, with spells of sunshine likely, especially in the east, and it will be very mild.

(*Guardian*, 10.2.98, p. 15)

[3] Caring 38yo romantic – profess, caring & attract – with love of the arts & travel. WLTM attract, romantic & interesting n/s M 28–40. Ldn.

TDH, profess M 42 into romantic evenings & country walks, GSOH, WLTM intellig F 25–35 E.Mids.

(*Guardian*, 'Guide', 7.2.98, pp. 61–3)

Each of these texts requires some deciphering, if you are not a regular reader of such items. They each have a very specific function and a restricted vocabulary. The first [1] is the report of a game of chess, where the moves of the chess pieces are numbered (1, 2, 3 ...), the chess piece being moved is identified (Nf3, Nb5, etc.), and the square to which it is being moved is indicated (e6, d6). The second text [2] is more readily recognizable as a weather forecast, with its lows and highs, its positions and directions (NW, north-east, south-west), its abbreviations (max/min temp, C, F), and its typical vocabulary and collocations (moderate south-west wind, drizzle, spells of sunshine, mild). The third text [3] contains a pair of advertisements seeking friendship with a member of the opposite sex. Besides the conventional abbreviation found in small ads ('attract' for 'attractive', 'profess' for 'professional', 'Ldn' for 'London'), these particular advertisements contain their own set of conventions: 'M' and 'F' for 'male' and 'female', 'yo' for 'year-old', 'WLTM' for 'would like to meet', 'TDH' for 'tall, dark and handsome', 'GSOH' for 'good sense of humour', and 'n/s' for 'non-smoker'.

Other restricted languages can be found in recipes, knitting patterns, birth and death notices, card games. Some restricted varieties of English are used in international communication, e.g. 'airspeak' between aeroplane pilots and air traffic controllers on the ground, or 'seaspeak', its equivalent at sea (see Crystal (1987), pp. 56–7 and Crystal (1995), pp. 390–1). The restricted language of airspeak and seaspeak may be the only English that a pilot, captain or navigator has command of, rather than being just a particular variety of English that they know as part of a wider command of the language. Its very restrictedness is meant to facilitate communication between air and ground and between sea and land, both by being a limited set of words to learn and speak, and by being a limited set of words and combinations of words to hear and understand in radio transmission.

EXERCISE 6/6

Look at the following text, taken from an advertisement for a personal computer (PC), and try to work out exactly what the potential buyer is being offered by the specification:

> 400MHz AMD K6–2 3D Processor. 10.1Gb hard disk. 64Mb SDRAM. 8Mb ATI 3D AGP×2 Graphics. 3D Now! Technology. SoundBlaster 64v 3D PCI Wavetable sound. 4× DVD ROM drive (also functions as fast CD ROM). 15" digital colour screen. 512k cache. Plus 56K PCI modem.

6.7 Summary

In this chapter, we have tried to show that the vocabulary of English is in reality a collection of 'vocabularies'. While all speakers of the language share a 'common core' of words, each one also has access, either solely as a reader/listener, or additionally as a writer/speaker, to a number of 'specialist' vocabularies.

The specialist vocabularies can be identified along a number of dimensions of variation, including: geography, giving national and regional (dialect) varieties; occupation and interest, giving 'jargons'; sub-culture, giving types of 'slang'; and formality.

The chapter concluded with a brief look at restricted languages, such as those used for air and sea navigation.

7 Investigating Vocabulary

Before we look at how lexical information is recorded in dictionaries, in Chapter 8, we need to consider how lexicologists find out about words, meaning and vocabulary. Where do they go for their information? What techniques do they use in exploring the lexical resources of a language? The investigation of vocabulary has been revolutionized in recent years by the computer, especially as storage capacity and processing speed have increased. Much of this chapter will concentrate on the electronic resources and tools now available to students of vocabulary.

7.1 What might we want to find out?

Lexicologists are interested in ascertaining what the extent of the current vocabulary of a language is, or what constituted the vocabulary of the language at some point in the past. A lexicologist may be particularly interested in the new words or expressions that are being coined and what word-formation processes (Chapter 4) are currently productive in the language. But a lexicologist will also want to know how extensive the currency of a new word is, whether it is accepted and used by a wide spectrum of speakers or whether it is restricted in its use to particular sub-groups of speakers.

For new words, a lexicologist will need to ascertain their pronunciation and spelling, whether they have variants and whether there is a standard form. The spelling and pronunciation of existing words also need to be monitored for any changes or new variants, or the perceived preference between existing variants. For example, many of the words with 'ae' in their spelling (*mediaeval, encyclopaedia*) are now more routinely spelt simply with 'e' (*medieval, encyclopedia*); some words with /juː/ in their pronunciation have dropped the /j/ (*lute, suit*) and others are continuing the change (*news, student*).

Some lexicologists have an interest in the (restricted) vocabulary used by specific social groups, age groups, sub-cultures or occupations. Eric Partridge, for example, was a great collector of slang, from the armed forces, the criminal underworld and so on (Partridge 1984). Others (e.g. Hudson

1978) have concentrated on the vocabulary developed by particular occupational groups, often to mystify their profession and create a barrier for outsiders. Such lexicologists need access to the speech and writing of people who are the inventors and users of these restricted vocabularies.

For a number of lexicologists their interest is in the origin and history of words, and in the birth and death of words. This applies not only to tracing the etymology of well-established words, but also to discovering and explaining the occasions that give rise to neologisms (see Knowles and Elliott (eds) 1997), both in everyday language and in the terminologies of professional and specialist groups.

Lexicologists are inevitably interested in the meanings of words, in the lexical environments in which they typically occur, in the grammatical structures they are able to enter, and in situational contexts to which they may be restricted or in which they may be typically found. In other words, lexicologists are interested in the semantics, grammar and pragmatics of words.

These are some of the areas that lexicologists want to investigate, some of the information about words that they want to find out about. The question is: How do they find out about words?

EXERCISE 7/1

Find out as much as you can, from whatever sources you have available, about one or more of the following words:

Aga-saga, mickle, presenteeism, stakeholder, waif.

7.2 How do we find out?

Linguists generally, including lexicologists, have recourse to three sources of linguistic data (Jackson and Stockwell 1996: 9): introspection, elicitation, and corpora. Introspection occurs when lexicologists use their own knowledge of a language as the data for describing words, meaning and vocabulary. While such a method might work to an extent for a grammarian, though that is arguable, it is unlikely that a lexicologist would have a sufficient range of intuitive data to support a worthwhile lexical description. This is not to discount a lexicologist's knowledge of the language; it can often be important as a filter for interpreting data from other sources; but it will prove inadequate as the sole or primary source of data.

Linguists use the method of elicitation when they have quite specific data to collect about some aspect of language. The method usually involves the construction of a questionnaire, which is then administered to a sample of speakers of the language. Much sociolinguistic research has used the elicitation technique; so have dialect surveys (e.g. the *Survey of English Dialects*, Orton *et al.* 1962–71), where researchers have often concentrated on the words that dialect speakers use for particular kinds of objects (e.g. foods, implements, plants) and their pronunciation. Some dictionary publishers have used a panel, usually of carefully chosen 'experts', to advise them on the accepted or 'correct' usage of words. Currently a large-scale elicitation, the 'Langscape Survey', is being carried out through the journal *English Today* of a number of variable features of spelling, grammar and usage. Elicitation has an important role to play in finding out about identifiable aspects of lexical usage in particular, but it is unlikely to be the lexicologist's sole, or even primary, source of data.

The primary source of a lexicologist's data will be corpora of various kinds. A corpus is a 'body' of material, from which linguists can extract the data they require. For a lexicologist, the corpus may consist of a dictionary, or more likely a collection of dictionaries; or of a citation collection; or of a collection of texts; or it may consist of some combination of these.

Dictionaries now exist in both printed and electronic form. Electronic dictionaries are available on CD-ROM (Compact Disc – Read Only Memory) for use with personal computers (7.3); some are available on the internet (7.6). Citation collections are also likely to be stored in an electronic medium these days, though the most famous citation corpus was collected painstakingly over years and stored on slips of paper. This was the collection of five million citations amassed by James Murray and the other editors for the *Oxford English Dictionary* (OED) in the second half of the nineteenth century (Murray 1977), and still being added to. Citations, in the OED sense, are usually single-sentence extracts from a text, which either illustrate the typical usage of a word or serve to explain its meaning. The extraction has been performed by a human being reading a text, so that the selection reflects to a degree the subjective judgment of that person.

Text corpora, which we shall discuss in the next section, are collections either of whole texts or of substantial extracts from texts. Text corpus is nowadays synonymous with electronic storage, but text corpora preceded electronic media. One such text corpus is the Survey of English Usage, begun in the 1950s under the direction of Randolph Quirk and located at University College in London. It has more recently been converted into electronic form as the London-Lund Corpus.

Corpora, whether general or specialist, form the bedrock of the lexicologist's data. Only with such resources is it possible to be sure of capturing sufficient and reliable information on the meaning and usage of words. We will now examine some of these sources in more detail, particularly as they are found in their electronic form.

EXERCISE 7/2

(a) Without consulting any sources, write down what you know about the usage of the following words: dependent, dependant.

(b) Ask three or four colleagues or friends to explain the difference in usage between these words to you, and note their replies.

(c) Now consult one or more dictionaries and, if you have access to one, a computer corpus, and check your information from (a) and (b).

Other pairs of words you could try this with are: complement/compliment, militate/mitigate, principal/principle, stationary/stationery, statue/statute.

7.3 Electronic resources

As the previous section has indicated, the two primary electronic resources available to the lexicologist are electronic dictionaries and computer corpora.

7.3.1 Electronic dictionaries

A number of monolingual English dictionaries, besides a range of bilingual dictionaries, are now available in the CD-ROM format. These include the 20-volume OED (2nd edn), as well as single-volume desk dictionaries, such as *Collins English Dictionary, the Concise Oxford Dictionary (Ninth Edition)* and *Longman Dictionary of the English Language*. Additionally, learner's dictionaries, such as the *Oxford Advanced Learner's Dictionary* (OALD), *Longman Dictionary of Contemporary English* (LDOCE) and *Collins COBUILD Dictionary*, have been made available in electronic form.

For the lexicologist, one of the chief advantages of an electronic dictionary over its printed counterpart is that it allows more sophisticated searching. Finding information in a printed dictionary is achieved almost exclusively through the alphabetical list of headwords. You could not, for example, discover all the words that have been borrowed into English from Hungarian, except by examining every etymology of every word in the dictionary. Electronic dictionaries allow searching of other 'fields of information', so that the answer to the previous query could be ascertained quickly by searching the etymology in the electronic versions of the OED (2nd edn) or the *Concise Oxford Dictionary (Ninth Edition)*. The latter notes the following fifteen items as having a Hungarian origin: biro, cimbalom, coach, csardas, forint, goulash, hussar, Kaposi's sarcoma, paprika, Rubik's cube, sabre, shako, soutache, tzigane, vampire.

Similarly, the definition 'field' of an electronic dictionary can be searched for all manner of information. A lexicologist who is investigating a particular lexical field (see 6.3) can search for terms connected with that field in the definitions. If the field consists of specialist terms that are likely to be marked with a subject or domain label, then that label can be searched for. A search for 'prosody', which is a subject label in the *Concise Oxford Dictionary*

(Ninth Edition), finds 46 items belonging to this lexical field. Many definitions of the 'genus + differentiae' type allow the identification of items in a
lexical field by searching for the 'genus' term in the definition field. For
example, a search for 'mollusc' identifies 48 items with this term in their
definition field, including *squid* 'any elongated fast-swimming cephalopod
mollusc of the order Teuthoidea, with eight arms and two long tentacles'.
Not all the items are using 'mollusc' as a genus term, but these can be easily
examined and excluded.

Electronic dictionaries do allow some extensive and rapid searching of
the dictionary text, and they yield much information that is of use to a
lexicologist; but there is no certainty that the information obtained is
comprehensive and completely reliable. The problem arises from the fact
that electronic dictionaries are currently merely the printed dictionary
transferred without any modification to the electronic medium. As a result,
all the inconsistencies of labelling and defining are replicated in the
electronic version, with consequences for the reliability of search results. It
is highly likely that the words making up the lexical field of molluscs will
have a definition of the style given above for *squid*, but there is unlikely to be
the same consistency in defining all the members of the lexical field of
containers, for example. The members of the lexical field of prosody may be
all marked with a subject label, but subject labelling tends to be restricted to
particular jargons; for example, it is unlikely that the terms associated with
forestry will be specially labelled.

However, there is no reason why electronic dictionaries should be stored
in the same way as their print counterparts (McArthur 1998). The space
restrictions of a printed book are not replicated in the CD-ROM medium.
Nor is the need for an alphabetical ordering. Words could be stored both as
an alphabetical list and by lexical field, with appropriate cross-referencing
and hyper-links (enabling immediate access to the cross-reference). The
dictionary could be browsed alphabetically, as with a conventional print
dictionary, or the vocabulary could be examined by lexical field or even sub-
field, with the same information presented for each item, irrespective of the
mode of lookup. With more systematic coding, which the less restricted
capacity of an electronic dictionary would allow, the amount and variety of
lexical information could be greatly increased, though not necessarily
displayed unless requested, to the advantage of the student of lexicology, if
not to the general user. Similarly, more extensive illustration of meanings
and uses should be possible. *Collins COBUILD on CD-ROM* (1994), for
example, already contains a five-million-word database of examples, integrated with the dictionary.

7.3.2 Text corpora

We have already suggested that computer corpora of texts represent a
fundamental source of data for the lexicologist these days (Rundell and Stock
1992). The first recognized computer corpus was assembled in the 1960s at

Brown University in the USA by Nelson Francis and Henry Kucera; it became known as the 'Brown Corpus'. It consists of five hundred 2000-word samples (one million words in all) from a wide variety of printed American English texts, all published in the year 1961. The text extracts include newspaper reports, editorials and reviews; essays and articles from a variety of non-fiction sources; government documents; academic writing; and an assortment of fictional writing. These are ordered in fifteen uneven-sized categories, ranging from nine texts for Category R (Humour) to 80 texts for Category J (Learned and Scientific Writing). In the 1970s, the Brown Corpus was replicated for British English (of 1961) by the Lancaster-Oslo/Bergen (LOB) Corpus, for which Geoffrey Leech and Stig Johansson were primarily responsible. This has enabled a large number of comparative studies of British and American English to be undertaken. The Brown and LOB corpora have again been replicated, using texts published in 1991, at the University of Freiburg (under the direction of Christian Mair), with the aim of providing corpora (FROWN and FLOB) for examining changes in British and American English over the thirty-year period between 1961 and 1991.

Each of the corpora so far mentioned contains one million words of text. Corpora of the same size are being constructed in the International Corpus of English (ICE) project, the brainchild of the late Sidney Greenbaum. The ICE project will eventually encompass around twenty one-million-word corpora of different varieties of English from around the world, though with a different text selection policy from that of the Brown and LOB corpora (see Leitner 1992). A text corpus of this size has proved useful for examining many features of the grammar of English (e.g. Coates 1983, Thomas and Short, eds, 1996, *ICAME Journal* 1977–), but it has limited use for lexical research. High-frequency words (most determiners and pronouns, and many conjunctions and prepositions) occur in abundance, but many items of interest to a lexicologist occur either with such low frequency that they provide insufficient data, or not at all.

The need for a large corpus for lexical research was recognized by John Sinclair and his team when they started the COBUILD project at the University of Birmingham in the 1980s. The aim of the COBUILD project, which was co-sponsored by Collins Publishers and Birmingham University, was an advanced learner's dictionary based entirely on evidence from a text corpus. For the first edition of the dictionary in 1987, the lexicographers had access to a corpus in excess of 20 million words. Besides its size, its distinctive feature was that it was composed of whole texts and not text extracts, and the texts were contemporary 1980s texts. The COBUILD team has continued to add to the corpus year by year, and the Bank of English, as it was renamed, had in excess of 200 million words of text for the second edition of the dictionary in 1995. Sinclair comments in the Introduction to the second edition:

> In general, the new analysis confirms the picture of the language that we gave in 1987, but the larger corpus enables us to make statements about meanings, patterns, and uses of words with much greater confidence and accuracy of detail. (p. viii)

The Bank of English continues to be added to, and in mid-1998 stood at well over 300 million words.

The COBUILD project was the pioneer in the compilation of a dictionary based on a computer corpus of texts. The editions of all four of the learner's dictionaries published in 1995 claimed to have used a text corpus in their compilation. The *COBUILD Dictionary* used the Bank of English; the OALD and the LDOCE used the 100-million-word British National Corpus, as well as other sources; and the *Cambridge International Dictionary of English* (CIDE) used the 100-million-word Cambridge Language Survey corpus. Dictionaries for native speakers also claim to have consulted the computer corpora: the fourth edition of *Collins English Dictionary* (1998) refers to the Bank of English as one of its sources, and the *New Oxford Dictionary of English* (1998) refers to the British National Corpus as having been used in its compilation.

There is, however, no automatic process that will convert a computer text corpus into a finished dictionary. In compiling the first edition of the *Collins COBUILD English Dictionary*, the recording of the data that would compose the dictionary article was done manually on slips of paper (Krishnamurthy 1987). Rundell and Stock (1992) envisage a continued central role for the lexicographer:

> Some corpus enthusiasts now predict an ever-diminishing role for human intervention and human introspection: as corpora grow ever more massive, and the tools of analysis become ever more powerful, what in future will be the lexicographer's role, beyond faithfully reporting the 'insights' that the corpus will supply automatically at the touch of a button? The truth is that we can only speculate on how things will develop. But it is possible to take a less apocalyptic view and to envisage a future in which the human lexicographers retain a very central role. As computers perform more and more of the routine work *and* make possible increasingly fine-grained analyses of the language, lexicographers will simultaneously be liberated from drudgery and empowered to focus their creative energies on doing what machines cannot do. (p. 14)

Not only is the lexicographical process not fully able to be automated, but it needs a partnership between human and machine, there are also questions about the nature of the corpus itself. We have mentioned already the question of size, how big a corpus needs to be in order to provide sufficient data for the lexicologist and lexicographer. A question is also raised about how representative a corpus must be, in terms of the range of media, genres and subject areas that it takes in. Sinclair (1985) provocatively suggests that if a particular sense of a word (the example given was the grammar sense of *decline*) does not occur in a 7.3 million-word-corpus of English, then it has no place in the dictionary. But it may just be the case that this sense does not occur because the corpus does not contain a text which has the appropriate examples. The question of balance and representativeness will continue to be discussed, as will more generally the nature of the ideal corpus for lexical studies.

We may conclude that, while text corpora must constitute the primary source of a lexicologist's data, it cannot be the only one. Citation corpora will continue to play a part. And the lexicologist's own experience, reading, intuition and knowledge are all necessary both for supplementing the data found in corpora and for evaluating that data. This raises the question of how data is extracted from corpora, to which we now turn.

EXERCISE 7/3

If you have an electronic dictionary on your computer, what information can you search for, apart from the headword?

If it allows you to search definitions or labels, find all the words belonging to a specialist vocabulary, such as 'music' or 'genetics'. Or search for a definition term such as 'instrument' or 'musical instrument'.

7.4 Tools of analysis

The essential tool of analysis, in the form of a computer program, for the lexicological investigation of corpora is the concordancer. For any search requested, of a word, phrase or any string of letters, a concordancer produces a list of each occurrence of the string, together with a specified amount of context, in what is known as a KWIC (key word in context) display. Here is an example of a KWIC concordance of the word *invited* as used in the 124,000 or so words of Jane Austen's *Pride and Prejudice*, generated by the MonoConc concordance program (Barlow 1996), with 40 characters of context either side of the keyword:

> oin his regiment, unless they are first [[invited]] to Longbourn; and I understand from
> of her intended civility, and they were [[invited]] and engaged to dine at Longbourn in
> remarkably good spirits. Mrs. Bennet [[invited]] him to dine with them; but, with
> and though Mrs. Wickham frequently [[invited]] her to come and stay with her, with
> ously closed his book. He was directly [[invited]] to join their party, but he declined
> on taken leave, than a glance from Jane [[invited]] her to follow her up stairs. When
> whole party at loo, and was immediately [[invited]] to join them – but suspecting them
> ension, wished them a good journey, and [[invited]] them to come to Hunsford again
> account that he has been so frequently [[invited]] this week. You know my mother's
> at had happened in London, Mr. Collins [[invited]] them to take a stroll in the garden,
> declaration that, though he had been [[invited]] only to a family dinner, she would tak

Such a list enables a lexicologist to understand how a word is used. For instance, it is clear from these few examples from a single text that *invite* has a human issuer and recipient, and may request someone either to (go to) a place (*Longbourn*) or occasion (*a family dinner*), or to do something (*to dine, to join, to come*).

As a further example, consider the following lines for the adjective *infectious*, from the 476 occurrences of the word in the British National Corpus, generated by the SARA program, which is used for searching the British National Corpus (Aston and Burnard 1998), at the British National Corpus website (http://thetis.bl.uk/). They illustrate the kinds of noun that *infectious* may be used with. Note that SARA gives whole sentences as context.

> The discharge may interfere with feeding and is highly *infectious* to anyone who comes into contact with it, apart from its mother.
> By lessening your own tension, you help to relax others in your sphere; relaxation and tension are *infectious*.
> ... mortality is only a good indicator of the overall health of a population when *infectious* diseases are a major problem.
> Our last good clerk, Miss Cameron, died of one of our worst fevers, *infectious* meningitis.
> Such people are *infectious*, however ...
> But you won't be *infectious* and most people are able to carry on just as normal.
> McCrea's smile was *infectious*.
> Her gaiety and enthusiasm for work was *infectious*; nothing seemed to get her down.
> No *infectious* agent was found in 30% of 77 patients at stage IV with diarrhoea ...
> Despite the *infectious* music and Pierre Le Rue's exhortations to the audience to rise from their seats and come towards the stage, precious few did so.

From these few examples, we can see that, in medical uses, 'diseases' may be infectious, 'discharges' and 'agents' may be infectious, and so may 'people'. In a metaphorical sense, moods and emotions may be infectious, or their manifestations (*smile*), or things that stimulate them (*music*).

Besides listing each occurrence of a word with its context, concordancers usually also give information on the overall frequency of occurrence of words, which can be a useful indicator of how core a word is in the vocabulary, though we need to be mindful of the caveats relating to the size and representativeness of a corpus. The highest frequency words are members of the grammatical classes (determiners, pronouns, prepositions and conjunctions). For example, the conjunction *and* occurs 2,689,689 times in the 100-million-word British National Corpus; *but* occurs 461,477 times, and *if*, 261,497 times. By contrast, in the area of 'political' adjectives, *political* itself occurs 30,565 times, *democratic*, 5951, *socialist*, 3396 (some of which could be a noun), *liberal*, 5554 (some of which may not be political in reference at all), *conservative*, 7110 (the same caveat applies as for *liberal*), *republican*, 1812. The word *caveat*, which I have used twice in this paragraph, occurs just 125 times in its singular form and a further 71 times in the plural, in the British National Corpus. And the noun *declension* occurs a mere four times, but two of them are in the grammar sense!

A further set of information that lexicologists are interested in and that concordancers can often provide is the general collocational behaviour of a word. Consider the following collocation table for the verb *bring*, generated by MonoConc (Barlow 1996) from the one-million-word LOB Corpus, in which the verb occurs 106 times. Only collocates that occur five times or more in the context of *bring* have been included.

bring, brings, bringing, brought

2nd left		1st left		1st right		2nd right	
14	and	90	to	54	the	50	the
12	the	21	had	47	to	42	to
7	would	20	be	35	about	21	by
7	that	20	and	29	up	21	a
6	have	17	was	23	in	13	and
6	which	15	been	22	him	11	in
5	had	11	will	20	out	10	from
5	enough	11	have	20	a	9	up
5	of	11	has	17	her	9	bear
5	has	9	would	13	back	8	back
		9	were	13	them	6	him
		8	not	12	it	6	out
		8	that	11	you	6	into
		7	which	10	us	5	more
		7	he	10	into	5	light
		7	it	10	home		
		7	in	9	his		
		6	are	7	me		
		6	of	6	on		
		6	is	5	with		
		5	He				
		5	I				
		5	can				

The columns indicate those words occurring immediately to the left (1st left) and immediately to the right (1st right) of the verb *bring*, as well as those that are two positions to the left and right of the keyword. Most of the words occurring to the left are auxiliary verbs (*was, have, will*), the infinitive marker *to*, personal pronouns (*he, it, I*), the conjunction *and*, and relative pronouns (*which, that*). More interesting are the collocates to the right of the keyword, which is usually the case with verbs. Here, besides the highest frequency word *the*, *bring* is followed by the preposition *to* (presumably in the 'carry' or 'deliver' sense of *bring*), by the adverbs (usually as part of phrasal verbs) *about, up, in, out, back, home* and *on*, and by personal pronouns (*him, her, them, you, me*), functioning presumably as direct objects of *bring*. The other prepositions with high frequency in 2nd right position are *by*, possibly in the phrase 'brought up by', and *from*, possibly in the combination 'bring out from'. Some clear patterns of usage and their relative frequencies thus begin to emerge from this table of collocations.

The corpora that we have used to illustrate the use of concordancers have been 'plain text' corpora. While much of interest to the lexicologist can be extracted from such corpora, there are some kinds of information that are more easily accessed if the corpus is pre-analysed in some way. For example, you may have noticed in the previous discussion on the collocation table that the word *to* was identified on one occasion as the 'infinitive marker' and on another as a 'preposition'. The identification was done solely on the position of *to* in relation to the verb keyword (as an infinitive marker to the left, and as a preposition to the right); but, in the end, this is an assumption, it is not based on an analysis of each of the occurrences. A further tool of analysis is a tagger or parser, which is a computer program (or rather, set of programs) that is applied to a corpus in order to give, as a minimum, the word class of each item in the corpus. Such an analysis would distinguish the two uses of *to*. Here is a brief sample of the tagged version of the LOB Corpus:

> ^ his_PP$ first_OD books_NNS of_IN short_JJ stories_NNS were_BED as_QL clear_JJ as_CS only_RB crystals_NNS of_IN poison_NN can_MD be_BE, _, and_CC the_ATI horrors_NNS he_PP3A held_VBD up_RP to_IN our_PP$ inspection_NN were_BED almost_RB too_QL recognisable_JJ to_TO be_BE faced_VBN. _. ^ but_CC, _, since_ IN then_RN, _, \0Mr_NPT Wilson_NP has_HVZ widened_VBN both_ABX his_PP$ medium_NN and_CC his_PP$ heart_NN. _.

Each word, and punctuation mark, is followed by a word class tag, though each word class is further sub-divided. Note that *to* as a preposition is tagged '_IN', and as an infinitive marker it is tagged '_TO'. You may also note that a distinction is made between an 'adverb particle' _RP (*up*), a 'nominal adverb' _RN (*then*) and the general run of adverbs _RB (*only, almost*). This enables a lexicologist to use a concordancer to search for items by tag, as well as or at the same time as, by letter string. For example, a search for 'attributive only' adjectives (tagged _JJB) in part of the LOB Corpus yields as the predominant examples, leaving aside expressions like 'three-year-old': chief, entire, front, further, inland, inner, joint, lone, maiden, main, overseas, past, principal, sheer, teenage, top, upper. A search for adverbs that modify adjectives, the tag sequence '_RB _JJ', identifies items occurring with some regularity such as the following: almost, always, brilliantly, completely, equally, essentially, extremely, highly, often, once, particularly, perfectly, quite, rather, unusually, utterly. There are of course many more; this is just a snapshot from part of the LOB Corpus. What it illustrates is the use of a concordancer with a tagged corpus to investigate the lexical co-occurrence of classes of items.

Another tool of analysis that may be of interest to lexicologists is one that measures the lexical density or the richness of vocabulary in a text. Lexical density is measured by the Type/Token Ratio (Crystal 1992). The tokens are the running words of the text, e.g. the word count produced by a word processor. The types are the number of different words in the text. For example, the item (type) *and* may have several hundreds, even thousands of occurrences (tokens) in a text, whereas the type *disingenuous* may occur only once, i.e. have only one token. Since the number of types is always smaller than the number of tokens, the Type/Token Ratio is expressed as less than 1. However, the higher this figure is, i.e. the closer to 1, the greater the lexical density, indicating that a text has a higher proportion of low-frequency words. Following are the Type/Token Ratios of a number of well-known novels, calculated on the first 10,000 words of each text, using a program called PC-LitStats (Reimer 1989), and listed in order of increasing lexical density:

Daniel Defoe: *Moll Flanders*	0.1523
Robert Louis Stevenson: *Treasure Island*	0.1880
Jane Austen: *Persuasion*	0.2015
Mark Twain: *Tom Sawyer*	0.2320
Charles Dickens: *Sketches By Boz*	0.2454
Joseph Conrad: *Heart of Darkness*	0.2534
Walter Scott: *Ivanhoe*	0.2640

Besides giving an, admittedly crude, indication of the size of an author's vocabulary, the Type/Token Ratio is also one of the indicators of the degree of difficulty that a text might present for a reader, a contribution to a text's readability score. It should be noted that the Type/Token Ratio for a text will vary depending on the sample on which it is caculated: the larger the sample, the lower will be the score. Compare the following scores for *Ivanhoe*, the highest scoring text in the list above:

Sample:	1000 words:	0.4390
	2000 words:	0.3740
	5000 words:	0.3208
	10,000 words:	0.2640
	15,000 words:	0.2443

It is important, therefore, to know the relevant sample sizes when evaluating Type/Token Ratio scores.

EXERCISE 7/4

(a) Examine the following concordance list for the adverb *highly*, taken from Jane Austen's *Persuasion*. What can you conclude about Jane Austen's usage of *highly* from this data?

she was a most dear and [[highly]] valued god-daughter, favourite, and
She rated Lady Russell's influence [[highly]]; and as to the severe
general air of oblivion among them was [[highly]]important from what
This meeting of the two parties proved [[highly]] satisfactory, and
thought such a style of intercourse [[highly]] imprudent; but she had
at Uppercross, it was [[highly]] incumbent on her to clothe her
and it would be [[highly]] absurd in him, who could be of no use ...

an officer, whom he had always valued [[highly]], which must have
friend of his, a Colonel Wallis, a [[highly]] respectable man,
perfectly could not know herself to be so [[highly]] rated by a
able man, and in many respects I think [[highly]] of him,'' said Anne;
and only superior to her in being more [[highly]] valued! My dearest
of Lady Russell, and insinuations [[highly]] rational against Mrs Clay.
half her accomplishments, and too [[highly]] accomplished for modesty to
The language, I know, is [[highly]] disrespectful. Though

(b) Do similarly for the verb *expect* from the following collocation
table, derived from the LOB Corpus:

2nd left		1st left		1st right		2nd right	
13	might	48	be	79	to	34	to
9	one	18	is	17	the	14	be
9	I	14	I	15	a	12	the
8	can	13	to	12	that	9	find
8	to	11	had	11	from	5	a
7	have	11	would	8	him		
7	what	9	you	8	and		
7	than	9	was	7	of		
6	we	9	been	7	in		
5	he	8	are	6	it		
5	could	7	the	5	her		
5	you	7	not	5	me		
5	would	6	have				
		6	might				
		6	we				
		5	never				
		5	don't				

7.5 MRDs, LDBs and LKBs

The electronic medium opens up a number of possibilities not only for
exploring vocabulary, but also for arranging the descriptions of vocabulary.
We have already noted (7.3.1) that electronic dictionaries hold potential
both for their design and for searching them that their print counterparts
do not possess. Linguists working in the areas of artificial intelligence and
natural language engineering are interested in computer-based lexical
descriptions, since they are essential to much of their research, for example
in machine translation, speech synthesis, automatic text analysis (see Atkins
and Zampolli, eds, 1994, Walker *et al.*, eds, 1995, Wilks *et al.* 1996).

As a first recourse, computational linguists turned to dictionaries already
available in electronic form, so-called Machine Readable Dictionaries (MRD).
One of the first to be made available as an MRD was LDOCE (1978), which
has been used in a variety of projects as a lexical resource (Wilks *et al.* 1996).
In fact, the electronic version contains additional information, e.g. labels for
lexical fields, that was not included in the print version.

One of the difficulties that computational linguists have found with MRDs is that some information about words is either missing completely or not entered in a structured and consistent manner. Definitions, for example, are often phrased without any overall consistency of pattern: some words have full, analytical definitions, while others merely have a synonym. Labelling (of subject domain, formality, style and the like) is often erratic and unsystematic. There is usually little indication of the morphological composition of words. For computational purposes, the lexical description needs to be more explicit, systematic and structured, with appropriate links marked between words. The construction of Lexical Databases (LDBs) has been proposed for this purpose. Calzolari (1995) sets out the requirements for an LDB as follows:

> an LDB must be able to represent computationally the very complex system of relations, between and within lexical entries, which constitutes our knowledge of 'lexical facts'. The LDB should provide a means of expression of lexical knowledge integrating the various aspects (phonological, morphological, syntactic, semantic, and why not pragmatic) which can be associated with lexical entries. (pp. 339–40)

The construction of an LDB fulfilling these requirements is a major undertaking, if the database is to be at all comprehensive and usable in real applications. Ways have been investigated to derive such a database, in part at least, from existing MRDs. One of the most extensive such databases has, however, been developed from scratch: WordNet. This project was begun in the mid-1980s at Princeton University (USA), under the direction of George Miller (Miller, ed., 1990). WordNet is described as 'an online lexical database' or 'an online lexical reference system'. In it, the nouns, verbs and adjectives of English are organized into synonym sets, each based on a single underlying lexical concept. The synonym sets are linked by a number of different kinds of relation. The organization of WordNet is based on word association theories deriving from psychology, Miller's own discipline; it is based on word meanings rather than word forms, though it is recognized that lexical relations, like synonymy and antonymy, hold between word forms, and some account has also to be taken of inflectional variants. Information on WordNet and how to obtain it is available online at: *http://www.cogsci.princeton.edu/ ~ wn/*.

For some computer applications, e.g. machine translation, it is thought that an LDB would provide insufficient information, since some of the analysis that the computer would be required to make may well extend beyond straightforward lexical information to more complex knowledge about the meanings of lexical items, their interrelationships, and their interpretation in context. The term Lexical Knowledge Base (LKB) has been used to refer to the computational capture of such knowledge (Ooi 1998: 94). The LKB could well include an LDB, and it is fair to say that the distinction between the two is not yet very clearly drawn. There is still much to be done in computational lexicology and lexicography.

7.6 WWW

We have mentioned already a number of electronic resources of use to a lexicologist, including dictionaries in CD-ROM format. In this section we consider additional resources available on the World Wide Web (WWW), or internet. A caveat must be entered at this point: internet addresses are subject to change, so that, while the author has accessed these websites at the addresses given, there is no guarantee that six months or a year later the address will be the same.

There are three kinds of site of interest to a lexicologist: those concerned with documenting lexical resources and lexical research; those documenting and giving access to computer corpora; and those related to dictionaries and lexicography.

In terms of lexical resources, we have mentioned already the WordNet site at the Cognitive Science Laboratory of Princeton University (USA). This site gives information on obtaining and accessing WordNet, as well as links to other sites where interfaces to WordNet have been developed. Among these, a particularly accessible one is the 'WordNet 1.6 Vocabulary Helper', developed by Greg Petersen at the Notre Dame Women's College in Kyoto (Japan): *http://www.notredame.ac.jp/cgi-bin/wn/*. A list of lexical resources with links can be found at the Consortium for Lexical Research site at the Computing Research Laboratory of New Mexico State University (USA): *http://crl.nmsu.edu/Resources/clr.htm/*. The Special Interest Group on the Lexicon of the Association of Computational Linguistics has a similar resource on its site at: *http://www.clres.com/siglex.html/*. And the Dutch Centre for Lexical Information has a site at: *http://www.kun.nl/celex/*, with lexical databases for English, German and Dutch; online access is restricted to Dutch scholars, but a CD-ROM is available for others.

Many of the classic computer corpora of English are distributed by the International Computer Archive of Modern and Medieval English (ICAME) at the Norwegian Computing Centre for the Humanities in Bergen. The ICAME site can be found at: *http://www.hit.uib.no/icame.html/*. The corpora are available on CD-ROM, a new edition of which was published in Summer 1999. ICAME also publishes an annual journal, which contains accounts of corpus research and reports on corpora under development (*ICAME Journal* 1977–). The British National Corpus has a site currently housed on the British Library's computer (*http://thetis.bl.uk/*), which contains information on the corpus, its availability, and the possibility of conducting simple online searches. Information on the Bank of English, the corpus underlying the COBUILD dictionaries, can be found on the Collins site at: *http://www.cobuild.collins.co.uk/boe_info.html/*. And information about the International Corpus of English can be found on the Survey of English Usage site at University College London (UK): *http://www.ucl.ac.uk/english-usage/*.

The following three internet sites provide an index or structured list of online dictionaries. The 'Index of Online Dictionaries' at the University of Paderborn (Germany) has links to monolingual, bilingual and specialist dictionaries, and to thesauruses: *http://www-math.uni-paderborn.de/dictionaries/ Dictionaries.html/*. 'A Web of On-line Dictionaries', developed by Robert Beard at Bucknell University (USA), claims to be linked to 800 dictionaries in 150 different languages: *http://www.falstaff.bucknell.edu/rbeard/diction.html/*. It also features a 'quick lookup' for English, based on *Merriam-Webster's Collegiate Dictionary* (10th edition). The 'OneLook Dictionaries' site claimed in January 1999 to have 449 dictionaries indexed, including WordNet: *http://www.onelook.com/*.

The *Oxford English Dictionary* has a site at: *http://www.oed.com/*, which gives all kinds of information about the dictionary and regular reports on progress with the third edition. A prototype online version of the second edition is being developed at: *http://proto.oed.com/*. Merriam-Webster's have an online dictionary at: *http://www.m-w.com/home.htm/*. The *Collins COBUILD Student's Dictionary* can be consulted online at the Ruhr University of Bochum (Germany): *http://www.linguistics.ruhr-uni-bochum.de/ccsd/*.

Of related interest are the various regional lexicography associations, whose websites have links to other sites useful to lexicologists. The European Association of Lexicography (EURALEX) resides at the University of Stuttgart (Germany): *http://www.ims.uni-stuttgart.de/euralex/*. The African Association (AFRILEX) site is located at the University of Pretoria (South Africa) Department of African Languages: *http://www.up.ac.za/academic/ libarts/afrilang/homelex.html/*. The Australian and the Asian Assocations (AUSTRALEX and ASIALEX) are both sited at the Australian National University: *http://www.anu.edu.au/linguistics/alex/* for AUSTRALEX, and *http://www.anu.edu.au/linguistics/alex/asialex.html/* for ASIALEX, though each can be accessed from the other's site. The Dictionary Society of North America is currently at the University of Wisconsin: *http://polyglott.lss.wisc.edu/dsna/index.html/*.

Finally, mention should be made of the Dictionary Research Centre at the University of Exeter (UK): *http://www.ex.ac.uk/drc/*, and its counterpart at Maquarie University in Sydney (Australia): *http://www.ling.mq.edu.au/drc*.

EXERCISE 7/5

If you have access to the internet, visit some of the sites mentioned in this chapter and explore the vast range of information that the World Wide Web can provide for lexicologists.

7.7 Summary

This chapter has examined the sources that lexicologists use in order to obtain data relevant to their concerns, as well as some of the tools of analysis that are available for extracting and analysing lexicological data.

We saw that lexicologists, in common with other linguists, need to rely on corpus data as their primary source, and to use elicitation and intuition as supplementary sources. For lexicologists, corpus data may be in the form of dictionaries, as well as the large computer corpora now available.

Tools of analyis of particular use to lexicologists are those that provide statistical information about word frequency, concordances for displaying the usage of words, and collocation tables for examining the combinatorial regularities of words.

The chapter concluded with a survey of some of the resources available on the internet which would be of interest to lexicologists.

8   Words in Dictionaries

If you wanted to find out something about a word, for example its spelling or its meaning, you would reach for a dictionary and search through the alphabetical list of headwords until you located the item you wanted to know about. Dictionaries contain information about words. They are the most systematic and comprehensive lexical descriptions that we have. Yet dictionary making – lexicography – has a history and a tradition that, until the latter half of the twentieth century, was quite independent of developments in linguistics. This chapter considers dictionaries as lexical descriptions and evaluates how adequate they are as such.

8.1 Repositories of words

Dictionaries – and we are concerned largely with monolingual dictionaries of English produced by British publishers – come in many shapes and sizes, and are aimed at different groups of users. No dictionary is totally comprehensive, in the sense that it contains all the words in the language. Even the great twenty-volume second edition of the *Oxford English Dictionary*, with its 291,500 entries (Berg 1993: 195), needs to be reviewed and updated for new senses of existing words as well as new words. The major dictionary publishers are constantly surveying material for new words and new meanings (e.g. Ayto 1990, Knowles and Elliott (eds) 1997). Each new edition of a dictionary has to make a selection from the words of current English and decide which to include and which to leave out.

8.1.1 Dictionaries classified by purpose and size

The number of words that a dictionary contains will depend on its size and purpose. Let us propose, first of all, three major categories of English dictionary according to purpose:

1. general-purpose dictionaries, aimed at native speakers of the language;
2. children's dictionaries, aimed at those acquiring English as their first language or through English-medium education;

3. learner's dictionaries, aimed at those learning English as a second or foreign language, usually in adolescence or adulthood.

Children's dictionaries come in various sizes, from large-format picture book dictionaries for infant school children to school dictionaries and dictionaries for teenagers that begin to resemble adult dictionaries. Learner's dictionaries are often seen as a progression from bilingual dictionaries in the language learning process, and they are therefore usually aimed at learners either at the intermediate or at the advanced stage of language learning. Some publishers produce a learners' dictionary for each of these levels; e.g. the *Oxford Student's Dictionary* (1998) for intermediate learners and the *Oxford Advanced Learner's Dictionary* (ed. Crowther 1995) for advanced learners; *Collins COBUILD Learner's Dictionary* (1996) for intermediate learners and *Collins COBUILD English Dictionary* (1995) for advanced learners. As it happens, Oxford also have a learner's dictionary for the 'beginner to pre-intermediate' stage, the *Oxford Elementary Learner's Dictionary* (1994).

General-purpose dictionaries, which will be the focus of our considerations in this chapter, come in three main sizes:

1. desk size (equivalent to college dictionaries in the USA), e.g. *Collins English Dictionary (CED), Longman Dictionary of the English Language (LDEL)*, the *New Oxford Dictionary of English*;
2. concise size, e.g. the *Concise Oxford Dictionary (COD), Collins Concise English Dictionary, Longman Concise English Dictionary*;
3. pocket size, e.g. the *Pocket Oxford Dictionary*, etc.

Publishers also produce dictionaries smaller than the 'pocket', e.g. 'gem' dictionaries, but their usefulness is questionable, except to check on the spelling of the commonest words.

8.1.2 How many words?

Difference in size is reflected partly in difference of format and page size, but more importantly from a lexical perspective, difference of vocabulary selection and information about words. It is very difficult to ascertain exactly how many 'words' a dictionary contains, because dictionaries count their contents in different ways and will clearly wish to maximize any count (Jackson 1998). Few dictionaries announce how many 'headwords' they have, and even if they do, there are two factors to bear in mind. First, 'headwords' may include the following in modern dictionaries: abbreviations (*MP*); prefixes (*mis-*), suffixes (*-ment*), and combining forms (*mal-*, *-mancy*); open compounds (*metal fatigue*); and encyclopedic entries, i.e. names of people and places. Second, dictionaries differ in their policy on multiple entries where a word belongs to more than one word class; for example, *middle* may be used as an adjective, a noun and a verb, and some dictionaries (e.g. LDEL 1991) have three headwords *middle*, whereas others (e.g. the *New Oxford Dictionary of English* 1998) include all three word classes under a single headword.

Another way of counting the contents of dictionaries is to express them in terms of the number of 'definitions' or 'meanings'. In most current dictionaries, where a word has more than one 'meaning', they are numbered, usually with figures (1., 2.), but sometimes additionally with sub-divisions by letter (1a., 1b.). It is not clear whether a definition total includes the sub-divisions or just the major divisions. A more significant consideration is the fact that dictionaries, even of the same size, do not agree on how many meanings they distinguish for any particular word. For example, the noun *monkey* has five numbered meanings in the LDEL (1991), but it has ten numbered meanings in *Collins Electronic Dictionary* (1992). Few dictionaries use definitions as the sole count of their contents.

The preferred way of expressing the quantification of a dictionary's contents is in terms of 'references'. This method of counting derives from American practice, and it is 'a system designed to maximise the number of entries one can claim' (Landau 1989: 84). References include: the headword; any additional word class a word belongs to that is defined separately; any inflected forms given; run-on derivatives without definitions; idioms and other fixed expressions included within an entry; variant spellings; words given in lists at the bottom of the page that are derived by prefixation. In fact, virtually anything in a bold typeface is counted as a 'reference'.

The desk-size CED (1994) claims to contain 180,000 references; its concise equivalent, *Collins Concise English Dictionary* (1995), claims 125,000 references; and the *Collins Compact English Dictionary* (1994) claims 68,000 references. These are all, of course, estimates, based on counting a sample of pages; but they give a good idea of how dictionaries differ in size in respect of the quantification of their contents.

8.1.3 Selection of vocabulary

We have already made the point that any dictionary contains only a selection of current vocabulary. As lexical records of the language, they must contain the everyday words, what the original editors of the *Oxford English Dictionary* identified as the 'common core' of the vocabulary (see 6.1.1). For most dictionary users, these words are of little interest, because they will rarely, if ever, have occasion to look them up. What is of more interest is the selection policy of a dictionary beyond the common core. H.W. and F.G. Fowler state in the Preface to their first edition of the COD (1911): 'if we give fewer scientific and technical terms, we admit colloquial, facetious, slang, and vulgar expressions with freedom'. That is a clear policy, but not one that would be credible at the end of the twentieth century.

All dictionaries nowadays would claim to pay particular attention to the vocabulary of science and technology. Other areas that often receive special mention are: information technology, the environment, business and finance, medicine, sport, and popular culture. Dictionaries are products of

their age, and the vocabulary selection policy inevitably reflects the interests, concerns and culture of the time. Dictionaries are also concerned to be
seen as up-to-date, which is usually reflected in the inclusion of recently
coined words or meanings. The ninth edition of the COD (1996) (COD9)
claims 'over 7,000 new words and senses in a wide variety of areas' (Preface),
including such neologisms as *spin doctor, bhaji, greening, hyperspace,* and
repetitive strain injury.

8.1.4 Arrangement of vocabulary

We associate dictionaries with an alphabetical arrangement of words.
Indeed the expression 'dictionary order' is synonymous with 'alphabetical
order'. An alphabetical arrangement, which is common to a large number
of reference works (directories and indexes of all kinds), enables a user to
quickly find a word that is being looked up. However, few dictionaries
operate with a strict alphabetical order of the lexical items entered in them.
This is because all dictionaries use some degree of 'nesting', where a lexical
item may be included within the entry for another word, so that only the
latter has headword status. Alphabetical ordering applies primarily, if not
exclusively, to headwords.

Dictionaries vary in their nesting policies. Most dictionaries will nest (or
'run on') words derived from a headword by suffixation, where the derived
word does not need separate definition, because a user can be assumed to
be able to deduce the meaning from the headword and the suffix, e.g.
folksiness is a run-on under *folksy* in COD9, but *folksy* has headword status,
separate from its root *folk.* Similarly, *cellist* is a run-on under *cello,* even
though *cellist* precedes *cello* in the alphabetical order. Dictionaries vary in
their treatment of defined derivatives: some will accord headword status
only to those derivatives whose meaning has diverged significantly from the
root; others routinely give headword status to any derivative that is deemed
to merit separate definition. Words derived by prefixation (e.g. *be-friend, en-
code*) are always accorded separate headword status, because a user would
not otherwise be able to find them in the alphabetical listing. An alphabetically arranged dictionary, especially one with minimal nesting, thus
obscures the picture of the derivational relationship between words.

Most dictionaries will also nest fixed phrases and idioms usually under the
headword of the first main word in the phrase; in COD9 'everything but the
kitchen sink' is found under *kitchen,* and 'before you can say knife' under
knife. But it is not always clear where you should look for such expressions;
for example, 'that one could cut with a knife' is entered under *knife* and not
cut, while 'cut one's coat according to one's cloth' is under *cut* and not
under *coat* or *cloth.*

Nesting policy differs most in the treatment of compound words. Compounds may be spelt either solid (*landmark*) or hyphenated (*land-law*) or
open (*land mass*). There may be some variation especially between hyphenated and open compounds: *land-crab* appears hyphenated in COD8 (1990)

but open (*land crab*) in COD9, and *land-mine* is hyphenated in COD8 but solid (*landmine*) in COD9. Some dictionaries, usually those which nest all suffixed derivatives, nest all compounds, though this is not normally the practice these days. An alternative is not to nest any compounds, but to accord them all headword status: this is the policy followed by COD9 and is the one that fits best with strict alphabetization. Intermediate between these two extremes is the policy that accords headword status to solid compounds but nests hyphenated and open compounds (followed by COD8) or that nests only open compounds, treating them like phrases, while giving headword status to solid and hyphenated compounds.

Arguably, a lexical description (in the shape of a dictionary) that arranges in alphabetical order the words it selects for treatment does not provide a very revealing account of the vocabulary of the language. First, it obscures in many cases morphological relationships between words. This is the case, as we have already noted, for prefixed derivatives: there is normally no indication at the entry for the root that particular prefixes may apply. It is also the case for a number of words where the 'derived' item has a different etymology from the root, especially where an adjective has a Latinate origin and the root an Old English one, e.g. *mind – mental, church – ecclesiastical, lung – pulmonary, heart – cardiac.* Second, and more significant, an alphabetical arrangement obscures the semantic relations between words (discussed in Chapter 5). Not only are relations of synonymy, antonymy and hyponymy not revealed, we can also not perceive which words are available in English to refer to particular phenomena in the world or in aspects of our experience. What words are available to us in English, for example, to talk about the processes of cooking (see Lehrer 1974), or mental states, or making evaluations? How do we distinguish between 'mugs' and 'cups' and 'beakers', or between 'arguing', 'debating' and 'disputing'?

The alternative to an alphabetically arranged dictionary is one arranged thematically or by lexical field, like *Roget's Thesaurus*, though this work does not have the full range of lexical information; in particular it lacks any definitions. There is no general-purpose dictionary arranged thematically, though thematic lexicography has a long tradition, going back to Francis Bacon's taxonomy of knowledge in the late sixteenth century (McArthur 1986: 110ff). Many lexicographers still find the thematic arrangement a useful and revealing way of arranging words, either for the purposes of language teaching (Godman and Payne 1979, McArthur 1981) or for describing the vocabulary of a particular age or region, e.g. *A Thesaurus of Old English* (Roberts, Kay and Grundy 1995), *The Scots Thesaurus* (McLeod, ed., 1990). It is to be regretted that no publisher has yet ventured a general-purpose dictionary with a thematic arrangement.

EXERCISE 8/1

Using a desk or concise size general-purpose dictionary, read carefully the entries for the following words: face, narrow-minded, soap, walleye. Note for each item:
(a) how many entries (headwords) your dictionary has;
(b) whether your dictionary uses nesting (run-ons), and for which kinds of item;
(c) how your dictionary treats compound words.

8.2 Information about words

Let us return to the general-purpose dictionaries that we do have and consider the kinds of information that they provide about words, and whether that information constitutes a revealing and comprehensive lexical description. Let us review, first of all, what might constitute such a description. Professor Dick Hudson, in a seminal article entitled 'The Linguistic Foundations for Lexical Research and Dictionary Design' (Hudson 1988), provides a checklist of 'types of lexical fact' under eight headings:

1. Phonology: the pronunciation of a word and variants.
2. Morphology: a word's morpheme composition, and any irregular inflections.
3. Syntax: the word class and particular structures a word may enter.
4. Semantics: the 'meanings' of a word and the semantic structures it may enter.
5. Context: restrictions on social context and style in which a word may be used.
6. Spelling: the normal and any variant spellings of a word.
7. Etymology: the origin and history of a word.
8. Usage: frequency of use, when acquired, any taboos.

This is an abbreviation of Hudson's more comprehensive list, but it will serve our purpose, which is to examine current general-purpose dictionaries for the types of lexical information that they contain. We can use Hudson's list as a starting point.

8.2.1 Phonology

All general-purpose dictionaries give a transcription of the pronunciation of words, as spoken in isolation, and including the accentual pattern of polysyllabic items. This is usually situated immediately after, or very close to, the headword. In most current dictionaries the transcription system used is the International Phonetic Alphabet (IPA), though the LDEL (1991) continues to use a respelling system. Arguments used against the IPA focus on its unfamiliar symbols, and the necessity of having to consult a chart to interpret it. A respelling system usually uses a large number of digraphs, which equally need a chart to interpret; the symbols, as letters of the alphabet, are familiar, though the schwa symbol /ə/ is often added. The IPA has the advantage of a one-to-one correspondence between sound and symbol. In any case, few people learn the pronunciation of unfamiliar words by figuring out the transcription in a dictionary, but rather by hearing others say the word or by guessing a pronunciation from the spelling.

A more significant question than that concerning the transcription system is: whose pronunciation is represented in dictionaries? Since Daniel Jones first coined the term to describe the public-school accent that he knew best, 'Received Pronunciation' (Jones 1917), or some version of it, has been the pronunciation represented in dictionaries, though a term such as 'Educated British English' is used rather than 'Received Pronunciation' these days. This means that *grass* is transcribed (in IPA) as /gra:s/ rather than /græs/, the Midland and Northern pronunciation, and *cup* is transcribed /kʌp/ rather than /kʊp/. While it would be impossible to represent all regional variations, some acknowledgement could be made of the few common differences between Southern and Midland/Northern British speech. After all, variations in the Southern-based standard are noted, e.g. the initial vowel in *economics* /i:k.. ɛk../. Interestingly the *New Oxford* (1998) gives pronunciation only for words it deems to be unfamiliar or problematical.

8.2.2 Morphology

There are two aspects of the morphology of words that need to be taken into account, indicated by the traditional terms 'inflectional' and 'derivational'. The inflections of words are mostly regular (e.g. -(e)s for plurals of nouns, -(e)d for past tense of verbs) and thus derivable from general rules of grammar: they need not be stated in the dictionary. A dictionary needs to indicate inflections where they are irregular and may be specific to one or a small number of words, e.g. plural *mice* for *mouse, teeth* for *tooth*, or past tense *saw* for *see, thought* for *think*. Other words for which dictionaries indicate inflections are where an inflectional suffix causes a change in the spelling and/or pronunciation of the root to which it is added, e.g. *spy – spies, travel – travelled*.

Derivational morphology relates to the morphemic composition of a word, whether a word is a simple root (*long*), or derived (*longish, prolong*), or a compound (*longhouse, year-long*), or a combination of compound and derived (*long-jumper*). Dictionaries do not explicitly indicate the morphemic structure of a word. Where a word is a run-on derivative contained within the entry for the root, or where nesting of compounds and derivatives occurs, the morphemic relationship is implicit. The alphabetical arrangement of dictionaries allows a word derived straightforwardly by suffixation (i.e. with minimal spelling alteration) to be found in the immediate vicinity of its root word, and a compound may be in proximity to the first root from which it is formed. But where a word is derived by prefixation (*prolong*) or in the case of a second or subsequent root of a compound (*lifelong*), then there is no necessarily deducible morphemic relationship.

Even more so is this the case where the morphemic relationship is not immediately obvious from the spelling or pronunciation, e.g. *long – length*, or where a spelling alteration removes a derivative from the vicinity of its root, e.g. *empire – imperial, poor – pauper*. In English, it would also be useful to show the relationship between particularly nouns and adjectives, where the noun has an Anglo-Saxon origin and the equivalent adjective has a Latinate origin, e.g. *mind – mental, lung – pulmonary, mother – maternal*; or where both have a Latinate origin but were borrowed at different times and have diverged in spelling, e.g. *uncle – avuncular, enemy – inimical.*

The morphological aspects of lexical description are not systematically covered by dictionaries. Where morphemic relationships are indicated, they are evident more from the alphabetical ordering and nesting practices of dictionaries, rather than from any consciously explicit treatment. In mitigation, it should be said that general-purpose dictionaries do now include the major prefixes, suffixes and combining forms as headwords, though this still leaves all the analytical work to the dictionary user.

8.2.3 Syntax

The general rules of sentence structure – the possible patterns and the possible orders of elements – are contained in a grammar book. Which rules apply to individual words or which patterns a word may appear in will not usually be comprehensively described in a grammar but only be mentioned incidentally by way of exemplification. Grammar descriptions vary in their level of detail; some (e.g. *COBUILD English Grammar*) pay more attention to individual words than others; none can possibly deal with the syntactic operation of every lexeme, and certainly not from the perspective of the lexemes rather than the grammatical patterns. A dictionary, on the other hand, as a lexical description, needs to include information about where each lexeme individually fits into the syntactic system of the language.

The most basic item of syntactic information is the word class, or part-of-speech, to which a lexeme belongs. Designating a word as a 'noun' or 'verb' or 'preposition' indicates how the word may operate in syntactic structure. If a word is designated 'adjective', then you would expect to be able to use it only in certain positions: before nouns, the attributive position (a *large* suitcase, a *suitable* boy), or after a copular verb, the predicative position (the suitcase is *large*, the boy seems *suitable*). In many dictionaries, the word class label represents the limit of syntactic information, except that verbs are usually sub-classified into 'transitive' (followed by a syntactic Object) and 'intransitive' (not followed by an Object), and nouns that are singular in form but used as plurals (e.g. police).

The syntactic operation of words encompasses far more than word class membership. Learner's dictionaries aim to provide a comprehensive and systematic account of syntax, but native-speaker general-purpose dictionaries do not yet, by and large, see this as part of their function. What kinds of syntactic information do we mean? For nouns, for example, we need to know whether they are 'countable' (bean) or 'uncountable' (bread). Not only does this determine whether a plural inflection is possible (*beans* but not *breads*), but it also determines what types of determiner (articles and quantifiers) may precede it (*many* beans but *much* bread). In the case of adjectives, most can appear in both attributive and predicative positions, but a small number are restricted to one or other position: they need to be marked as such in the dictionary (e.g. *main* is only attributive – the *main* argument, while *asleep* is only predicative – the baby is *asleep*).

The class of words that needs the most extensive syntactic information is that of verbs. The simple transitive/intransitive distinction does not do justice to the variety of syntactic patterns that verbs may enter, as the pivotal elements in the structure of sentences. For example, some transitive verbs may have a clause as their syntactic object, and the clause may be a *that*-clause or an infinitive clause, or some other type; e.g. *hope* may enter constructions such as 'I hope that you feel better soon', 'We hope to visit you next week'. Some verbs may have more than one object (*give*, *send*), others may be followed by an object and a complement (*appoint*, *consider*). Some verbs are associated with specific prepositions (*rely on*, *accuse ... of*). A few verbs have quite complex and restricted syntactic operation (e.g. *matter*).

General-purpose dictionaries are not very good at providing syntactic information. It is, arguably, information that users will generally not need to refer to. As a native speaker you learn how to use a word grammatically by observing and imitating someone else's use of it, rather than by consulting a dictionary. But that argument holds for other information given in dictionaries (pronunciation, for example). The syntactic operaton of words is as much an idiosyncratic lexical fact as pronunciation.

EXERCISE 8/2

Examine the following entry for *discriminate*, taken from CED (1998):

discriminate *vb* (dɪ'skrɪmɪ,neɪt). **1** (*intr*, usu. foll. by *in favour of* or *against*) to single out a particular person, group, etc., for special favour or, esp., disfavour, often because of a characteristic such as race, colour, sex, intelligence, etc. **2** (when *intr*, foll. by *between* or *among*) to recognize or understand the difference (between); distinguish: *to discriminate right and wrong; to discriminate between right and wrong.* **3** (*intr*) to constitute or mark a difference. **4** (*intr*) to be discerning in matters of taste. ♦ *adj* (dɪ 'skrɪmɪnɪt). **5** showing or marked by discrimination. [C17: from Latin *discriminare* to divide, from *discrimen* a separation, from *discernere* to DISCERN] ➤ **dis'criminately** *adv* ➤ **dis'crimi,nator** *n*

What information does it give about: pronunciation, morphology, syntax?

8.2.4 Semantics

Here we are on more familiar dictionary ground. This is what we think dictionaries are primarily about: giving us the meanings of words, by providing definitions. First, though, lexicographers have to decide how many 'meanings' or 'senses' a word has (see 3.3), which they usually do on the evidence of examples of the word in use. It is a matter of judgment how finely to differentiate meanings. COD9, for example, along with other dictionaries, has the following senses for the verb *sing*: 'bring to a specified state by singing (sang the child to sleep)'; 'usher (esp. the new or old year) in or out with singing'. It is debatable whether significant distinguishable meanings of *sing* are being described here that could not be deduced from the general meaning of *sing* in the specific context. Dictionaries not only draw the line more or less finely, but you will also find that dictionaries draw the lines for polysemous words in different places.

Definitions are an attempt to characterize the denotation (3.2) of words. The most common type of definition is the analytical definition, based on the classical schema of 'genus' and 'differentiae'. The 'genus' word in the definition assigns the word to a class (genus) of items, and the 'differentiae' distinguish the meaning of this particular word from those of others in the class. For example, COD9 gives as its first definition of *window*: 'an opening in a wall, roof, vehicle, etc., usu. with glass in fixed, sliding, or hinged frames, to admit light or air etc. and allow the occupants to see out'. The genus in this definition is *opening*; so a window is a type of opening; and it is differentiated from other kinds of opening by its position (wall, roof, vehicle, etc.), its structure (glass in a frame), and its function (let in air and light, enable people to see out). Definitions of words with more abstract reference that are not readily cast in an analytical form often use a synonym or synonym phrase, e.g. *inconsequential* is defined in COD9 simply as 'unimportant'.

As we might expect, dictionaries are quite good at describing these semantic lexical facts. But, as we have seen (Chapter 5), meaning is more than denotation or reference: it encompasses in particular semantic (sense) relations like synonymy and antonymy, as well as collocational relations. In these respects, dictionaries do not do quite so well, although, as in the case of syntax, learner's dictionaries do much better – for example, synonyms and antonyms are included systematically, along with grammatical informa-tion, in the *Collins COBUILD English Dictionary's* 'extra column'. Among the general-purpose dictionaries, the LDEL (1991) contains a number of 'syno-nym essays', in which words that share a similar area of meaning are differentiated.

Collocation is a more difficult area to cover systematically, partly because we do not have sufficient information about the regular company that words keep (see Chapter 7) and partly because collocation is a matter of degree. One of the definitions of the verb *fake* in COD9 is given as: 'make a pretence of having (a feeling, illness, etc.)', where 'feeling' and 'illness' are cited as typical collocations of *fake* in this sense. But such information is accidentally given, rather than systematically (see Benson, Benson and Ilson 1997).

EXERCISE 8/3

Examine the entries for the following words in two or three dictionaries of a similar size: height, nucleus, subjective.

How many numbered meanings does each dictionary identify, and do they identify the same range of meanings?

8.2.5 Context

We have seen (in Chapter 6) that some words are restricted as to the types of text or discourse in which they may occur or as to the appropriate social contexts and occasions in which they may be used. Dictionaries traditionally have the function of being our guides to usage in these respects; consequently, we find that contextual information is systematically recorded in dictionaries. Such information includes both the level of formality for words that are marked as either 'formal' or 'informal', 'colloquial' or 'slang', and specialist subject domains that words may be restricted to.

Examples of formality marking from COD9 include the following:

  formal: postprandial, potation, prevenient, psittacism, repast
  colloq(uial): parky, prezzie, pronto, pudgy, pushy
  slang: party-pooper, perisher, pie-eyed, pillock, poppycock
  coarse slang: fart, piss-up, plonker, shitbag, tosser.

Dictionaries do not always agree how to categorize such words, and they may use alternative category labels (e.g. 'informal' for 'colloquial', 'vulgar' for 'coarse slang'). Related to these categories are labels such as 'derog(atory)' (or 'pejorative'), 'joc(ular)', 'iron(ical)' and 'euphem(istic)'. Marked as 'derog' in COD9 are: papist, paramour, pelf, pleb, puritanical; as 'joc': pate, peregrinate, pinguid, proboscis, purloin; as 'iron': big deal, dearie, fat (chance), plaster saint, pundit; and as 'euphem': challenged, cloakroom, departed, derrière, ethnic cleansing.

Among the many examples of subject domain marking in COD9 are the following:

  Computing: peripheral, port, reboot, screen saver, search engine
  Ecol(ogy): ecad, quadrat, sere, sustainable, xeric
  Med(icine): parenteral, paresia, parotitis, percuss, percutaneous
  Psychol(ogy): paramnesia, parasuicide, preconscious, schizothymia, superego.

As noted, dictionaries do well at marking these kinds of lexical fact.

8.2.6 Spelling

After meaning, the most frequent reason for consulting a dictionary is to check the spelling of words (Jackson 1988: 194). As a printed, alphabetically ordered reference work, a dictionary is inevitably based on spelling; so that information about spelling is a given. However, there are two particular and less obvious kinds of spelling information that need to be given, and dictionaries usually provide these. First, as we saw under 8.2.2, adding a suffix to a root may cause a spelling change in the root, not only with irregular inflections (buy – bought, bad – worse), but also with regular ones. For example, final 'y' changes to 'i' with the addition of a plural or past tense suffix (lorry – lorries, reply – replied), some consonants double when a suffix is added (sin – sinning, stop – stopped), a final 'e' may elide before a suffix (give – giving) or the elision may be optional (judge – judgment/judgement).

Second, quite a number of words in English have alternative spellings. In some cases, these reflect continuing differences between British and American English (centre – center, colour – color). In other cases, American spellings are becoming accepted alternatives in British English: the '-ize' for '-ise' ending (personalise/ize); the 'e' instead of 'ae' in words like *archaeology, encyclopaedia, mediaeval*. In yet other cases, alternatives exist in British English, some of which are systematic, e.g. the '-er'/'-or' alternation in *adviser/or* or the '-ie'/'-y' alternation in words like *auntie/y*; while others are idiosyncratic, e.g. *baloney/boloney, botch/bodge, camomile/chamomile*. All these are faithfully recorded in dictionaries.

8.2.7 Etymology

One of the motivations that led to the development of dictionaries as representative collections of vocabulary in the seventeenth century, including the common words, was the recording of etymologies. Arguably, the etymology of words is irrelevant to the functioning of the vocabulary system in current English. The history and origins of words is not part of our linguistic knowledge that enables us to communicate successfully with our English-speaking fellow-citizens. A grammar book describing current English does not give a history of English syntax at the same time. In the same way, etymology is misplaced in dictionaries, if they purport to be descriptions of current vocabulary. Nevertheless, Hudson (1988) lists etymology among his 'lexical facts', and all general-purpose dictionaries include it, though, interestingly, learner's dictionaries do not.

Dictonaries vary in the amount of detail that they provide for etymologies. All give the immediate origin of each word, whether from English's Anglo-Saxon (Old English) base, or borrowed from another language at a specified period in the history of the language. Some trace the origin of the word further back to its ultimate origin, as far as etymological study can determine it, and sometimes cognate words in related languages are also given. A couple of examples will suffice to show the kind of information given. Here is the etymology for *camomile* as given in COD9:

> [Middle English via Old French *camomille* and Late Latin *camomilla* or *chamomilla* from Greek *khamaimelon* 'earth-apple' (from the apple-smell of its flowers)]

It was borrowed into Middle English from Old French, and then its origin is traced via Late Latin back to Greek. Here now is the etymology for *fill* from the CED:

> [Old English *fyllan*; related to Old Frisian *fella*, Old Norse *fylla*, Gothic *fulljan*, Old High German *fullen*.]

Its origin is traced to Anglo-Saxon, and its cognates are given in other older Germanic languages. It is not clear what level of detail is appropriate to represent this lexical fact for a description of the current language.

8.2.8 Usage

Restrictions on the usage of words, such as level of formality or subject domain, are covered by Hudson (1988) under 'Context'. His 'usage' category is reserved for a ragbag of information, little of which is conventionally entered in dictionaries. The first concerns the frequency of use of a word. Until recent studies using computer corpora (see Chapter 7), reliable information on frequency of use was difficult to ascertain. Such information is now included in two of the learner's dictionaries (*Longman Dictionary of Contemporary English* (1995), *Collins COBUILD English Dictionary* (1995)), but no native-speaker dictionary has yet entered it.

The second piece of information included in this category by Hudson is the age at which a child usually acquires the word. While there is much interest in vocabulary acquisition and psychological aspects of vocabulary storage and access (e.g. Aitchison 1994), this is not informaton that dictionaries pay any attention to. The third piece of information concerns particular occasions of use, which, presumably, have become culturally significant. This information is sometimes reflected in the citations that may be included as illustrative quotations and the source acknowledged. One of the learner's dictionaries (*Cambridge International Dictionary of English* (1995)) consciously includes memorable sayings containing particular words, e.g. under *potent* ' "Extraordinary how potent cheap music is" (from Noel Coward's play *Private Lives*, 1930)'.

The fourth piece of information under this category involves clichés containing the word, which are rarely noted in dictionaries. And the final piece of information relates to taboos on words. Some dictionaries no longer use the 'taboo' label (e.g. COD9, which uses the 'coarse slang' label instead), perhaps in recognition that no subject or mode of speech is any longer proscribed, but may merely be contextually inappropriate. Dictionaries that continue to mark words as 'taboo' (e.g. *Collins Electronic Dictionary*

1992) do so for those considered blasphemous, or those that refer collo-quially to body parts and functions associated with defecation and sexual intercourse. This particular area of 'usage' is related to contextual restrictions on formality and status, mentioned in 8.2.5. Apart from this area, dictionaries pay little attention to 'usage' in Hudson's terms.

EXERCISE 8/4

(a) Look up the words given in 8.2.5 under 'formal' in a dictionary other than the COD. Does the dictionary use the same or alternative labels for these words? In particular, is the 'taboo' label used?

(b) Discuss with your fellow students whether you think that etymological information should be included in a dictionary aiming to describe the contemporary language. How might its inclusion be justified? After all, Hudson includes it in his list of 'lexical facts' and we have included a chapter (Chapter 2) in this book on the origins of English vocabulary.

8.3 How do dictionaries decide?

It is not exactly dictionaries that do the deciding: it is the lexicographers who compile them. We have noted already that, as lexical descriptions, dictionaries make a selection from the vocabulary of English; they decide how to arrange that selection; they decide what information to include about it, and they decide how to present or 'word' that information. The question we ask in this section is: are there any agreed or understood principles on which those decisions are taken, or are they at the whim of the individual lexicographer?

8.3.1 Selection of vocabulary

While they are selective, dictionaries are also 'comprehensive', in the sense that they aim to include words from across the range of different types of vocabulary. The common core will be included, if only for the sake of spelling and etymology. This will most likely be taken over from one edition of a dictionary to the next, with due attention being paid to the balance of distribution of entries among the letters of the alphabet (Landau 1989: 241). Some specialist vocabulary, for example from science, technology and medicine, as well as from the arts and social sciences, will be of longstanding and incorporated as a matter of course. For smaller size dictionaries (concise, pocket), a selection from this vocabulary will be made, on the basis of its currency and usefulness. Words from newer specialist areas, e.g.

computing, environment and popular culture, will be identified by an extensive reading programme of books, newspapers and magazines, both by dictionary editorial staff and members of the public (see Ayto 1990, Knowles and Elliott, eds, 1997), and also by searching computer corpora (see Chapter 7). The lexicographers will need to make a judgment about the balance of representation from the vocabulary of the various areas, as well as about how well-established some of the newer words might be.

8.3.2 Homographs

Decisions about homographs determine whether a dictionary may contain more than one entry for the same spelling, and how many. A dictionary could decide to base its arrangement on a single entry for each different orthographic word, i.e. one entry per spelling (e.g. *Collins COBUILD English Dictionary* 1987, 1995). This is unusual. More usual is the decision to have an entry for each spelling that can be shown to have a unique etymology; so that if a spelling can be traced back to more than one origin, there will be as many entries as there are origins.

On this basis, for example, *ear* has two entries in most dictionaries: one for the 'organ of hearing', and one for the 'head of a cereal plant'. The first of these derives from Old English *eare*, the second from Old English *ear*. Similarly, *sound* has four homographs (in COD9): the first, relating to 'noise', is traced back to 'Middle English via Anglo-French *soun*, Old French *son*'; the second, meaning 'healthy', has its origin in 'Middle English *sund*, *isund* from Old English *gesund*'; the third, relating to 'measuring depth', derives from 'Middle English from Old French *sonder*, ultimately from Latin *sub-* + *unda* "wave"', and the fourth, referring to a 'passage of water connecting two seas', has its origin in 'Old English *sund*', cognate with 'Old Norse *sund* "swimming, strait"'.

In some cases, homographs are distinguished even where the ultimate origin is the same, if the route into English has been different. On this basis, *mite* has two entries (in COD9): the 'insect' meaning derives from 'Old English *mite*, from Germanic'; the 'small coin' or 'small child' meaning has the same Germanic origin but came into 'Middle English via Middle Low German, Middle Dutch *mite*'. In other cases, homographs are distinguished even where there is an assumed relation between the origins of the two words. For example, *graze* has two entries (in COD9): the first relates to the grazing of grass by animals, and its origin is traced to 'Old English *grasian* from *græs* grass'; the second relates to the scraping of the skin, and its origin is presumed to be 'perhaps a specific use of *graze 1*, as if "take off the grass close to the ground" (of a shot etc.)'. It then becomes unclear why these are not treated as two senses of one lexeme, the second as an extension of the first.

Etymology is not an intuitive basis for homograph distinction for the contemporary user; but it is a more certain basis for the lexicographer than its more slippery alternative, perceived difference in meaning. One other basis for homograph distinction is word class membership, where a different word class means a separate entry. The LDEL (1991) operates this criterion, making, for example, separate entries for *skin* (verb) and *skin* (noun).

8.3.3 Polysemy

After the actual writing of definitions, the lexicographers surveyed by Kilgarriff (1998) had most difficulty with splitting the meaning of words into senses. We have noted already (8.2.4) that some dictionaries may have a tendency to overdifferentiate senses. Examine the entries for a multiply polysemous word in any two dictionaries, and you will find a different number and arrangement of senses. Consider the following entries for the noun *sound* from the *Collins Electronic Dictionary* (1992) and COD9:

Collins Electronic Dictionary 1992

1. a. a periodic disturbance in the pressure or density of a fluid or in the elastic strain of a solid, produced by a vibrating object. It has a velocity in air at sea level at 0°C of 332 metres per second (743 miles per hour) and travels as longitudinal waves. b. (*as modifier*): a sound wave.
2. (*modifier*) of or relating to radio as distinguished from television: sound broadcasting; sound radio.
3. the sensation produced by such a periodic disturbance in the organs of hearing.
4. anything that can be heard.
5. a particular instance, quality, or type of sound: the sound of running water.
6. volume or quality of sound: a radio with poor sound.
7. the area or distance over which something can be heard: to be born within the sound of Big Ben.
8. the impression or implication of something: I don't like the sound of that.
9. *Phonetics.* the auditory effect produced by a specific articulation or set of related articulations.
10. (often pl) *Slang.* music, esp. rock, jazz, or pop.
11. *Rare.* report, news, or information, as about a person, event, etc.

COD9

1. a sensation caused in the ear by the vibration of the surrounding air or other medium.
2. a. vibrations causing this sensation. b. similar vibrations whether audible or not.
3. what is or may be heard.
4. an idea or impression conveyed by words (don't like the sound of that).
5. mere words (sound and fury).
6. (in full *musical sound*) sound produced by continuous and regular vibrations (cf. noise n. 3).
7. any of a series of articulate utterances (vowel and consonant sounds).
8. music, speech, etc., accompanying a film or other visual presentation.
9. (*often attrib.*) broadcasting by radio as distinct from television.

The two dictionaries not only recognize a different number of senses, but there is very little direct correspondence between the senses identified. The following clear correspondences can be observed:

CED Sense	2	=	COD Sense	9
	3	=		1
	4	=		3
	8	=		4

Possibly, a correspondence exists between CED Sense 9 and COD Sense 7, but it is not so clear as those above. Beyond that, it may be possible to identify some overlap between some of the senses, e.g. CED 10 and COD 6, but a number of senses are unique to one or other of the dictionaries.

How does such a situation arise? Lexicographers have to make judgments on the evidence that they, and the dictionary's staff, have collected. Traditionally, besides the treatment in previous editions of the same or other dictionaries, the evidence has been a collection of citations, often of single sentences, illustrating the meaning and context of the word. More recently, such evidence is supplemented or even replaced by concordance lines produced from a search of computer corpora. A lexicographer has to sift through this evidence, decide which citations belong together as examples of the same sense, and expect, or hope, that a division into senses emerges from the sorting process. Previous treatments may provide a check on the process and the lexicographer's judgment. What the user is then presented with in the dictionary they buy is the output of the evidence collected, filtered by the lexicographer's judgment. It is not a mechanistic process; it

is dependent on the quality of the evidence and the skill of the lexicographer.

8.3.4 Order of senses

Having decided how many senses to recognize in the case of a polysemous
lexeme, the lexicographer must then decide the order in which to present
them. Dictionaries have general principles that lexicographers follow. In
simplest terms, dictionaries order senses either on the basis of supposed
frequency or commonness of use, or historically from the earliest to the
latest sense.

Since large computer corpora have only very recently been able to yield
accurate information on the frequency of use of different senses of a word,
ordering by frequency of use has in the past been based on the intuitions of
lexicographers. Even with computer corpora, lexicographers need to look
at the number and range of texts that are included in the corpus and their
representativeness, before they rely too readily on any frequency information derived from it. For example, Sinclair (1985) found no examples of the
grammatical sense of *decline* in his 7.3-million-word corpus, and so concluded that this sense should not even be included in a dictionary of current
English.

Dictionaries usually have a more complex set of principles on which to
decide the ordering of senses. They attempt to make an entry have a
measure of coherence and progression in its treatment of the meaning of a
lexeme. The progression is often from central meanings to peripheral ones,
or from concrete meanings to more abstract and figurative ones. Very often
such a progression will mirror either or both of historical development and
frequency of use. The LDEL (1991: xvi), for example, states its policy as
follows:

> Meanings are ordered according to a system which aims both to show the main
> historical development of the word and to give a coherent overview of the relationship
> between its meanings. Meanings that are current throughout the English-speaking
> world are shown first; they appear in the order in which they are first recorded in
> English, except that closely related senses may be grouped together regardless of strict
> historical order. They are followed by senses whose usage is restricted, such as those
> current only in informal use or in American English. Senses which have become
> archaic or obsolete are shown last.

The *CED* (1986: xii) has a rather different policy:

> As a general rule, where a headword has more than one sense, the first sense given is
> the one most common in current usage. Where the editors consider that a current
> sense is the 'core meaning', in that it illuminates the meaning of other senses, the core
> meaning may be placed first. Subsequent senses are arranged so as to give a coherent
> account of the meaning of the headword ... Within a part-of-speech block, closely
> related senses are grouped together; technical senses generally follow general senses;
> archaic and obsolete senses follow technical senses; idioms and fixed phrases are
> generally placed last.

8.3.5 Derivatives, compounds and multiword lexemes

In this section, we will consider lexemes that do not automatically qualify for headword status, and which dictionaries treat differently. Besides derivatives and compounds, we are concerned with phrasal verbs, idioms and other kinds of fixed expression (see Chapter 3 of this book, Gramley and Pätzold 1992: 53ff).

As we have already noted (8.2.2), the treatment of derivatives is not uniform in dictionaries. Where a derivative differs significantly in spelling from its root, it will usually have a separate entry: this applies to all prefixed derivatives (*anti-racist, bipolar, rediscover, self-delusion*); it also applies to derivatives where the suffix causes a change in the spelling of the root (*breadth, height, strength, vanity*). If a suffixed derivative is considered to need separate definition, either because its meaning has diverged from that of its root, or because it has acquired additional or specific meanings, then it is usually given headword status in the dictionary (*fabricate, glamorize, milky, parliamentary*). If, on the other hand, the derivative is considered not to need separate definition, because its meaning can be readily deduced from the root, then it is usually included within the entry for the root word as a run-on (*glamorous, happiness, kidnapper, optimistic*).

Compounds may be spelt in three different ways: solid (*sandbank*), hyphenated (*sand-bath*), open (*sand dune*) – all examples from COD9. In COD9 all compounds have headword status, but that is not the case in all dictionaries. The eighth edition of the same dictionary (COD8, 1990) accorded headword status only to solid compounds; the other two types were included as run-ons under the first element (*sand*).

Phrasal verbs are composed of a verb word and an adverb particle (or an adverb and a preposition), e.g. *point out, run down, take off, wrap up, give up on, put up with*. Such verbs are usually included within the entry for the verb word, along with any other expressions or multiword lexemes based on the verb. Because the verb words concerned are themselves usually very common and highly polysemous, and so have long entries, it is often difficult for a user to locate items such as the phrasal verbs. Some dictionaries, e.g. CED (1992), do give headword status to phrasal verbs, recognizing that they usually have separate meanings, sometimes unrelated to that of their verb word.

Idioms, on the other hand, never have headword status, not least perhaps because of their length. But they are not always easy to locate in a dictionary: dictionaries have different policies about where to place them. COD8 expresses its policy as (p. xxxii):

> They are normally defined under the earliest important word in the phrase, except when a later word is more clearly the key word or is the common word in a phrase with variants (in which case a cross-reference often appears at the entry for the earliest word).

The LDEL (1991: xiv) has a far more complex policy:

An idiom is entered at the first noun it contains . . . If it contains no noun, it is entered at the first adjective . . . If it contains no adjective, it is entered under the first adverb; if no adverb, under the first verb; if no verb, under the first word. In any case, cross-references to the entry where the idiom appears are given at the entries for other major words in it.

Idioms may indeed not be easy to find, nor may it necessarily be evident that a particular lexeme enters one or more idiomatic phrases. For a comprehensive treatment of idioms, users must turn to the specialist dictionaries devoted exclusively to idioms and to the explanation of their meaning and origin (e.g. Clark 1988, Long, ed., 1979).

EXERCISE 8/5

(a) Would you expect the following words to be entered more than once in a dictionary (as homographs), or to be treated in a single entry (as a case of polysemy)? First make a guess, then consult a dictionary.

coach (bus, give training); cobble (stone for paving, mend shoes); fence (round a field, sport using a sword); mount (ascend, mountain); rook (bird, chess piece); stable (firmly fixed, place for horses); table (piece of furniture, of figures); whim (fancy, machine used in mining).

(b) Find the following idioms in your dictionary. Which word are they under? Are they cross-referenced from the entries for any of the other words in the idiom?

fly in the ointment; fly off the handle; turn in one's grave; turn over a new leaf; spill the beans; full of beans.

8.4 Meaning

In this section, we want to expand on the discussion in 8.2.4 by considering how dictionaries describe the meaning of words. The most obvious way is by means of the definition; but, as we noted earlier, meaning encompasses the sense relations that a lexeme or sense of a lexeme enters, as well as its typical collocations, and perhaps even the usage restrictions that apply to it.

8.4.1 Definition

A definition usually consists of a single phrase, which is substitutable for the word being defined in a given context. This means that if the word being defined is a noun, the definition will be a noun phrase, with a noun as the central, 'head', element. For example, *crime* is defined in COD9 as 'a serious offence punishable by law', where the head noun is *offence*. Similarly, where the word to be defined is a verb, a verb will head the definition phrase; *crush* is defined in COD9 as 'compress with force or violence, so as to break, bruise, etc.', where the head verb is *compress*.

The *Collins COBUILD Learner's Dictionary* introduced an alternative style of definition, in the form of whole sentences; so for *crime*, 'A crime is an illegal action for which a person can be punished by law'; and for *crush*, 'If you crush something, you press it or squeeze it very hard so that you break it or destroy its shape.' The aim was to produce readable definitions that would sound like the teacher explaining the meaning of the word in the class-room. Nevertheless a number of formulae are favoured, such as the two illustrated in these examples: 'A something is . . .' for nouns, 'If you . . .' for verbs.

The definitions considered so far conform to the 'analytical' type dis-cussed in 8.2.4. Definitions in the smaller dictionaries or for words with a more abstract meaning often use synonyms or brief synonym phrases as a means of definition. In the case of smaller dictionaries, this is more economical on space than analytical definitions; for abstract words analyt-ical definitions are often difficult or impossible to formulate. In COD9 *cursory* is defined as 'hasty, hurried', *daunt* as 'discourage, intimidate', *decompose* as 'decay, rot; disintegrate, break up', *distress* as 'severe pain, sorrow, anguish, etc.'.

Some definitions, especially of natural phenomena, e.g. flora and fauna, go beyond a simple explanation and tend towards the 'encyclopedic'. Consider the following definition of *elephant* in CED (1992): 'either of the two proboscidean mammals of the family *Elephantidae*. The African ele-phant (*Loxodonta africana*) is the larger species, with large flapping ears and a less humped back than the Indian elephant (*Elephas maximus*), of S and SE Asia.' Not only does the definition contain the Latin biological names, but the entry contains an explanatory sentence in addition to the definition phrase, such as might be found in an encyclopedia.

Definitions are an attempt to characterize the 'meaning' of a lexeme or sense of a lexeme and to distinguish the meaning of the lexeme concerned from the meanings of other lexemes in the same semantic field, for example the 'elephant' from other large mammals. There is a sense in which a definition characterizes the 'potential' meaning of a lexeme; the meaning only becomes precise as it is actualized in a context. Since the division of the meaning of a lexeme into senses is based on the variation of meaning perceived in different contexts, a tension exists in lexicography between the recognition of separate senses and the potentiality of meaning found in definitions. This may well account in large part for the divergence between similar-sized dictionaries in the number of senses recorded and in con-sequent differences of definition.

8.4.2 Meaning relations

We have noted (Chapter 5) that the semantic relations which a lexeme enters into with other lexemes in the vocabulary make a contribution towards the characterization of the lexeme's meaning. Meaning relations – synonymy, antonymy, hyponymy, meronymy – are rarely treated explicitly in dictionaries. There are two notable exceptions: in the first edition (1987) of the *Collins COBUILD English Dictionary*, and to a lesser extent in the second edition (1995), synonyms, antonyms and hypernyms are regularly noted in the dictionary's 'extra column'. The second exception is the LDEL (1991), which contains around 400 'synonym essays' within boxes throughout the dictionary, and which discuss the often subtle distinctions between words with closely related meanings, e.g. lethargy, sluggishness, lassitude, languor, listlessness, laziness, sloth, indolence.

Meaning relations are more indirectly indicated in dictionaries through the form of definitions. We have noted (8.4.1) that some definitions take the form of synonyms, thus signalling this meaning relation. Much less frequently, antonymy is used as a means of definition, e.g. *absent*, 'not present', *aloud*, 'not silently', *awake*, 'not asleep'.

The analytical definition is formed using the meaning relation of hyponymy: the 'genus' term is the hypernym, the superordinate term, of which the lexeme being defined is a hyponym, e.g. *mammal* and *elephant* in the definition cited in 8.4.1. However, the analytical definition does not always use a natural or obvious hypernym as the genus term, and there is no description of co-hyponyms. Consider the following definition of *musk* in COD9: 'a strong-smelling reddish-brown substance produced by a gland in the male musk deer and used as an ingredient in perfumes', where the hypernym is the very general word *substance*. The CED (1992) definition of *musk* reads: 'a strong-smelling glandular secretion of the male musk deer, used in perfumery', where the hypernym is now the more specific *secretion*.

The meaning relation of meronymy also finds expression in some analytical type definitions, e.g. *abdomen*, 'the part of the body containing the stomach, bowels, reproductive organs, etc.', *carriageway*, 'the part of a road intended for vehicles'. Where the expression 'the part of' occurs in a definition, this is a signal of the meronymy relation. Again, the co-meronyms of the defined lexeme are not given.

Where meaning relations are used for the purposes of definition, the intention is not to give information about the meaning relations that the defined lexemes enter into, but rather merely to exploit the meaning relations for the purposes of defining. In that case, the dictionary is not describing meanings relations, and so we can conclude that this is an area where dictionaries give scant information.

8.4.3 Collocation

Partly constitutive of the meaning of a word is the regular lexical company that it keeps: its collocates (5.6). Reliable information on collocation is only now becoming available with the computational analysis of large text corpora (Chapter 7). It is not surprising that collocation information is not yet routinely recorded in dictionaries, though it is an area to which learner's dictionaries in particular are paying increasing attention (LDOCE (1995), *Cambridge International Dictionary of English* (1995)). A specialist dictionary of collocations for learners has also been published: Benson, Benson and Ilson (1986a, 1997).

In general-purpose dictionaries, any descriptions of collocation are quite limited. So-called 'grammatical' collocation (Benson *et al.* 1986a), e.g. the preposition that usually follows a verb, noun or adjective (*grieve for, annoyance at, afraid of*), is generally given, but collocation proper, i.e. 'lexical' collocation, is less usually indicated. However, there are cases in which, for example, the restriction on the subjects or objects that a verb collocates with, or the typical nouns that an adjective associates with, are indicated.

One of the senses of *abort* in COD9 is defined as: 'abandon or terminate (a space flight or other technical project) before its completion, usu. because of a fault'. Here the bracketed expression proposes a typical object of *abort* in this sense. A sense of the verb *rise* is defined as '(of buildings etc.) undergo construction from the foundations (*office blocks were rising all around*); (of a tree etc.) grow to a (usu. specified) height'. The bracketed items indicate typical subjects of this sense of the verb. Three of the eight senses of the adjective *organic* in COD9 have collocation information (in the brackets): 'Med. (of a disease) affecting the structure of an organ'; '(of a plant or animal) having organs or an organized physical structure'; 'Chem. (of a compound etc.) containing carbon'.

The 'collocates' shown in these examples are quite general in nature, and in that sense not collocations in the strict sense, certainly not in the sense of the *Collins COBUILD English Collocations on CD-ROM* (1995), which is based on the 'Bank of English' corpus. This CD-ROM informs us, for example, that the ten most frequent collocates of *organic* in the corpus are, in order: matter, material, farming, food, wine, wines, compound, molecules, gardening, chemistry. Such specific collocational information has not yet found its way into general-purpose dictionaries.

EXERCISE 8/6

Examine the entries in your dictionary for the following words. What style of definition (analytical, synonym) is used? If the definition is analytical, what is the 'genus' term (hypernym)?

  contusion, galloglass, lading, muesli, pendent, stencil

8.5 Dictionaries and vocabulary

General-purpose dictionaries contain a selection of words from the current vocabulary of English, and they are arranged more or less in alphabetical order. We have already noted (8.1.4) that alphabetical ordering not only obscures some morphological (e.g. derivational) relations between words, but, more significantly, completely ignores the semantic relationships and connections in the vocabulary, such as are described by lexical field theory (5.5.3). No general-purpose dictionary has been published using a lexical field, or 'thematic' approach. The nearest example is the *Longman Lexicon of Contemporary English* (McArthur 1981), based on the LDOCE (1978) and aimed at learners (see 5.5.3).

The perspective that dictionaries give of the vocabulary tends to be atomistic, treating each word as if it exists and has developed as an item isolated from all other words. In reality, the vocabulary is a system, in which the value of one element is determined by the values of related elements in the system. Some of those interconnections (synonymies, hyponymy relations, registers, collocations) are indicated in current dictionaries, but either accidentally and indirectly or sporadically and unsystematically. The alphabetical ordering inevitably inhibits systematic treatment of such connections.

The dictionary-buying public has an expectation of what a dictionary should look like and what it should contain. Alphabetical ordering is part of that expectation. Dictionary publishers are probably only confident enough to make small, incremental changes, e.g. the introduction of 'encyclopedic' information (on people and places) in CED (1979), since imitated by other dictionary publishers. A thematic dictionary would be too great a departure from the current expectations and thus too great a publishing risk. Thematic dictionaries are also much less economical on space, since for many words, which belong to more than one lexical field, the same information has to be repeated. McArthur (1981) is about two-thirds the size of the LDOCE (1978), but it treats less than one-third of the number of lexemes (around 15,000 to the LDOCE's 55,000).

An answer to the problems of both expectation and space may well be found in the new generation of electronic dictionaries (COD9, CED 1992). Space is no longer the consideration that it is for a printed dictionary: the whole of the twenty printed volumes of the second edition of the *Oxford English Dictionary* are contained on a single CD-ROM. The new electronic medium should also give publishers confidence to present dictionary information in new ways: the ordering of information in this medium does not have the same significance as in the print medium. If words are coded for lexical field information, as they are already in part by means of register or domain labels, then it should be possible to enable users to view the vocabulary for a particular field. Up to now, however, publishers have simply transferred their print dictionaries to the electronic medium in the same alphabetical format and with the same information, though allowing more extensive searching of both the headword list and the whole text of the dictionary (see further Chapter 7). The potential of the electronic medium for dictionaries has not yet been fully exploited (Byrd 1995).

8.6 Lexicology and lexicography

Lexicology is the branch of linguistics that investigates, describes and theorizes about vocabulary (Chapter 1). Lexicography is concerned with the making of dictionaries: it is both what dictionary makers – lexicographers – do, and also the theorizing about dictionaries and their compilation. In a sense, lexicography is applied lexicology: the lexicographer takes the insights of lexicology and applies them in making their particular description of the vocabulary of a language. Increasingly, the interaction between the linguistic discipline of lexicology – and semantics, and grammar – and the practice of lexicography is bearing fruit in the structure and content of dictionaries. In particular, this has been seen in learner's dictionaries, but not only there: most dictionary publishers seek the advice of one or more eminent scholars of language, and many of their staff will have been trained in linguistics.

Nevertheless, the practice of lexicography has a long and independent tradition, which predates by many centuries the rise of the modern linguistic disciplines. It is a tradition that has developed and refined the general purpose dictionary into the product that we use today. It is a tradition on which the linguistic disciplines, including lexicology, have only just begun – in the last forty years – to make an impact. It should be clear from this book that lexicology will be able to offer much to lexicography in the future, and especially as dictionary publishers begin to exploit the potential of the electronic medium for their products.

EXERCISE 8/7

Using the knowledge that you have gained from studying lexicology and bearing in mind the issues raised in this chapter, write a brief critique of the dictionary that you regularly use. How adequate is it as a description of the words, meaning and vocabulary of English?

8.7 Summary

This chapter has looked carefully at the information that dictionaries contain, as the most complete lexical descriptions that we have. We used Hudson's (1988) categories to examine the various kinds of information that are recorded in dictionaries, and we identified a number of areas where dictionaries have yet to meet the lexicologist's requirements. Some comments are made on the merits of thematic lexicography by comparison with the traditional alphabetical ordering of headwords, and the chapter concludes by drawing attention to the relationship between lexicology and lexicography.

Key to Exercises

Chapter 1

1/1

Definitions 1, 3 and 4 agree that lexicology is about the meaning and use/behaviour of words. 1 and 4 also agree that it is about the nature/form of words/word elements. 1 and 2 mention history of words/vocabulary. But 2 is different from the others in its focus on 'vocabulary' rather than 'words' and in mentioning the 'structure' of vocabulary. 1 also mentions the critical relation of lexicology to lexicography. So, while there is some agreement about the scope of lexicology, there are also considerable differences. This book encompasses most of what is mentioned in all these definitions.

1/2

Collins English Dictionary (CED) (1998) gives the following etymology for *bridegroom*: [C14: changed (through influence of GROOM) from Old English *brydguma*, from *bryd* BRIDE[1] + *guma* man; related to Old Norse *bruthgumi*, Old High German *brutigomo*]. The folk etymology is mentioned in the phrase 'through the influence of GROOM'.

The same dictionary gives the etymology of *adder* as: [Old English *nædre* snake; in Middle English *a naddre* was mistaken for *an addre*; related to Old Norse *nathr*, Gothic *nadrs*]. The folk etymology was to transfer the 'n' from the noun to the indefinite article.

Again from CED (1998), *snake* has the etymology: [Old English *snaca*; related to Old Norse *snakr* snake, Old High German *snahhan* to crawl, Norwegian *snok* snail]. Everything in this etymology after 'related to' is about cognate words in other languages.

1/3

1. There are some odd word selections in this sentence. The syntax is alright. It reads like a notice: you would expect 'kindly' rather than 'aggressively', and 'entering' rather than 'leaving'.
2. This is syntactically deviant. A reordering of the words will form a grammatical and meaningful sentence: 'You can put the bread you have bought on the table.'
3. This sentence comes from the 'Jabberwocky' song in Lewis Carroll's

Alice's Adventures in Wonderland: the syntax is fine, you could assign word classes to each of the words; it is the words themselves that are 'nonsense'.

4. These are the first two lines of an e.e.cummings poem: the syntax is more or less alright; but a number of words have been reclassified, e.g. 'anyone' is used as a proper name, 'how' as an adjective, 'up' as an intensifer like 'ever'.

5. This looks like the kind of 'nonsense' in No. 3, but it in fact contains two items of rhyming slang: apples and pears = stairs, uncle ned = bed.

1/4

1. These words all belong to a sub-field of verbs concerned with human movement. Specifically, these verbs denote various kinds of 'walking aimlessly'.

2. These words represent the forms of the verb 'speak'.

3. The words here do not have a common meaning, as do those in 1., or relate to a common form, as do those in 2. But they could be regarded as belonging to a lexical field of 'telephone communication'.

4. These words are synonyms, denoting the possession of wealth. They differ in the formality of the context in which they might be used and their connotations; e.g. 'wealthy' and 'rich' are fairly neutral; 'affluent' is formal, even euphemistic; 'well off', 'well-heeled' and 'loaded' are more informal, tending to the colloquial; and 'oofy' is a slang term.

1/5

(a) 1st person pronouns: I, me, mine; we, us, ours.
2nd person pronouns: you, yours.
3rd person pronouns: he, him, his; she, her, hers; it, its; they, them, theirs.
You may also have included the reflexive pronouns: myself, ourselves; yourself, yourselves; himself, herself, itself, themselves.

(b) Adjectives generally attribute descriptions or characteristics to people, objects and ideas. Many adjectives can form a 'comparative' form (bigger, slower) and a 'superlative' (biggest, slowest). Adjectives either precede the noun they are describing (an excellent suggestion, the big red balloon) or they come after a verb like 'be' or 'become' (Your suggestion is excellent, That balloon has grown big).

Chapter 2

2/1

The *New Oxford Dictionary of English* (1998) has the following entry for 'English':

English > **adjective** of or relating to England or its people or language.
> **noun 1** [mass noun] the language of England, now widely used in many varieties throughout the world. **2** [as plural noun **the English**] the people of England.

English is the principal language of Great Britain, the USA, Ireland, Canada, Australia, New Zealand, and many other countries. There are some 400 million native speakers, and it is the medium of communication for many millions more; it is the most widely used second language in the world. It belongs to the West Germanic group of Indo-European languages, though its vocabulary has been much influenced by Norman French and Latin.

– DERIVATIVES **Englishness** noun
– ORIGIN Old English *Englisc* (see **ANGLE, -ISH**). The word originally denoted the early Germanic settlers of Britain (Angles, Saxons, and Jutes), or their language (now called **OLD ENGLISH**).

2/2

Here is a fairly literal translation of the lines (inserted words in brackets):

Thence evil broods all were born:
Ogres and elves and goblins
Likewise (the) giants who against God strove
(for a) long time he them their reward paid.

You may have made some connection between 'ealle' and 'all', 'ond' and 'and', 'ylfe' and 'elf', 'gigantas' and 'giants', 'lange' and 'long' – but not necessarily. 'He' is clearly still 'he', and 'Gode' is 'God'; 'wið' corresponds to 'with'. For the rest, we largely have words that have not survived into modern English.

2/3

Here is a fairly literal translation. There are probably few words that you had to struggle over:

Now awoke Wrath, with two white eyes
And with a snivelling nose, and nipped his lips.
'I am Wrath,' quoth that man, 'would gladly smite
Both with stone and with staff, and steal upon my enemy
To slay him (with) slyest tricks I think (up) ...'

The lines come from the section in *Piers Plowman* on the Seven Deadly Sins.

2/4

Apart from the word 'mased' (mad, compare 'amazed') and the meaning of 'fonde' (stupid), the vocabulary is probably familiar, though the spelling does not always correspond to modern English (hee, putt, noe, etc.), nor the use of capital letters or '&' for 'and'.

2/5

cousin:	developed from a Latin word denoting specifically 'mother's sister's child', but now denoting any child of either parent's siblings.
hose:	an OE word originally referring to a male's garment that covered the whole of the lower part of the body; now restricted to leg coverings; and extended to a flexible pipe for transferring liquids.
knight:	an OE word originally denoting a 'servant', developing into its medieval sense of a 'soldier, from the nobility, in the service of his lord', and thence to the 'rank' meaning; and adopted as the name for a piece in the game of chess.
nice:	from a Latin word meaning 'ignorant', thence to 'foolish/simple', and to 'precise/subtle'; and now a general term of approval.
span:	from an OE word denoting the distance between the tips of the thumb and little finger; extended to cover all kinds of distances (e.g. span of a bridge), and to periods of time (e.g. attention span).
spell:	from an OE word meaning 'speech/story' (e.g. 'gospel'), thence to a magical incantation, and to the correct ordering of letters in a word.
starve:	from an OE word meaning 'die', then specialized to denote 'die from hunger' or 'make to die from hunger'; and metaphorical extensions (e.g. 'starved of love and attention').
train:	from a Latin word meaning 'drag/draw', and so to many things that are dragged or pulled (e.g. of a dress or cloak) and specifically to railway coaches; metaphorically a series (train) of events; the 'teach/educate' meaning also has the sense of 'following' (instructions).

2/6

You should have found that the proportion of OE words in the text (b) is higher than the proportion from the dictionary count (a), because many of the common and grammatical words of English (of OE origin) occur more frequently than subsequently borrowed words.

2/7

Each of you will end up with different lists, so a key here would be superfluous. You might, however, like to compare your list with those made by your fellow students.

2/8

addendum (plural, addenda):	Latin
baguette:	French
cannelloni:	Italian
con brio:	Italian
criterion (plural, criteria):	Greek
id est (i.e.):	Latin
in loco parentis:	Latin
mañana:	Spanish
sang-froid:	French
vis-à-vis:	French
zucchini:	Italian

Chapter 3

3/1

(a) There are 34 orthographic words, i.e. sequences of letters bounded by spaces.
(b) There are 23 grammatical words (or 24 if you count 'at' and 'once' separately). 'A' occurs 6 times, 'is', 3 times, 'and', twice, 'in', twice, and 'world', twice.
(c) There are 19 lexemes: 'is' and 'are' are separate grammatical words but belong to the same lexeme; and the following have both a singular and a plural form: 'container', 'tool', 'weapon'.

3/2

1. The 'bull' is literal, a male bovine animal.
2. 'Bull' means simply 'male' in relation to elephants, whales, etc.
3. The use of 'bull' in the fixed phrase 'bull in a china shop', usually as a simile, compares a person who is being clumsy or lacking sensitivity.
4. A 'bull market' is one where prices rise fast because there is a lot of buying of shares in anticipation of profits.
5. In the game of darts, the centre circle is called the 'bull's eye'.
6. Here 'bull' is a more polite version of 'bullshit', and means 'nonsense' or 'lame excuses'.
7. 'Take the bull by the horns' is an idiom, meaning '(have the courage to) deal with someone or something directly'.

3/3

The connotations are (intended to be) as follows: (1) poetic, (2) slang, (3) baby talk, (4) biblical, (5) colloquial, (6) humorous (reference to oneself), (7) legal, (8) literary.

3/4

The following meanings (senses) are given for *lemon* in *Collins Electronic Dictionary* (1992): (1) the tree, (2) the fruit, (3) the colour, (4) the flavour, (5) the 'useless' person. And the following are given for *review*: (1) look at again, (2) look back on, (3) formally inspect, e.g. troops, (4) look over for correction, (5) re-examine judicially, (6) write a critical assessment (of a book, play, film, etc.).

3/5

   barge: polysemy
   court: polysemy
   dart: polysemy
   fleet: homonymy
   jam: homonymy
   pad: homonymy
   steep: homonymy
   stem: homonymy
   stuff: polysemy
   watch: polysemy

These are the decisions made by the editors of *Collins Electronic Dictionary* (1992), who will have used etymology as their primary criterion (see 8.3).

3/6

There are three major things lacking from this definition, though, it must be said, it is probably unreasonable to expect these to be incorporated in a dictionary definition, and so this is not a criticism as such of the Collins dictionary.

(1) No clear distinction is drawn, though it is hinted at, between orthographic/phonological words, grammatical words, and lexemes.
(2) No mention is made of homonymy and its attendant problems.
(3) No account is taken of multiword lexemes (e.g. phrasal verbs, open compounds, idioms), which would seem to be excluded by the definition. The dictionary does, though, pay full attention to these in its lexicographical treatment.

Chapter 4

4/1

beadiness: bead + -y + -ness (the addition of -ness changes the 'y' to 'i')

coagulative: coagulate + -ive (we could recognize -ate as a morpheme, but we have nothing to which we can relate 'coagul(e)')

deactivators: de- + (active + ate) + -or + -s (the brackets indicate the -ate must be added to 'active' before the de- prefix applies)

forbearingly: for- + bear + -ing + -ly

half-deafened: half + deaf + en + ed (probably 'half' and -en could be applied in any order)

left-handedness: (left + hand + -ed) + ness ('left' and -ed apply together)

noncombatant: non- + combat + -ant

readability: read + able + ity (note spelling and pronunciation changes here as morphemes are added)

temporarily: temporary + -ly (-ary looks like a morpheme, and 'temp' has some association with time, but it is not an identifiable morpheme in English)

weedkiller: weed + (kill +-er)

4/2

bring: brings (3rd singular present), brought (past tense), bringing (present participle), brought (past participle)

cow: cows (plural), cow's (singular possessive), cows' (plural possessive)

forget: forgets (3rd singular present), forgot (past), forgetting (present participle), forgotten (past participle)

guest: guests (plural), guest's (singular possessive), guests' (plural possessive)

have: has (3rd singular present), had (past), having (present participle), had (past participle)

high: higher (comparative), highest (superlative)

stop: stops (3rd singular present), stopped (past), stopping (present participle), stopped (past participle)

tall: taller (comparative), tallest (superlative)

tooth: teeth (plural), tooth's (singular possessive), teeth's (plural possessive)

weary: wearier (comparative), weariest (superlative)

4/3

covariance: co- (meaning 'with'), vary, -ance (changing verb to noun)

enactable: en- (changing noun to verb), act, -able (changing verb to adjective)

ungracious: un- (negative meaning), grace, -ous (changes noun to adjective)

preconnection: pre- (meaning 'before'), connect, -ion (changes verb to noun)

depressive: de- (negative meaning, 'down'), press, -ive (changes verb to adjective)

incriminatory: in- together with -(n)ate (changes noun to verb), crime, -ory (changes verb to adjective)

proconsulship: pro- (means 'instead of'), consul, -ship (changes concrete to abstract noun)

officialdom: office, -al (changes to someone who holds the office), -dom (changes person noun to abstract noun)

declassify: de- (negative meaning), class, -ify (changes noun to verb)

troublesome: trouble, -some (changes noun to adjective)

4/4

Here are a few examples for one element from each list:

heart: heartache, heart attack, heartbeat, heartbreak(ing), heartburn, heart failure, heartland, heart murmur, heart-rending, heart-searching, heartstrings, heart-throb, heart-warming.

push: pushball, push-bike, push button, pushcart, pushchair, push fit, push money, pushover, pushpin, pushrod, push-start.

quick: quick assets, quick-change artist, quick fire, quick-freeze, quick grass, quicklime, quick march, quicksand, quickset, quicksilver, quick-step, quick-tempered, quickthorn, quick time, quick-witted.

front: front bench, front door, front-end, front line, front loader, front man, front matter, front-page, front-runner.

4/5

This exercise is intended to make you appreciate the continuing productivity of English word-formation processes. For further evidence, see Tulloch (1991), Knowles and Elliott (eds) (1997).

Chapter 5

5/1

The synonym essay for these words from LDEL (1991) reads:

Plentiful, plenteous, ample, abundant, and **copious** may all suggest 'more than enough, but not too much'. **Plentiful** is generally used with concrete things, and suggests a comparison with need or demand <*plentiful food and drink*> <*a plentiful supply of matches*>. **Plenteous** is a poetic or formal synonym for **plentiful**. **Ample** suggests something between *enough* and **plentiful**; it often implies a generous supply for a particular need <*ample reward for all her trouble*> <*ample room for one, but not for two*>. **Abundant** is usually preferred to **plentiful** to describe abstracts <*abundant praise*>. With concrete objects, it describes natural rather than man-made things <*abundant vegetation*>. **Copious** suggests abundant flow or volume <*copious tears*> <*a copious vocabulary*>; otherwise it is linked with such expressions as *supply of* or *store of* to suggest great abundance <*a copious crop of tomatoes*>.

5/2

1. Formality; 2. Connotation; 3. Dialect (Scots); 4. Formality; 5. Connotation; 6. Dialect (Australian); 7. Formality; 8. Dialect (Scottish and Northern English); 9. Dialect and Formality; 10. Connotation.

5/3

    emigrate: immigrate (converse)
    equine (no antonym)
    freedom: captivity (complementary)
    frothy (probably no antonym)
    new: old (gradable)
    proud: humble (gradable)
    simple: complex (gradable)
    speak: listen to (converse) or: be silent (complementary)
    straight: crooked (complementary)
    triangular (no antonym)

5/4

Here is a suggested outline structure for a hyponymy tree for *crockery*:

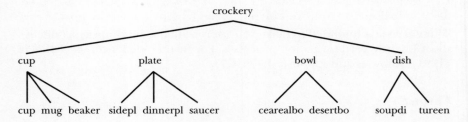

5/5

Here is a suggested outline structure for a meronymy tree for *bicycle*:

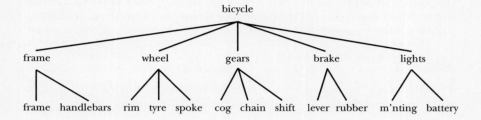

5/6

Here is a matrix using only binary components as follows: WATER to indicate where water is the liquid used in the cooking process, then FAT for where this is used (a minus for both will indicate dry cooking); IMMERSED for whether the cooking liquid covers the food being cooked or not; OVEN, with a plus value for inside the oven and a minus value for on the hob or under the grill, COVERED for whether the vessel used for cooking has a covering or lid.

	cook	bake	boil	fry	braise	stew	grill	poach
WATER	+/−	−	+	−	+	+	−	+
FAT	+/−	−	−	+	+	−	−	−
IMMERSED	+/−	−	+	+/−	−	+	−	+
OVEN	+/−	+	−	−	+	+/−	−	−
COVERED	+/−	−	+/−	−	+	+	−	−

For multivalued components we could propose: LIQUID, with the terms WATER, FAT, NONE; IMMERSED with the terms COMPLETELY, PARTIALLY, NOT; HEAT SOURCE with the terms OVEN, HOB, GRILL; and COVERED with the terms COMPLETELY, PARTIALLY, NOT. This would allow us to dispense with one component and to provide a more precise and differentiated componential description.

	cook	bake	boil	fry	braise	stew	grill	poach
LIQUID	ANY	N	W	F	W/F	W	N	W
IMMERSED	ANY	N	C	C/P	P	C	N	C
HEAT	ANY	O	H	H	O	O/H	G	H
COVERED	ANY	N	C/P	N	C	C	N	P/N

As far as componential analysis is able to, this arguably provides a more illuminating description of these cooking terms. You may like to try adding others to either matrix.

5/7

The field might be organized in a number of ways: by the material used to make the vessel; by the drinks the vessel is used for; and so on.

Material:
Earthenware: cup, mug, beaker
Glass: glass, tumbler, wineglass, goblet, beer glass, sherry glass, balloon, snifter
Metal: tankard, goblet

Drinks:
Hot (e.g. tea, coffee): cup, mug, beaker
Non-alcoholic: glass, tumbler
Beer: beer glass, tankard
Wine: wineglass, goblet
Spirits: balloon, snifter, sherry glass

5/8

The following suggestions are taken from the *Collins COBUILD English Collocations on CD-ROM* (1995):

fundamental: change, problem, issue, question, right, principle
spend: (expressions of) time, money
trauma: childhood, emotional, physical, psychological, major, severe
unite: party, people, world, country, nation, community: behind, against, around
behave: well, badly, differently, better, like ...
boost: confidence, morale, economy, market, sales, profits, prices.

Chapter 6

6/1

Here are some suggestions. You may well have alternatives, depending on where you live.

gym shoe: plimsoll, sandshoe
bread roll: bap, cob
sandwich: butty, sarnie
attic: loft
broom: brush, besom
beautiful: bonny
left-handed: cack-handed, cag-handed

excellent: champion, A1
tired out: fagged out, jiggered
lavatory: loo, netty, privy
nothing: nowt, zilch

6/2

It is not always easy as an 'insider' to know whether a word that you are familiar with is in fact a specialist term of your sport or hobby. The test on an 'outsider' will usually help to settle the matter.

6/3

apples and pears	stairs
bird (lime)	time (in prison)
butcher's (hook)	look
china (plate)	mate
half-inch	pinch (i.e. steal)
jam jar	car
pig's ear	beer
porky (pie)	lie
raspberry (tart)	fart
Rosie Lee	tea
tea leaf	thief
tit for (tat)	hat
trouble and strife	wife
Uncle Ned	bed
whistle (and flute)	suit

6/4

hitherto	until now
incumbent	necessary
inveracity	lie, untruth
laudation	praise
lavation	washing
lubricious	lewd
manifold	different kinds of
mariner	sailor
natation	swimming
yesteryear	last year, the past

6/5

cold feet	loss of nerve/confidence
floozie	girl/woman (possibly disreputable)

footling	trivial
gamp	umbrella
(play) hookey	truant
lughole	ear
miffed	offended
piddle	urin(at)e
slaphead	person with little or no hair
stroppy	bad-tempered, awkward
twerp	a stupid person (one of over 70 such terms in COD9)
unfazed	untroubled
veggie	vegetarian
wag	(play) truant
zilch	nothing
zit	pimple

6/6

Computer jargon has spawned a large number of abbreviations and acronyms, and specifications have developed their own ordered restricted language. You may have understood very little of this specification. You are probably not meant to: it is there as much to impress as to inform. If you are still curious, please consult a computer expert for a detailed interpretation.

Chapter 7

7/1

Aga-saga. An 'Aga' (the word is an acronym of the name of the original Swedish manufacturer) is a type of heavy cooking stove, designed as a form of heating as well as cooking. It is associated with a middle-class, often rural, lifestyle. In this context, 'saga' is another name for 'story'. So, 'Aga-saga' denotes a particular kind of 'popular novel set in a semi-rural location and concerning the domestic and emotional lives of middle-class characters' (Knowles and Elliott, eds, 1997: 9). It is especially associated with the author Joanna Trollope.

Mickle. Probably only now used in the phrase 'many a mickle makes a muckle', in the sense that many small amounts make a big one. However, this is based on a misunderstanding, motivated possibly by the symbolism of the respective vowel sounds: /i/ has connotations of 'smallness', and /ʌ/ connotations of 'bigness'. 'Mickle' is an archaic word, persisting in the Scottish dialect, meaning 'much, great' or 'a large amount'. The saying is supposed to be: 'many a little makes a mickle'.

Presenteeism. This is a word popularised in the 1980s and 1990s when job insecurity motivated many office workers to stay at their desks for far longer hours than they were contracted for, in order to show their loyalty to the job and the firm. It is formed by analogy with 'absenteeism', and is, in effect, its opposite.

Stakeholder. The origin of this word is in gambling: the 'stakeholder' is a neutral non-participant who holds the gamblers' 'stakes' while the event that they are betting on takes place. Its more modern meaning denotes anyone who has a 'stake' in an enterprise, perhaps as an investor, or it may be as a user or customer, or even employee. In the UK, there has been talk of a 'stakeholder economy', and universities have been encouraged to identify their 'stakeholders' – students, their parents, future employers, and so on.

Waif. Traditionally, this word has been used primarily in the phrase 'waifs and strays'. It has been applied especially to a neglected or abandoned child. More recently, the word has been used in the context of fashion to refer to a particular 'look' cultivated by some supermodels: the look involves extreme slenderness, childlikeness, and an appearance of fragility and vulnerability.

7/2

You will probably have found that the information gained from (a) and from (b) is in some respect or other deficient by comparison with the information gained from (c) – unless you or your informants are very knowledgeable.

7/3

You have discovered, no doubt, that for the lexicologist the electronic version means that a dictionary becomes a much richer source of information about words, especially for establishing the kinds of lexical relations explored in Chapter 5 and for realizing that the vocabulary of a language is structured in many ways.

7/4

Highly is used in two main ways in this data. First, it is used as an 'intensifying' adverb, like *very* or *extremely*, before a whole range of adjectives, from those like 'important' and 'satisfactory' with a fairly general meaning, to those like 'incumbent', 'rational' and 'disrespectful' which are not often intensified. Secondly, it is used as a 'degree' adverb with verbs like 'rate', 'think' and 'value', to indicate how much or to what degree someone or something is valued.

Expect in this data is frequently preceded by a personal pronoun (I, you, we, he, one) or an auxiliary verb, mostly a form of 'be' or 'have', or a modal (can, could, might, would). More interestingly, *expect* is frequently followed by an infinitive verb (with 'to'), of which the two most frequent are 'to find' and 'to be'. It is also followed by 'that', presumably introducing a *that*-clause, and by the prepositions 'from' and 'of'. Otherwise, the next item after the verb is a noun (introduced by 'the' or 'a') or a pronoun ('him', 'her', 'me').

Chapter 8

8/1

We are not used to reading whole entries through in dictionaries. We are usually searching for some specific information, and once we have found it we ignore the rest. This exercise should have given you a good impression not only of how your dictionary handles the various types of lexical information, but also of some of the considerations that lexicographers have to weigh up in deciding how to present the information.

8/2

Pronunciation: the full IPA transcription, including primary and secondary stress, is given for the verb headword and for the adjective, which has a different stress pattern from the verb, resulting in a different final vowel. The run-on adverb and noun have their stress pattern indicated in the spelling.

Morphology: the verb and adjective are shown to have the same form, the adverb and noun derivations are given as run-ons. No inflectional information is given.

Syntax: word classes are given for all forms. Senses 1, 3 and 4 of the verb are marked as 'intransitive'; by implication sense 2 may be used both intransitively and transitively. The typical following prepositions are given for senses 1 and 2, and the examples for sense 2 illustrate the absence and presence of the preposition *between*.

8/3

Here are the figures for three dictionaries. The figures in brackets include a count of sub-divisions (e.g. 1a, 1b, etc).

	CED (1998)	LDEL (1991)	COD8 (1990)
Height	10	4 (6)	7 (9)
Nucleus	10 (11)	3 (6)	6 (7)
Subjective (adj)	6	3 (8)	3
(n)	1 (2)	1	1

The CED tends to provide a greater differentiation of senses; the LDEL uses sub-divisions extensively. The same basic meanings are identified, but there is still considerable variation.

8/4

(a) The words are marked as follows in *Collins Electronic Dictionary* (1992):
Postprandial: unmarked; listed without definition at the bottom of the page; Potation: unmarked; Prevenient: unmarked; Psittacism: not entered; Repast: unmarked.
Parky: informal; Prezzie: informal; Pronto: informal; Pudgy: unmarked; Pushy: informal.
Party-pooper: informal; Perisher: not entered; Pie-eyed: slang; Pillock: slang; Poppycock: informal.
Fart: taboo; Piss-up: slang; Plonker: slang; Shitbag: not entered; Tosser: slang.

(b) There are arguments both for including and for excluding etymology from dictionaries. You might ask yourself and others how often you look up etymological information, except for academic purposes, and then you would most likely go to an historical dictionary or a specialist etymological dictionary. Ellegård (1978) argues that etymology should be included in learner's dictionaries, from which it is excluded, on the basis that it may provide useful clues that will help in learning new vocabulary items.

8/5

(a) In COD8 (1990), *cobble, mount, rook, stable* have two entries, and so are treated as homographs, with different etymologies. The other words (*coach, fence, table, whim*) have a single entry, and so are treated as cases of polysemy with a single etymology. You have probably found that etymology does not always coincide with your intuitions about whether the meanings of a word form are related or not.

(b) In COD9 (1996):
fly in the ointment: is under *fly* (n), and not under *ointment*
fly off the handle: is under *fly* (v), and not under *handle*
turn in one's grave: is under *grave*, and cross-referenced from *turn*
turn over a new leaf: is under *turn*, but not under *leaf*
spill the beans: is under *spill*, but not under *bean*
full of beans: is under *bean*, but not under *full*
It is hard to detect what principles, if any, are operating here.

8/6

The answer will depend on your dictionary. The following are based on CED (1998).

contusion: both analytical (hypernym 'injury') and synonym ('bruise')

galloglass: analytical (hypernym 'soldier'), together with some encyclopedic information
lading: synonym ('load', 'cargo', 'freight')
muesli: analytical (rather general hypernym 'mixture')
pendent: synonym ('dangling', 'jutting', etc.)
stencil: analytical (general hypernym 'device')

8/7

You have probably found that overall your dictionary provides a fair lexical
description, but that it has a few gaps (especially in grammatical and usage
information), and perhaps even some superfluous information.

References

Abdullah, K. and Jackson, H. (1999) 'Idioms and the Language Learner', *Languages in Contrast*, Vol. 1(1): 89–109.

Ahulu, S. (1995) 'Hybridized English in Ghana', *English Today*, No. 44: 31–6.

Aitchison, J. (1994) *Words in the Mind*, 2nd edn, Blackwell.

Aston, G. and Burnard, L. (1998) *The BNC Handbook: Exploring the British National Corpus with SARA*, Edinburgh University Press.

Atkins, B.T.S. and Zampolli, A. (eds) (1994) *Computational Approaches to the Lexicon*, Oxford University Press.

Awonusi, V.O. (1990) 'Coming of Age: English in Nigeria', *English Today*, No. 22: 31–5.

Ayto, J. (1990) *The Longman Register of New Words, Volume 2*, Longman.

Bamiro, E.O. (1994) 'Innovation in Nigerian English', *English Today*, No. 39: 13–15.

Barlow, M. (1996) *MonoConc for Windows*, Athelstan.

Bauer, L. (1983) *English Word Formation*, Cambridge University Press.

Bauer, L. and Nation, P. (1993) 'Word Families', *International Journal of Lexicography*, Vol. 6(4): 253–79.

Baumgardner, R.J. (1990) 'The Indigenization of English in Pakistan', *English Today*, No. 21: 59–65.

Bede (731) *Historia Ecclesiastica Gentis Anglorum (Ecclesiastical History of the English People)*.

Benson, M., Benson, E. and Ilson, R. (1986a) *The BBI Combinatory Dictionary of English*, John Benjamins.

Benson, M., Benson, E. and Ilson, R. (1986b) *Lexicographic Description of English*, John Benjamins.

Benson, M., Benson, E. and Ilson, R. (1997) *The BBI Dictionary of English Word Combinations*, John Benjamins.

Berg, D.L. (1993) *A Guide to the Oxford English Dictionary*, Oxford University Press.

Bloomfield, L. (1933/5) *Language*, George Allen and Unwin.

Bones, J. (1986) 'Language and Rastafari', in Sutcliffe, D. and Wong, A. (eds) *The Language of the Black Experience*, Blackwell, pp. 37–51.

Branford, J. and Branford, W. (eds) (1991) *A Dictionary of South African English*, Oxford University Press.

Brook, G.L. (1981) *Words in Everyday Life*, Macmillan.

Burchfield, R. (ed.) (1986) *The New Zealand Pocket Oxford Dictionary*, Oxford University Press.

Byrd, R.J. (1995) 'Dictionary Systems for Office Practice', in Walker, D.E., Zampolli, A. and Calzolari, N. (eds), pp. 207–219.

Calzolari, N. (1995) 'Structure and Access in an Automated Lexicon and Related Issues', in Walker, D.E., Zampolli, A. and Calzolari, N. (eds), pp. 337–56.

Cambridge International Dictionary of English (CIDE) (1995), ed. Paul Proctor, Cambridge University Press.

Cannon, G. (1987) *Historical Change and English Word-Formation: Recent Vocabulary*, Lang.

Cassidy, F.G. (ed.) (1985) *Dictionary of American Regional English*, Harvard University Press.

Chafe, W. (1970) *Meaning and the Structure of Language*, University of Chicago Press.

Chomsky, N. (1957) *Syntactic Structures*, Mouton.

Clark, J.O.E. (1988) *Word Wise: A Dictionary of English Idioms*, Harrap.

Coates, J. (1983) *The Semantics of the Modal Auxiliaries*, Croom Helm.

Collins COBUILD English Collocations on CD-ROM (1995), HarperCollins.

Collins COBUILD English Dictionary (1987/1995), 1st/2nd edns, Harper-Collins.

Collins COBUILD English Grammar (1990), Collins ELT.

Collins COBUILD Learner's Dictionary (1996), HarperCollins.

Collins COBUILD Student's Dictionary (1990), HarperCollins.

Collins COBUILD on CD-ROM (1994), HarperCollins.

Collins Compact English Dictionary (1994), 3rd edn, HarperCollins.

Collins Concise English Dictionary (1995), 3rd edn revised, HarperCollins.

Collins English Dictionary (CED) (1979/1986), 1st/2nd edns, ed. Patrick Hanks, Collins.

Collins English Dictionary (CED) (1994), 3rd edn updated, HarperCollins.

Collins English Dictionary (CED) (1998), 4th edn, HarperCollins.

Collins Electronic Dictionary and Thesaurus (1992), Reference Software International.

Collins Thesaurus (1995), ed. Lorna Gilmour, HarperCollins.

The Concise Oxford Dictionary (First Edition) (1911), eds H.W. and F.G. Fowler, Oxford University Press.

The Concise Oxford Dictionary (Eighth Edition) (COD) (1990), ed. R.E. Allen, Clarendon Press, Oxford.

The Concise Oxford Dictionary (Ninth Edition) on CD-ROM (COD) (1996), Oxford University Press.

The Concise Oxford Thesaurus: A Dictionary of Synonyms (1995), ed. Betty Kirkpatrick, Oxford University Press.

Cook, W. (1969) *Introduction to Tagmemic Analysis*, Holt Reinhart and Winston.

Cruse, D.A. (1986) *Lexical Semantics*, Cambridge University Press.

Crystal, D. (1964) *Linguistics, Language and Religion*, Burns and Oates.

Crystal, D. (1987) *The Cambridge Encyclopedia of Language*, Cambridge University Press.

Crystal, D. (1992) *An Encyclopedic Dictionary of Language and Languages*, Blackwell.

Crystal, D. (1995) *The Cambridge Encyclopedia of the English Language*, Cambridge University Press.

Crystal, D. and Davy, D. (1969) *Investigating English Style*, Longman.

Delacroix, H. (1924) *Le Langage et la Pensée*, Paris.

de Saussure, F. (1959) *A Course in General Linguistics*, ed. C. Bally and A. Sechehaye, Peter Owen.

de Wolf, G.D. (1996) 'Word Choice: Lexical Variation in Two Canadian Surveys', *Journal of English Linguistics*, Vol. 24(2): 131–55.

Donovan, P. (1976) *Religious Language*, Sheldon Press.

Ellegård, A. (1978) 'On Dictionaries for Language Learners', *Moderna Språk*, Vol. LXXII: 225–44.

Fellbaum, C. (1995) 'Co-occurrence and Antonymy', *International Journal of Lexicography*, Vol. 8(4): 281–303.

Fernando, C. and Flavell, R. (1981) *On Idiom*, Exeter University Press.

Goddard, C. and Wierzbicka, A. (eds) (1994) *Semantic and Lexical Universals: Theory and Empirical Findings*, John Benjamins.

Godman, A. and Payne, E.M.F. (1979) *Longman Dictionary of Scientific Usage*, Longman.

Gramley, S. and Pätzold, K.-M. (1992) *A Survey of Modern English*, Routledge.

Gyasi, I.K. (1991) 'Aspects of English in Ghana', *English Today*, No. 26: 26–31.

Halliday, M.A.K. (1985) *An Introduction to Functional Grammar*, Edward Arnold.

Halliday, M.A.K. and Hasan, R. (1976) *Cohesion in English*, Longman.

Hjelmsler, L. (1963) *Prolegomena to a Theory of Language*, University of Wisconsin Press.

Hudson, K. (1978) *The Jargon of the Professions*, Macmillan.

Hudson, R. (1988) 'The Linguistic Foundations for Lexical Research and Dictionary Design', *International Journal of Lexicography*, Vol. 1(4): 287–312 (updated version in: Walker, D.E. *et al.* (eds) (1995), pp. 21–51).

ICAME Journal (1977–) International Computer Archive of Modern and Medieval English, The HIT-centre – Norwegian Computing Centre for the Humanities, Bergen.

Jackson, H. (1985) *Discovering Grammar*, Pergamon Press.

Jackson, H. (1988) *Words and Their Meaning*, Longman.
Jackson, H. (1998) 'How Many Words in YOUR dictionary?', *English Today*, No. 55: 27–8.
Jackson, H. and Stockwell, P. (1996) *An Introduction to the Nature and Functions of Language*, Stanley Thornes.
Jespersen, O. (1954) *Growth and Structure of the English Language*, 9th edn, Blackwell.
Jones, D. (1917) *An English Pronouncing Dictionary*, J.M. Dent and Sons.
Katamba, F. (1994) *English Words*, Routledge.
Kilgarriff, A. (1998) 'The Hard Parts of Lexicography', *International Journal of Lexicography*, Vol. 11(1): 51–4.
Kirkpatrick, B. (1995) *The Original Roget's Thesaurus of English Words and Phrases*, Viking Longman.
Knowles, E. and Elliott, J. (eds) (1997) *The Oxford Dictionary of New Words*, 2nd edn, Oxford University Press.
Krishnamurthy, R. (1987) 'The Process of Compilation', in Sinclair, J.M. (ed.) 1987, pp. 62–86.
Landau, S.I. (1989) *Dictionaries, The Art and Craft of Lexicography*, Cambridge University Press.
Leech, G.N. (1969) *Towards a Semantic Description of English*, Longman.
Leech, G.N. (1981) *Semantics*, 2nd edn, Penguin.
Lehmann, A. and Martin-Berthet, F. (1997) *Introduction à la Lexicologie: Sémantique et morphologie*, Dunod.
Lehrer, A. (1974) *Semantic Fields and Lexical Structure*, North Holland Publishing Co.
Leitner, G. (ed.) (1992) *New Directions in English Language Corpora*, Mouton de Gruyter.
Lipka, L. (1990) *An Outline of English Lexicology: Lexical Structure, Word Semantics and Word Formation*, Max Niemeyer Verlag.
Long, T.H. (ed.) (1979) *Longman Dictionary of English Idioms*, Longman.
Longman Dictionary of Contemporary English (LDOCE) (1978, 1987, 1995), 1st/2nd/3rd edns, Longman.
Longman Dictionary of the English Language (LDEL) (1991), 2nd edn, Viking Longman.
Longman Language Activator (1993), ed. D. Summers, Longman.
Lynch, D.B. (1991) *Concise Dictionary of Computing*, Chartwell-Bratt.
Lyons, J. (1968) *Introduction to Theoretical Linguistics*, Cambridge University Press.
Lyons, J. (1977) *Semantics*, Vols. 1 and 2, Cambridge University Press.
Matthews, P.H. (1974) *Morphology*, Cambridge University Press.
McArthur, T. (1981) *Longman Lexicon of Contemporary English*, Longman.
McArthur, T. (1986) *Worlds of Reference*, Cambridge University Press.
McArthur, T. (1987) 'The English Languages?', *English Today*, No. 11: 9–13.
McArthur, T. (1992) 'Models of English', *English Today*, No. 32: 12–21.

McArthur, T. (ed.) (1992) *The Oxford Companion to the English Language*, Oxford University Press.

McArthur, T. (1998) *Living Words: Language, Lexicography and the Knowledge Revolution*, Exeter University Press.

McLeod, I. (ed.) (1990) *The Scots Thesaurus*, Aberdeen University Press.

Miller, G.A. (ed.) (1990) *WordNet: An On-Line Lexical Database*, Special Issue of *International Journal of Lexicography*, Vol. 3/4.

Murray, K.M.E. (1977) *Caught in the Web of Words: James A.H. Murray and the Oxford English Dictionary*, Yale University Press.

The New Oxford Dictionary of English (1998), ed. Judy Pearsall, Clarendon Press Oxford.

Nida, E.A. (1975) *Componential Analysis of Meaning*, Mouton.

Ooi, V.B.Y. (1998) *Computer Corpus Lexicography*, Edinburgh University Press.

Orton, H.B. and Dieth, E. (eds) (1962–71) *Survey of English Dialects*, Edward Arnold.

Oxford Advanced Learner's Dictionary (OALD) 5th edn (1995), ed. J. Crowther, Oxford University Press.

Oxford-Duden Pictorial English Dictionary (1981), ed. J. Pheby, Oxford University Press.

The Oxford English Dictionary (OED) (1933), ed. James A.H. Murray, Henry Bradley, W.A. Craigie and C.T. Onions, Vols. 1–12, Clarendon Press Oxford.

The Oxford English Dictionary (OED) (1989), 2nd edn, ed. J. Simpson and E.C. Weiner, Vols. 1–20, Clarendon Press Oxford (available on CD-ROM).

Oxford Elementary Learner's Dictionary (1994), Oxford University Press.

Oxford Student's Dictionary (1998), 2nd edn, ed. A.S. Hornby and C.A. Ruse, Oxford University Press.

Palmer, F.R. (1981) *Semantics: A New Outline*, 2nd edn, Cambridge University Press.

Partridge, E. (1984) *A Dictionary of Slang and Unconventional English*, 8th edn, ed. Paul Beale, Routledge.

Pyles, T. and Algeo, J. (1993) *The Origins and Development of the English Language*, 4th edn, Harcourt Brace Jovanovich College Publishers.

Quirk, R., Greenbaum, S., Leech, G. and Svartvik, J. (1985) *A Comprehensive Grammar of the English Language*, Longman.

Reimer, S. (1989) *PC-LitStats: A Statistical Package for Literary Study* Version 1.62, University of Alberta, Edmonton.

Roberts, J., Kay, C. and Grundy, L. (1995) *A Thesaurus of Old English*, King's College London.

Roget, P.M. (1852) *Roget's Thesaurus of English Words and Phrases*, Longman.

Rundell, M. and Stock, P. (1992) 'The Corpus Revolution', *English Today*, No. 30: 9–14, No. 31: 21–32, No. 32: 45–51.

Sinclair, J.M. (1985) 'Lexicographic Evidence', in Ilson, R. (ed.) (1985), pp. 81–94.

Sinclair, J.M. (ed.) (1987) *Looking Up: An Account of the COBUILD Project in Lexical Computing*, Collins ELT.

Strang, B.M.H. (1968) *Modern English Structure*, 2nd edn, Edward Arnold.

Sure, K. (1992) 'Falling Standards in Kenya?', *English Today*, No. 32: 23–6.

Sutcliffe, D. (1982) *British Black English*, Blackwell.

TACT (1990), Version 1.2, ed. J. Bradley and L. Presutti, University of Toronto.

Thomas, J. and Short, M. (eds) (1996) *Using Corpora for Language Research*, Longman.

Todd, L. and Hancock, I. (1990) *International English Usage* (pbk edn), Routledge.

Tripathi, P.D. (1990) 'English in Zambia', *English Today*, No. 23: 34–8.

Tulloch, S. (1991) *The Oxford Dictionary of New Words*, 1st edn, Oxford University Press.

Ullmann, S. (1962) *Semantics: An Introduction to the Science of Meaning*, Blackwell.

Walker, D.E., Zampolli, A. and Calzolari, N. (eds) (1995) *Automating the Lexicon*, Oxford University Press.

Webster's Third New International Dictionary of the English Language (1961), ed. Philip Gove, Merriam.

Wierzbicka, A. (1995) 'Universal Semantic Primitives as a Basis for Lexical Semantics', *Folia Linguistica*, Vol. XXIX(1–2): 149–69.

Wierzbicka, A. (1996) *Semantics: Primes and Universals*, Oxford University Press.

Wilks, Y., Slator, B.M. and Guthrie, L.M. (1996) *Electric Words: Dictionaries, Computers and Meanings*, MIT Press.

Index